KINGSTON OAK TREE
INSTITUTE

First published in Great Britain in 2022.

This edition published in Great Britain in 2022.

ISBN: 978-1-8384826-2-6

Designed by:
Hassan Ismaili

Table of Contents

Transliteration Guide

Alone	Romanization	English words having similar sounds
ء	ʾ	-
ا	ā	-
ت	t	true
ث	th	think
ح	ḥ	-
خ	kh	-
ذ	dh	this
ش	sh	show
ص	ṣ	-
ض	ḍ	-
ط	ṭ	-
ظ	ẓ	-
ع	ʿ(ayn)	-
غ	gh	-
ق	q	-
ه ، ة	t or h	-

Vowels and Diphthongs

ـَ	a	اَ	ā	ـِي	ī
ـُ	u	ـَى	ā	ـَوْ	aw
ـِ	i	ـُو	ū	ـَيْ	ay

Introduction

When choosing the best topic to write on; or indeed when deciding on the best path to walk upon, I thought that it is very important to first realise where we are and where we are heading. This is the fundamental question of any Muslim in this life. There are so many deeds out there; indeed, one might even spend their entire lifetime engaging in the noblest of acts which is to seek knowledge - in the general sense, and more specifically knowledge about Islam - only to gain no reward for their endeavour; and may even attain burden and sin.

For how many people study Islam, yet are ignorant of Allah ﷻ, or ignorant of what their purpose is!

We know that there will be a group of people who will come on the Day of Judgment having seemingly achieved high status in the Islamic realm, yet in reality they will be the first to be thrown into the Fire. Examples of those include someone like a *qārī*, or an *ʿālim* who desires a 'title' or superiority in the eyes of people rather than for the purpose itself.

The Prophet ﷺ said:

إنَّ أوَّلَ النَّاسِ يُقْضَى يومَ القِيامَةِ عليه رَجُلٌ اسْتُشْهِدَ، فَأُتِيَ به فَعَرَّفَهُ نِعَمَهُ فَعَرَفَها، قالَ: فَما عَمِلْتَ فيها؟ قالَ: قاتَلْتُ فيكَ حتَّى اسْتُشْهِدْتُ، قالَ: كَذَبْتَ، ولَكِنَّكَ قاتَلْتَ لأَنْ يُقالَ: جَرِيءٌ، فقَدْ قيلَ، ثُمَّ أُمِرَ به فَسُحِبَ علَى وجْهِهِ حتَّى أُلْقِيَ في النَّارِ، ورَجُلٌ تَعَلَّمَ العِلْمَ، وعَلَّمَهُ وقَرَأَ القُرْآنَ، فَأُتِيَ به فَعَرَّفَهُ نِعَمَهُ فَعَرَفَها، قالَ: فَما عَمِلْتَ فيها؟ قالَ: تَعَلَّمْتُ العِلْمَ، وعَلَّمْتُهُ وقَرَأْتُ فِيكَ القُرْآنَ، قالَ: كَذَبْتَ، ولَكِنَّكَ تَعَلَّمْتَ العِلْمَ لِيُقالَ: عالِمٌ، وقَرَأْتَ القُرْآنَ لِيُقالَ: هو قارِئٌ، فقَدْ قيلَ، ثُمَّ أُمِرَ به فَسُحِبَ علَى وجْهِهِ حتَّى أُلْقِيَ في النَّارِ، ورَجُلٌ وسَّعَ اللَّهُ عليه، وأَعْطاهُ مِن أصْنافِ المالِ كُلِّهِ، فَأُتِيَ به فَعَرَّفَهُ نِعَمَهُ فَعَرَفَها، قالَ: فَما عَمِلْتَ فيها؟ قالَ: ما تَرَكْتُ مِن سَبِيلٍ تُحِبُّ أنْ يُنْفَقَ فيها إلَّا أنْفَقْتُ فيها لَكَ، قالَ: كَذَبْتَ، ولَكِنَّكَ فَعَلْتَ لِيُقالَ: هو جَوادٌ، فقَدْ قيلَ، ثُمَّ أُمِرَ به فَسُحِبَ علَى وجْهِهِ، ثُمَّ أُلْقِيَ في النَّارِ

"Among the first people who will be judged on the Day of Resurrection is a man who was martyred. He will be brought forth, and he will be shown His blessings; and he will recognise it. He [Allah] will say, 'So, what did you do regarding it?'

He will say, 'I fought for You until I was martyred!'

He will say, 'You have lied! Rather you fought so that it would be said: he is brave. And it was said.'

He will then be commanded, and he will be dragged on his face and thrown into the Fire.

And [among the first will be] a man who learnt knowledge and taught it to others, and recited the Quran. He will be brought

forth, and he will be shown His blessings, and he will recognise it. He [Allah] will say, 'So, what did you do regarding it?'

The man will say, 'I learnt knowledge and taught it, and I recited the Quran for You!'

Allah will say, 'You have lied! Rather you learnt the knowledge so that it will be said: he is an *ʿālim*; and you recited the Quran so that it will be said he is a *qārī*. And indeed, it was said.'

He will then be commanded, and he will be dragged on his face and thrown into the Fire.

And [among the first will be] a man whom Allah expanded for him and gave him of an assortment of wealth. He will be brought forth, and he will be shown His blessings; and he will recognise it. He [Allah] will say, 'So, what did you do regarding it?'

He will say, 'I didn't leave any avenue in which You love to be spent on, except I spent in that avenue for You!'

Allah will say, 'You have lied! Rather you did that, so it will be said: he is generous. And it was said.'

He will then be commanded, and he will be dragged on his face and thrown into the Fire."[1]

In his explanation of Ṣaḥīḥ Muslim, Imam al-Nawawī comments on this hadith:

"The way these people were treated for doing things for other than Allah is an indication of the severity in the prohibition of showing-off and the intensity of the punishment therein. It also teaches us that the virtues of the good acts mentioned are all dependent on one doing these sincerely for Allah."

1 *Ṣaḥīḥ:* Hadith narrated by Imam Muslim

That is why it remains essential for us to understand the nature of what will give us success. This lies in understanding who we are, knowing where we are and knowing our purpose in life. And this can only happen by knowing Allah ﷻ and being aware of Him ﷻ.

I chose to dwell and interact with the text of Imam al-Nawawī ﵀, which is "Bustān al-ʿĀrifīn": Garden of the Aware. Imam al-Nawawī is renowned for being a *muḥaddith*, an expert hadith narrator. He has compiled a plethora of great works and authored many others in the field of hadith. Some are household names, like "Riyāḍ al-Ṣāliḥīn" (Gardens of the Righteous)-a book that has a place in most Muslim homes. Another example is the "40 Nawawī Hadith" a book that is owned by many, memorised by children, commented and explained by numerous. He also compiled an explanation and commentary of Ṣaḥīḥ Muslim, named: "Al-Minhāj fī Sharḥ Ṣaḥīḥ Muslim".

At the same time, he was a *faqīh*: someone who understood the *dīn* and learnt the fiqh, specializing in the *madhhab* of Imam al-Shāfiʿī ﵁ as well as being well versed in all the other *madhāhib*. In this field, he also compiled in-depth books that are considered some of the most authoritative works in the Shāfiʿī *madhhab*. These include titles like "al-Majmūʿ Sharḥ al-Muhadhdhab" and "Minhāj al-Ṭālibīn" (The Path of the Seekers) and "Rawḍat al-Ṭālibīn" (Garden of the Seekers).

In addition to these two fields, he compiled "Ṭabaqāt al-Shāfiʿiyyah" (The Levels of the Shāfiʿī Scholars) in the field of history and biographies. In the field of language, he produced "Tahdhīb al-'Asmā' wa al-Lughāt" (Abridgement of the Names and Dialects). In the area of *'adab* and *dhikr*: "Kitāb al-Adhkār" (Book of Remembrances) and "Al-Tibyān fī Ādāb Ḥamalat al-Quran" (The Explanation of the Etiquette of the Carriers of the Quran).

So, we have this aspect of Imam al-Nawawī, the *muḥaddith* and *faqīh*, almost like the university academic. However, in this book Bustān al-ʻĀrifīn, he comes out with his spiritual side. It is about the purification of the soul, about learning and knowing who Allah ﷻ is and realising one's path in this life.

He chose a similar title of this book to his other book "Riyāḍ al-Ṣāliḥīn" - *Riyāḍ* also having the meaning of gardens or meadows. It is a plural of the word *rawḍah*, which almost implies a place of entertainment and recreation. It is the gardens of the *Ṣāliḥīn* and that is the compilation relating to *aḥādīth*; in which he mentions verses from the Quran and narrates hadith related to different disciplines from understanding the core actions of the heart, the *akhlāq* and then he addresses *'adab* and the *faḍā'il* (virtues) amongst other topics. In this book, he has chosen a similar title, which is Bustān al-ʻĀrifīn. Bustān also means garden, not dissimilar to *riyāḍ*; however it is for those who are aware – a higher dimension, no doubt.

I use the word "aware", although "aware" is a poor translation of the word *ʻĀrifīn*, because an *ʻārif* is somebody who is not *just* aware. I have explored the different translations, and it is difficult to find a precise term. A *ʻārif* is somebody who is enlightened, having reached a realisation of knowing who they are, and that can only happen by realising their status in this life and by knowing Allah ﷻ. Whilst living this life, it becomes part of the nature of our lives to be engrossed in its day-to-day aspects, running after this or that, performing the daily chores, earning a living to stay alive, and to enjoy and to buy things that will be beneficial for us and things for our luxury and so on. Sometimes, we lose the whole aspect of taking time out and this is what the entire nature of *ṣalāh* is supposed to be about.

For some people, attending the congregational prayer in the *masjid* has become almost like a duty. Some people even come to the *masjid*, because it is like they are expected to go. They know that people are expecting to see them there: in the *masjid*. And if they don't come, the guilt they feel is not because they are missing out on the deed's virtue, but because they are missing out on not being seen by others in the *masjid*, and that becomes a problem in itself.

So, the theme of the book is about coming to a gathering where we can take time out, away from this whole materialistic aspect of life. It also takes us away from the dangers of the ego-centric life, seeking always to satisfy our egos in this way. As in the example of the person who comes to the *masjid*, he feels others will criticise him if he is not seen in the *masjid*. If they are not in the front row, even then, they feel it is a problem. Some people fight to be in the front row, not because of the reward but more for the status that comes with that, and that is a problem in itself. I have prayed in some *masājid*, where the front row is like a tin of sardines with everyone squeezed in. People miss the whole aspect of attaining concentration and focus in *ṣalāh*, at the expense of standing in the front row. And that's why I have refused – many a time – the generous offer by a kind brother to step into the front row, which is already densely packed. I always smile, place my hand on my heart to indicate my heartfelt appreciation, and firmly decline. Because for me, focus and concentration in *ṣalāh* are more important than standing in the front row. That said, some will step back into the second or third row to give me their space, which is always humbling for me to be respected in such a way, despite me not deserving of it.

Here I will mention a related incident, for the benefit of the narration, not for the sake of showing off. Once I came into the *masjid* and ended up in the fifth row. One brother saw me there and invited me to be a "sardine" in the front row. I smiled and expressed my appreciation but declined for the reason I mentioned previously. As the prayer was called, the regular imam was not present; and the attendees looked for someone to lead the prayer. They saw me and invited me forward. And so, I stepped forward the few lines to lead the prayer. The same brother seeing me come to the very front, smiled at me and said, "That is the blessing of Allah: He gives it to whom He wishes!" For me, this incident is quite a humbling one; to be allowed to step forward. I ask Allah to accept from us our good deeds.

I mention the example of those who come to the *masjid* for the wrong reason, because as you will note in this book, I very much bring the reader's attention to a category of Muslim who has completely missed the spirit of Islam, by focusing on the letter of the law. This category is a danger to themselves and society. May Allah guide us to the correct and proper understanding.

For someone to realise that their behaviour is tainted, and then to go back to correct it, is an immense process that can be painful. It is like the different animals (arthropods, snakes and some birds and mammals) that have to shed their outer body – a process known as moulting. Take the caterpillar, for example. When it wants to become a winged insect, it has to undergo the process of becoming a cocoon and dwelling about its reality and staying in that position, until it has the strength of realising it, and then to emerge a changed being. If it does not go through that stage, it will always remain a caterpillar. And in this life, we have that choice of either staying as a caterpillar: crawling on the ground, on the *dunyā*, just feeding and getting fatter and fatter; or we have the option of taking time out, secluding ourselves, going through an internal reflection within ourselves, so that we can then emerge into a butterfly which is free to fly and reach higher levels, that a caterpillar would never dream of achieving. [Some – however – will become moths, but that's another topic!]

It is from this perspective that this book Bustān al-ʿĀrifīn comes. It is about the garden: not the garden in the *Ākhirah: al-Jannah*, but it is a garden here in the *dunyā*. Because people who know Allah ﷻ and realise their place will live in happiness, much like a garden, much like *al-Jannah* in this life before they die. This is where the real pleasure is: the pleasure is in knowing Allah ﷻ. The joy is in being associated with Allah ﷻ through one's good deeds, and in realising one's position in life. For if you do that, you will feel happy, you will feel that contentment, you will feel that joy, and that is the garden; that is the *Bustān*.

Other people are striving to get joy and to realise happiness through achieving material gain. We know from not one or two stories, but repeated stories of wealthy and super-rich people, who have not achieved happiness nor have they realised it.

Consider the famous saying of 'Ibrāhīm ibn 'Ad-ham ﵀, who was a poor man. He didn't have much and was living the life of a *zāhid* (ascetic). He made an announcement, which had been engraved in the stone of history. He said, "We are in a state of happiness and contentment; if the kings and the princes knew what kind of happiness we are in, they would have fought us over this happiness with their swords." Meaning that they would have wanted to achieve that happiness, (even if it meant robbing it of others) because there are kings on their thrones, princes in their palaces and oil sheikhs in their skyscrapers who are not fulfilled in their happiness.

A similar realisation was vocalised by Ibn Taymiyyah ﵀ who said, "In this *dunyā* is a *Jannah*, who does not enter it; will not enter *al-Jannah* in the next life."

On another note: what a great reality to ponder upon. When we think about the righteous people of the past of how they spend time and effort in learning; compiling and writing for people to come later on to benefit from their works and to make *du'ā'* for them. If you told Imam al-Nawawī that there will be a group of people in the land of the non-Arabs[2], gathered in a *masjid* reading his

2 *al-Frenj*, as they use to call them

book, seven or eight centuries after him, he probably wouldn't have envisaged such a thing and would have thought that idea far-fetched. Yet, it is a blessing from Allah ﷻ, and it is indeed from His *barakah* for this great man, who is reaping the rewards many years after departing from the face of the Earth. This is also one of the motivations for me to put this book together, in an endeavour that Allah accepts it as a form of continuous charity in the format of useful knowledge for those who come after me.

In this book, I have taken the text of the Bustān and gone through the sayings and narrations with some explanations. In some cases, I have expanded greatly to emphasise the point; on other occasions, I have chosen not to comment, as the words have sufficient clarity.

On some topics, I have included some extended information to give the reader depth in certain points, in order that s/he can appreciate the vastness of knowledge. I have chosen to include Arabic words, which you will find in *italics* to relay important Islamic vocabulary to the reader. A full glossary can be found at the end of the book to aid comprehension. My intention is that you can expand your vocabulary and begin to use these words in your daily usage, so please do try.

To add some uniqueness to this book, I have included some personal stories and thoughts, as I believe that every individual has a story that will add to the human experience, either as motivation and inspiration or as pitfalls to avoid. However, I have tried my utmost to avoid mentioning names of others where that may cause issues.

Where I have quoted the Quran, Prophet Hadith or poetry, I have included the original Arabic text, as I believe there is educational benefit. In the case of poetry, there is much more eloquence for those who know Arabic to include the original text. The translated Quranic verses are placed in brackets ﴿﴾; the hadith is in **bold**; and the poetry in blue.

After completing the book, I found that some quotations and narrations would benefit from being collated together for similarity of the topic. I understand that Imam al-Nawawī's method of compilation was to make this book as "informal" or less complicated as possible, by omitting headings and subject categories. However, as this book is an explanation and not a translation, I felt it would be more beneficial for the reader to have similar topics collated. I am hopeful that this is the best approach, and Allah knows best. [For those wishing to access the translation alone, then that is available as a separate compilation].

The compilation of this book, referencing it, reviewing and revising it has taken many hours, as any book would take. And I ask Allah that this work has been in tune with the nature of this book, which is to have the correct intention and that this intention is sincere for Him. And my sincere request to you – my dear reader – is that if you have benefitted from a word or a phrase from this book, that you stop for a moment and make a *du'ā'* for me, even if short.

No doubt you will find many errors and mistakes in this book. Imam al-Shāfi'ī ﷺ passed on his compilation to his student al-Buwayṭī saying, "Take this book, despite the many errors in it!"

Surprised, his student responded, "O Aba AbdUllah, why don't you correct these mistakes?"

He said, "How can I, when Allah has said, 'and had it been from other than Allah, they would have found many disparities in it,' for Allah has denied that any book be perfect, save His."
So, I am grateful if you do find any errors; that you present them to me in the best of ways.

Lastly, I am grateful to all those who have participated in bringing about this book. Most of all, my friend Hassan Ismaili for his contribution to designing and publishing of this book. May

Allah reward him immensely and give him a great share in this reward. *Āmīn*.

In addition, I wish to extend my gratitude in the form of *du'ā'* to my brothers Mohammad Alfateh and Hazmi Sulami and my sister Nourine Ahmad for their contribution to proofreading my writings; as well as others who wished to remained anonymous. I know it has been hard for them to navigate through my style, but they did a great job. May Allah ﷻ bless them in their lives: their time, health and wealth. *Āmīn*.

Our Lord accept from us…
for You are the Most Hearing Most Knowing!

Biography of Imam al-Nawawī

Imam al-Nawawī (may Allah be pleased with him) is a fascinating character. He is someone who - in many ways - sets a very high standard for people who want to achieve in life. For children, he sets the bar, for the elders as well, and even amongst the scholars.

When he was at the age of seven, children would drag him to come and play, but he would refuse to play with them because he wanted to engage in learning. At that time, he was learning the Quran.

His father put him in his shop to work and sell, but he would just be occupied with learning and the Quran to the extent that customers would leave without being served. They left as he didn't give them any attention. Ergo, the shop was badly affected because of that.

Shaykh Yāsīn al-Marākashī had observed the devotion of young Yaḥyā to learning and his reluctance to play with other children. He said, "On observing his sagacity and profundity, special love and affection developed in my heart for young Nawawī. I approached his teacher and urged him to take exceptional care of this lad as he was to become a great religious scholar and a most pious saint of the future."

The teacher asked, "Are you a soothsayer or an astrologer?"

Yāsīn said, "I am neither a soothsayer nor an astrologer, but Allah caused me to utter these words!"

The teacher conveyed this incident to al-Nawawī's father, and that's the moment when his father realised how crucial it was to push his son towards knowledge and give him that ability. And from then on, his father assisted his son in the quest for knowledge.

Initially, young al-Nawawī wanted to study medicine. He purchased the book al-Qānūn[3]. He said that he felt his heart darken, and so, he abandoned this and went for Islamic studies.

He was born in 631AH and he lived for only 45 years. A very short life by any standards, even by the standards of the old times. It was a short life. But he spent those 45 years being dedicated to his work, his contributions and his efforts. Look out for a strange reference to this that will come towards the end of this book.

His Pursuit of Knowledge

Imam al-Nawawī lived in his birth town till the age of 18 years. In the year 649AH, his father took him to Damascus, which – at that time – was considered the centre of learning as it housed more than three hundred educational institutes.

He first began his education at the Sāramiyyah school in Damascus. This is where his father had left him. He had no housing there

3 Known in English as "The Canon of Medicine" is an encyclopaedia of medicine in five books compiled by Persian Muslim physician-philosopher Ibn Sīnā (Avicenna) and completed in 1025CE

whatsoever. After some time, he approached the school's head to ask if they had any accommodation, as many schools house their students. They had no housing for him, and it was suggested that he go to Rawāḥiyyah School.

At this stage, he left the Sāramiyyah school and went on hajj with his father in 650AH. Upon coming back, he enrolled with the Madrasah Rawāḥiyyah. There, he was given a very small room in which he lived for a number of years. It was stated that when one visited him, the room was so small and the books were so many, that the only way one could sit down was to remove the books and pile them on top of each other to make some room.

When he first joined this school, he memorised "al-Tanbīh"[4] in four and a half months; He read "al-Muhadh-dhab"[5] – from memory – during the remainder of that year to his teacher.

It has been reported that he had about 12 lessons every day in a variety of sciences including fiqh (jurisprudence), hadith, hadith terminology and Arabic. He studied with many great Islamic scholars some of whom he mentions in this book between your hands.

During this time, he lived a hard life, eating what bread was offered and sleeping rough.

He remained in that small room at the Rawāḥiyyah, until he was appointed the head of Dar al-Hadith Ashrafiyyah school, a number of years later. He assumed his role as the head in succession to Shaykh Abu Shāmah who had just died. This happened when the Imam was at the age of 24. He remained there as the head for eleven years, never accepting any compensation or salary.

4 This is a famous fiqh book of Imam al-Shīrāzī (d. 476AH), which is considered an important reference in the Shāfiʿī School.
5 Al-Muhadhdhab is the book compiled by Imam al-Shīrāzī, which was explained partially by Imam al-Nawawī. It is a book in comparative fiqh.

It was said about him that he would not waste any moment of the day or night, but he would spend it busy with attaining knowledge. Even when he was walking down the streets, he would be busy going over what he had remembered and reviewing his notes.

His reputation and excellence as a scholar began to be recognised by the scholars and inhabitants of Damascus. His pursuit of knowledge dominated his entire life. He would put all of his time into studying, learning and teaching. It is even stated that he would not sleep except when sleep would overtake him. He would rest on his book and sleep for a little, then he would be startled upon awakening and continue studying. He once said about himself, "I spent two years without lying on the ground [to sleep] on my side."

His Austerity

He led a very austere, simple and modest life although it would have been possible for him to live otherwise, given his teaching position and strong influence. Some narrations state that all the clothing he possessed were a turban and a long gown. He did not desire any of the pleasures of this world.

At one point in time, he would not eat anything except some cake and olives that his father would send him from time to time. One of the reasons for this was that he was not certain that such food came from permissible sources. He had a similar attitude to fruit, as he was certain that a lot of fruit came from endowment properties; and were not supposed to be handed out. The other reason for not eating fruit was what he said, "I'm afraid the fruit will make me a bit moist, and that will make me lethargic, and I won't be able to achieve much."

Every day he only used to have time for only one meal. Even with that one meal, he felt that he didn't have timc to eat. This might have been the reason why he died young, as well as due to the fact that he was not eating healthily. He spent and dedicated a lot of time and effort for his quest. Even though it was a short life, he produced so much to the extent that he is an authority up until today.

He did not accept a stipend for his teaching, and his only material possessions of this world were books, as his small room was like a warehouse of books. His goal was not simply to possess a large library for decoration nor display. Instead, he benefited greatly from those works and, from his lectures and writings, numerous people have benefited from them since then.

Al-Nawawī never married

Al-Nawawī never got married and the reasons for this was his desire for knowledge and disinterest in worldly pleasures. His life was filled with the desire to learn, teach and engage in acts of worship.

Some said that he did not marry because he feared that he would not be able to fulfil the rights of his wife due to his learning desires.

His Writings and Books

Al-Nawawī started writing in the year 663AH. Hence, in a span of twelve or thirteen years, he compiled some of the most important works in the history of Islam.

Some of his works that he completed in that short time, include:

1 - Riyāḍ al-Ṣāliḥīn (Gardens of the Righteous)

2 - Al-Minhāj fī Sharḥ Ṣaḥīḥ Muslim (His Commentary to Sahih Muslim)

3 - Al-Majmūʿ Sharḥ al-Muhadh-dhab (The Compiled in comparative fiqh)

4 - Minhāj al-Ṫālibīn (The Path of the Seekers)

5 - Tahdhīb al-'Asmā' wa al-Lughāt (Abridgement of the Names and Dialects)

6 - Forty *Aḥadīth*

7 - Kitāb al-'Adhkār (Book of Remembrances)

8 - Ṫabaqāt al-Shāfiʿiyyah (The Levels of the Shāfiʿī scholars)

9 - Rawḍat al-Ṫālibīn (Garden of the Seekers)

10 - Bustān al-ʿĀrifīn (Garden of the Aware)

11 - Al-Tibyān fī Ādāb Ḥamalat al-Quran (The Explanation of the etiquette of the carriers of the Quran)

Al-Nawawī and the Ruler

The leader of the Muslims during much of al-Nawawī's lifetime was al-Sultān al-Ẓāhir. He was the one who fought off the Mongols and handed them a great defeat. However, his status and popularity did not prevent al-Nawawī from standing up to him when he was wrong. On more than one occasion, al-Nawawī either reproached the ruler in the Hall of Justice or sent him letters concerning a particular matter that was of common interest to the people of Damascus.

On one occasion, al-Nawawī sent the Sultan a letter on behalf of the Muslim masses, co-signed by several other scholars. This letter was a request for the ruler to lessen the taxes that were placed on the inhabitants of Shām. The intention of al-Nawawī's letter was about correcting the wrong that was being done by the ruler. He did not bow down to the ruler, just because he was the ruler and just because he had done some excellent deeds in the past. However, he realised that he must advise the ruler to what's right. In his response, the ruler claimed that he needed to collect those taxes for the sake of *jihād*.

On his continuous encounters with the ruler through letters and his persuasion to urge the ruler for all the right reasons, the ruler became very upset with al-Nawawī. Hence, he decided to have him removed from Damascus. Al-Nawawī said that he would listen and obey, perhaps realising that in doing so would cause less harm and civil strife compared to him remaining in Damascus and opposing the ruler.

He commented: "As for myself, threats do not harm me or mean anything to me. They will not keep me from advising the ruler, for I believe that this is obligatory upon me and others."

Hence, he left Damascus and went to his hometown of Nawā. Scholars of that time went to try to bring al-Nawawī back to Damascus. However, he refused. He said that he would not enter Damascus if al-Ẓāhir was still there. After a few months, al-Ẓāhir Baibars died.

His Death

After returning to Nawā, al-Nawawī fell ill and passed away. He died on the 24th of Rajab, 676 AH (1277 AD), at the age of forty-five. However, by the grace and mercy of Allah, his accomplishments during his short life span were equal to or greater than many who lived even twice as long as he did.

When the news of his death reached Damascus, the people were very saddened. Tears flowed from their eyes. One of the greatest scholars and greatest leaders had died. Indeed, the one who was greatly beloved by almost everyone he touched in his life had passed away.

His Burial Place

Al-Nawawī was buried in his hometown of Nawā, Syria. He wished and advised that his grave would be according to the Sunna (i.e., to be levelled and not prominent). However, some people decided to build a dome over his grave. However, Allah willed that al-Nawawī's wish be fulfilled. Every time they tried to build something over his grave, it was destroyed. His grave, after many attempts, was finally left flat, slightly marked and according to the sunna. His grave is still well-known and recognised today.

May Allah reward this great man, a giant by all accounts for his efforts and striving for the sake of Allah.

01

The Imam's Introduction

Imam al-Nawawī (hereafter referred to as "the Imam") begins his book by praising Allah ﷻ. And in praising Allah, he reminds us about who Allah ﷻ is, as knowing Allah is the core of Islam.

He is the one who is the Almighty: Al-ʿAzīz, the One who forgives: Al-Ghāfir. These are the names that Allah ﷻ has described Himself with. Allah ﷻ is the one who alternates the night over the day, and folds the day into the night, and unfolds the night and the day; so He is the One who created time and is in control of time, and that's why He is angered with the one who curses time.

Allah said, as reported in a Divine hadith:

يُؤْذِينِي ابنُ آدَمَ يَسُبُّ الدَّهْرَ وأنا الدَّهْرُ، بيَدِي
الأمْرُ أُقَلِّبُ اللَّيْلَ والنَّهارَ

"The son of Adam harms Me[6]: he curses time; yet I am Time: in My Hands is the command: I alternate the day and the night."[7]

6 "harm Me" here means that he attributes false things to Me, as no one can harm Allah.
7 *Ṣaḥīḥ:* Hadith narrated by Imams al-Bukhārī and Muslim

More importantly, the Imam mentions here in praising Allah ﷻ that Allah is the One who awakens whomever He chooses from among His creation. Because the reality of this life is that it is a dream and humankind is sleeping. There is a saying attributed to 'Alī ibn Abī Ṭālib رضي الله عنه:

النَّاسُ نِيامٌ، إِذَا مَاتُوا انتَبَهُوا

"People are asleep. It is only when they die that they wake up."

It is only after death that they realise that they were sleeping, and now the *real* life begins. The Next Life is the LIFE, as Allah mentions in the Quran.[8]

If you consider most people: their default position is that they are asleep - meaning that they are unaware of what is happening: they do not see the reality of things. When someone is sleeping, he is having dreams (or nightmares), and he is living in those dreams, and they seem very real. He can hear things; he can even smell the smells and taste the foods. Everything that the sleeping person sees in a dream seems to be happening in real-time. However, the reality is that it is not there. For, when you open your eyes: the whole reality is a different one.

Praise is thus to Allah ﷻ who will choose people to awaken them, after they have been sleeping in this *dunyā*. And by waking them, He brings them amongst His ranks of those who are righteous, because to have that awakening is to have that awareness. That awareness is also a blessing from Allah ﷻ, it is a virtue from Allah, which is only gifted to the select.

When you consider people today, you just have to look outside and see how people are busy with their day-to-day lives: engaging in different activities, trying to achieve things. You don't even have to look outside the Muslim realm. When you look at Muslims in the

8 Holy Quran; Chapter of the Spider 29:64

communities around you: observe how they behave and see how they are striving. You will find some are willing to cheat others; they are eager to steal from others, lie or slander to get things. Others will kill to satisfy their whims. Those who have positions of authority want to make sure that they are fastened tightly on their chairs. They are bolted tightly to their thrones: they do not want anyone to shake them or remove them from their positions: they are corrupt.

It is all happening because they do not realise what their purpose is. So, to be awakened by Allah ﷻ is indeed a blessing, and it is not just about being a Muslim. Being a Muslim is in itself a blessing, but even from amongst the Muslims to be chosen by Allah ﷻ, to be awakened is a much greater blessing. For true belief and proper worship have light and warmth. Allah casts them in the hearts of whomever He chooses from among His servants.

That is why He ﷻ says that He grants success to whomever He chooses. And He places them amongst the people of right conduct. As for those He loves, He gives them insight into reality so that they become people who understand the reality of this world. And as a consequence, they don't entertain themselves in this life. That is the real realisation. That is why when you look at the people of the past, the people who achieved great lives, they didn't have that attachment to the *dunyā*, and this is essentially what this book is going to be addressing.

Then the Imam says: I testify that there is no God but Allah ﷻ and I testify that Muhammed ﷺ is His slave and Messenger, chosen from among His creation. And the Prophet ﷺ is the noblest of His creation, from the first to the last. He is the most perfect. The one with the most and greatest awareness of Allah, the one who has great knowledge of Allah, and there is no doubt in that. Because Allah gave that awareness to the Prophet ﷺ. He was the most fearing of Allah and the most pious. When you look at the life of the

Prophet ﷺ even when you see the context in which the Prophet ﷺ made this claim - and it is not a false claim – it is a supported and justified statement. It was said in the context where some people thought that the Prophet ﷺ was not behaving according to their ideals and their outlook. They judged that he was not behaving as a *zāhid* who abstains from the *dunyā*.

In the hadith, three men came searching for the Prophet ﷺ to enquire about his actions. They couldn't find him, so they searched and asked his wives. And when they pondered upon his actions, "they thought it was little," and they did not think these were significant actions.

Do you see their lack of awareness?

Due to their lack of realisation, they could not see things for what they are.

So, what did they say?

One of them said, "As for me, I will fast, and I will not break my fast", and the other one said, "I will pray throughout the night and not sleep." And the third one said, "I will not marry the women." They said these notions thinking that these actions will bring them that awareness, and will get them *taqwa*. On hearing this, the Prophet ﷺ was quick to correct them.

And he said in that famous hadith:

والله إنّي لأرجو أن أكونَ أخْشاكُم لله وأعلمَكُم بما أتّقى

"By Allah, I surely anticipate that I am the most fearing of Allah from among you and the most knowledgeable in that which I beware of."[9]

9 *Ṣaḥīḥ:* Hadith narrated by Imam Muslim

He is not boasting here, but he wants to reiterate that he is the one who knows Allah ﷻ, and he fears Him the most. And when you look at his actions, they don't contradict that. And again, this is an establishing principle that we will need to understand, as some people mistakenly think that being poor or not possessing wealth makes them closer to Allah ﷻ.

Others think that if they live a hard rough life, that brings them closer to Allah. Whereas the reality is not in how much you own or the quality of the clothes you wear, but it's about your heart, whether the *dunyā* is in your heart or whether it is in your hands. And that is something that is reiterated through the actions of the righteous people of before.

So, the Imam sends the salutations and prayers to the Prophet ﷺ.

Then, he reminds us that this world dwindles away. It is not the one that is going to endure. It is the abode that will pass, and we are just going to pass through it. It is not going to be a lasting delight. It is the abode of destruction. It's not something that's going to last forever. It's something that will just finish: it will come to an end, and sometimes, a sudden one.

Then he reminds us that if you look at the traditions and the narrations and observe the sound intellectual people who use their rationale: you will see that there are ample proofs therein for anybody who examines them. There are things that everybody realises, even those who don't believe in Allah ﷻ. Everybody – and everyone knows that there is no eternal life in the *dunyā*. There is a consensus amongst humanity that everybody will die. Nobody has ever lived for eternity. Everybody knows that there will come a time when they will die. They know that this life will end. They fully understand that their beauty, strength, or whatever they possess will not last forever. So, they know this already; and therefore, it does not even need proof. It doesn't need scientific evidence. It is there in front of everyone to see and observe. The elite, the commoners, the rich, the poor: they all possess this knowledge, and they all know this, without a doubt.

Both the mind and the eyes focus on it so that it cannot be any clearer. Some people argue about things, but the evidence for this is so clear. And that is the basis of anybody coming closer to Allah and learning who Allah is, to realise this fact. To see that there must be a purpose, because if there's nothing after this life, then this life has no meaning. And if it has no meaning, and it is so short, then it justifies that people can do whatever they want to achieve whatever they aspire for. But surely, as it is not going to last forever, it warrants that somebody questions: What is after this? Is there something else?

We are warned about this in the Quran. We are cautioned to always be on our guard, to be aware of relying on the *dunyā* or in allowing ourselves to be deluded, allowing ourselves to trust in the materialistic aspect. These same warnings, as mentioned in the Quran, have come through the Prophetic Hadith. And the same warnings have come through the wise sayings of the righteous people. That's why the best people in this life are those who are the slaves of Allah, for they have understood their position and status. The most intelligent amongst humans are those who have managed to abstain from this life by not indulging in the luxuries.

Imam al-Nawawī then brings forth some additional material in the form of eloquent poetry. He doesn't tell us who the poet is. I have inserted the Arabic for those who can read and understand, as the eloquence can very often be lost in translation.

The poet says:

انظر إلى الأطلال كيف تغيَّرتْ   من بعدِ ساكنها وكيف تنكرتْ
سحبَ البِلى أَذياله برسومه   فتساقطت أحجارها وتكسَّرت
ومضتْ جماعةُ أهلها لسبيلهم   وتغيَّبتْ أخبارُهم وتنكرت
لما نظرتُ تَفَكُّراً لديارهم   سَحَّتْ جفوني عَبْرةً وتحدَّرت
لو كنتُ أَعْقِلُ ما أفقتُ من البكا   حسبي هناكَ ومُقْلتي ما أبصرتْ
نصبتْ لنا الدنيا زخارفَ حُسْنها   مَكراً بنا وخديعةً ما فَتَرَتْ
وهي التي لم تَحْلُ قطُّ لذائق   إلا تغيَّر طعمُها وتمررت
خدَّاعةً بجمالها إنْ أقبلتْ   فجَّاعة بزوالها إنْ أدبرتْ
وهَّابةً سلاَّبةً لِهباتها   طلاَّبة لخراب ما قد عمَّرتْ
وإذا بنتْ أمراً لصاحبِ ثروةٍ   نصبتْ مجانقَها عليه فدمَّرتْ

Look at the ruins how they have changed
After their inhabitants, and how they are unrecognisable.

The wear extended its trails over its demarcations
Such that its stones have tumbled down and shattered.

The groupings of its people have departed on their ways
Their news has disappeard and become concealed.

Somehow when you think about this today: we go to the graves, we bury people, and at that time, everyone is emotional. The relatives of the deceased are emotional, and even those who are not related are emotional. But come to them after a few months or even after a few weeks [and sometimes even after a few days] and you will find them arguing about the inheritance: who gets what and how much. It is like their recently deceased relative has been completely forgotten. He or she are in their own world. So, what about when years have passed?

The poem continues:

When I look - in reflection – about their dwellings
Teardrops drown out my eyelashes; and flow.

Had I been wiser, I would not have awoken from crying
Enough therein for my eyes, as what it has seen.

The *dunyā* has erected for us the beauty of its ornaments
Out of deception for us and treachery, never ceasing.

It is that which never tastes sweet in the mouth;
Even after the sweetness, its taste alters: becoming bitter.

Deceiving in its beauty as it comes forth
Causing grief with its end, as it departs.

A giver who strips away his gifts
Seeking to ruin that which it has constructed.

When it constructs something for an owner of wealth
It [simultaneously] erects its catapults on it, and as such, destroys it.

When Hārūn al-Rashīd - the famous ʿAbbāsid Caliph built his palace, he built such a mighty well-constructed elegant palace. When the construction was completed, he invited people to come and inspect. Everyone who came congratulated him on such a magnificent piece of architecture and such a grand palace.

However, Abu al-ʿAtāhiyah - one of the famous ascetic poets of that time - came and remarked: "It is an extraordinary great palace;

however, it has two major flaws!"

Hārūn said, "Really? What are those defects?"

He said, "The owner will die, and the palace will come to an end and will no longer last."

It is quite possible that the same incident has been preserved in poetry form.

Abu al-ʿAtāhiyah said:

عِشْ مَا بَدا لَكَ   فِي ظِلِّ شَاهِقَةِ القُصُورِ
يَجري عَلَيكَ بِما أَردتَ   مَعَ الغُدُوِّ مَعَ البُكُورِ
فَإذَا النُّفُوسُ تَغَرغَرتْ   بِزَفِيرِ حَشرَجَةِ الصُّدُورِ
فَهُناكَ تَعلمُ مُوقِناً   مَا كُنتَ إِلا فِي غُرُورِ

Live as you wish
in the shade of the towering castles

Whatever you desire will come flowing to you;
in the morning and in the evening

Yet, when the souls gargle,[10]
as the chests wheeze

Only then, you shall know for sure,
that you were not living except in delusion!

So, Hārūn cried till he fainted.

That comment shook Hārūn because he was quite pleased with this

10 Signifying death, as the spirit leaves the body

palace, and didn't think about the *real* state of affairs. And that is the reality, if you go to Iraq now, you will not find the Palace of Hārūn al-Rashīd; and obviously, Hārūn has also passed away.

The Imam continues by giving other lines of poetry:

ومَنْ يَحْمدِ الدُّنيا لعيشٍ يَسُرُّه فسوف لَعمري عن قليل يلومُها

إذا أدبرت كانت على المرء حسرةً وإن أقبلت كانت كثيراً همومُها

When someone praises the *dunyā* for a pleasing life [he has]
By my life, soon he shall blame it when only little remains.

When it departs, it is grief for the person
And when it comes forth, its troubling worries are many.

Following this short introduction, the Imam defines the purpose of this book. So as an introduction it is to clarify how to travel this path: the path to the *Ākhirah*. It will show you how to take on the excellent qualities that he has described.

In this book, he tells us that he will mention some of the gems and realities of this awareness of Allah. The Imam told us that this book is not a textbook, which may bring about boredom, but rather it is compiled in a way that will be joyful to read. Because unfortunately, during the time that the Imam was compiling this book, people had lost enthusiasm in learning and researching.

Take for example, a book like Fatḥ al-Bārī which is the explanation of Ṣaḥīḥ al-Bukhārī by Imam Hadith Master Ibn Ḥajar al-ʿAsqalānī ﷺ. It is an extensive compilation: about 14 volumes explaining al-Bukhārī's book. When you read that book you will see that he goes into details, by examining the narrators of the hadith and explaining matters about each narrator. He extracts the hadith or similar wordings from other sources and explains everything, which includes dispelling ambiguities or confusions. He also deals with aspects of *ʿaqīdah* and fiqh and so on: a very intense and detailed book.

Prior to that, when the Imam compiled Ṣaḥīḥ Muslim, he went on to say, "I wanted to make this very wide and expounded, but then I saw people are not that bothered, not interested. So, I thought the best way is just to shorten it; at least some people will benefit."

And he takes a similar approach in this book. He has chosen to compose this book in a simplified way to help the average reader to benefit from it. There will be some uplifting sayings of the righteous *salaf*, the meaning of specific inspiring stories and some beautiful poems. In most cases, it will be demonstrated whether the hadith is sound {*ḥasan*} or authentic {*ṣaḥīḥ*}. In some instances, the chains of transmission will be inserted, because after all, Imam al-Nawawī is a *muḥaddith,* and he has to comment on the hadith. Unlike Imam al-Ghazālī, who when compiling this book "Iḥyāʾ ʿUlūm al-Dīn", didn't comment on the hadith transmission. He just narrated all the hadith; and it almost seemed like he gave a task for people to come later on to verify the hadith, which coincidentally: some took up the challenge like the Hadith Masters al-ʿIrāqī, Ibn al-Subkī and al-Zubaydī.

The Imam commits to explaining whatever may be obscure or hidden, by clarifying it and giving those necessary definitions to remove any distortion. Despite choosing to make the book concise, he could not escape mentioning certain chains of narration, especially for what might be considered problematic narrations.

This is to establish in the mind of the reader that indeed, our *dīn* is based on *ʾisnād*.

Hadith Master AbdUllah ibn al-Mubārak ﵀ said, "*ʾIsnād* is from the *dīn*. And had it not been for the *ʾisnād,* then anyone could have said anything."

He also said, "Between us and them are the lists", meaning the chains of transmission of narrators. And by "them", he is referring to those who are fabricators and liars.

Something similar was said by the Senior Follower Imam Muhammad ibn Sīrī ﷺ: "This knowledge is *dīn*, so look unto whom you are taking your *dīn* from."

The Imam said that this book is meant for worshippers and for people who are not in need of the science of narrators (*'ilm al-Rijāl*). You don't need to have a look at all the chains. And most of what will be quoted by the praise of Allah will have *'isnād* which is already famous in the well-known books, so don't worry about it in that regard. For the purpose of this book, I have removed the chains of transmission. However, you can find those chains in the original translation that I have completed of this book titled: Garden of the Aware.

In the main, the Imam has chosen not to give commentary on the sayings and narrations unless there are finer points that warrant explanation in order to remove potential ambiguity. This book will contain various sciences of the shari'a, some of the subtleties of hadith, some finer points of hidden fiqh and the mannerisms (*'adab*). It contains essential issues concerning belief and some gems of important principles. And it will include some subtle marvels which stimulate the remembrance of Allah and which should be mentioned in gatherings.

It deals with the awareness of the hearts, the illnesses, the remedies and the cure. Should something arise that would require an explanation, then the Imam says, "I will refer you to another book where you can get more insight". He adds an important point to clarify why he is doing this. He cautions the readers into thinking that he is trying to show off by mentioning all his compilations when he is referring them to another book. Instead, he is doing that for those who wish to seek further elaboration on the topic and hence be guided towards the good. Then he says: "I have brought these finc points to your attention because I see there are those who find fault with anyone who acts in this way. Those people do so, because of their ignorance, bad opinion, perversity, envy, incapacity and overall stubbornness. I want to establish this meaning and cleanse people of any false opinion."

Lastly, he asks Allah ﷻ to grant him success in his intention and to help in all manners of obedience, to make all obedience easy for him and to always guide him towards increasing in those acts until death. He ends with: I ask Allah for this for those who love Him, and for those who love me for the sake of Allah, and for all the Muslim men and women, to bring us together in the abode of His generosity in the highest station and to provide us with His pleasure and aspects of all goodness.

I have come to Allah seeking His protection, and I have sought the help of Allah. I have relied on Allah. There is no power, no strength except by Allah, the Most High, the Immense, the Most Splendour, and Allah is enough for us, and He is the best of Guardians.

And we say *Āmīn* to his *du'ā'* and also ask Allah to bless our Shaykh: Shaykh al-Islam Imam al-Nawawī, and to have mercy on him and to raise his status for the beautiful works that he has provided us with.

02

Intention

In this book, the Imam talks about some of the essential topics relating to spirituality. He starts by addressing a vital topic that anyone who is walking towards Allah ﷻ has to be aware of, and has to be practising; and that is intention.

No doubt there is so much to be said of intention. It is one of those matters that the scholars continuously refer to because they know that there is so much to attain within the scope of intention, so much to learn, and so much to achieve.

The Imam starts in a somewhat similar manner to his other book *Riyāḍ al-Ṣāliḥīn* in which he begins with some verses of the Quran, then followed by the hadith, then the sayings of the righteous. This method is also the favoured teaching of Imam al-Shāfiʿī, as we can see demonstrated in the *dhikr* after *ṣalāh*. For after ending *ṣalāh*, the recommended Shāfiʿī way is to begin by reciting the verses of the Quran (āyat al-Kursī[11] and the three quls[12]), then followed by the other *adhkār*.

He starts with Allah's saying:

﴿ وَمَا أُمِرُوا إِلَّا لِيَعْبُدُوا اللَّهَ مُخْلِصِينَ لَهُ الدِّينَ حُنَفَاءَ وَيُقِيمُوا الصَّلَوٰةَ وَيُؤْتُوا الزَّكَوٰةَ وَذَٰلِكَ دِينُ الْقَيِّمَةِ ﴾

11 Holy Quran; Chapter of the Cow 2:255
12 Referring to the last three chapters of the Quran, which being with "Qul".

﴾They were only ordered to worship Allah, to make their *dīn* sincere to Him, as people of pure natural belief, and to establish *ṣalāh* and pay *zakāh* - that is the upright *dīn*.﴿[13]

This verse teaches us that they (meaning humanity) were not ordered except for the following three things. As far as we are concerned, these are the essence:

1 - The first thing was to worship our lord Allah ﷻ with *ikhlāṣ*: to be sincere to Him in their *dīn*.

2 - That they should be *ḥunafā'*.

3 - That they establish *ṣalāh* and give *zakāh*.

The reality of all these matters is that Allah's basic request from any individual in this life is to worship Him with *ikhlāṣ*. And *ikhlāṣ* is usually translated as sincerity. However, one should know that it is derived from the root word kh-la-ṣa (خ ل ص). The Arabs talk about the honey being *khāliṣ* when it is free from any wax, so it is purified honey. And so, this is how a person's *īmān* should be. This is how a person's *'ibādah* should be and how his practice should be: it should be clear of any impurities that may impact (negatively) on that action.

Secondly, that they should be *ḥunafā'*. This word is taken from Allah's description of Prophet 'Ibrāhīm ﵇ whom Allah ﷻ names a *ḥanīf*.

Allah says:

﴿ثُمَّ أَوْحَيْنَا إِلَيْكَ أَنِ اتَّبِعْ مِلَّةَ إِبْرَاهِيمَ حَنِيفًا وَمَا كَانَ مِنَ الْمُشْرِكِينَ﴾

﴾Then We revealed to you that you should follow the religion of 'Ibrāhīm who was a *ḥanīf* and he was not of the idolators.﴿[14]

13 Holy Quran; Chapter of the Clear Proof 98:5
14 Holy Quran; Chapter of the Bees 16:123

Hanīf means someone who is diverted away, or inclined away. It has a different meaning from *'istiqāmah*, which is to be upright or to go straight. And in this context, it means that a person is inclined towards the *dīn* of Allah, diverted towards the *fitrah* which is the pure natural practice.

Some of the commentators said that this is why when we pray, and we sit down in the final *tashahhud*, we don't sit down straight. We sit down a little bit tilted towards the left, with the right foot upright. This mode of sitting is called *tawarruk*, and it is recommended to sit in this position in the last sitting of the obligatory prayers except for *al-Ṣubḥ* (as it is only a two-unit prayer). This tilt is symbolic of signifying the *Ḥanafiyyah* of our religion. Indeed, Allah wants us to practice the natural way, to be naturally inclined towards what is correct.

When you look at this verse, its message is quite basic. It is saying that the *dīn* is not difficult and that Allah ﷻ does not want much from you. We know from the Quran[15] that, on the Day of Judgment, Allah ﷻ will bring forth a person who is from the people of the Fire. That person had committed atrocities, lots of wrongdoings, and so he is heading for the Fire. Allah ﷻ will ask him, "If you – now – had all the treasures of the Earth, and all that which is in it, would you pay that as a ransom to save you from the punishment that you are heading for?"

And he will say, "Yes! Of course." He thinks there is an opportunity. "Of course, I will do it!"

Then Allah ﷻ will say, "Well, what I asked of you was easier than that. All I asked from you was that you do not associate anything with Me; yet you insisted on associating [others] with Me."[16]

15 Holy Quran; Chapter of the Thunder 13:18 and The Troops 39:47
16 *Ṣaḥīḥ:* Hadith narrated by Imam al-Bukhārī

Something simple. As Allah ﷻ is not asking you to give up *all* your money, or to give up *all* your wealth or treasures: just simply to worship Him sincerely.

In the hadith narrated by Jābir ibn AbdUllah ؓ who said that a man asked the Prophet ﷺ, 'Do you see that if I pray the five prescribed prayers, fast Ramadan, make *halal* what is *halal* and make *ḥarām* what is *ḥarām*, and do not do anything more than that, will I enter *al-Jannah*?'

The Prophet ﷺ said, '**Yes**.'[17]

"Yes!": it's that simple once again vocalised by the Prophet ﷺ.

The next verse is Allah's saying:

﴿وَمَن يَخرُج مِن بَيتِهِ مُهَاجِراً إِلَى اللهِ وَرَسُولِهِ ثُمَّ يُدرِكهُ المَوتُ فَقَد وَقَعَ أَجرُهُ عَلَى اللهِ﴾

﴾ And whoever leaves his home, emigrating to Allah and His Messenger, and death catches up with him, then his reward has become established with Allah. ﴿[18]

So again, another verse emphasizing that it is the intention that is more prominent than the action. Such that if you leave your house wanting to reach Allah ﷻ, meaning that you are going towards an act of worship or closeness, you are sacrificing, you are giving up, you are migrating to Allah and His Messenger, but death catches up with you on the way, before you manage to complete your journey and you did not reach your destination; you will still attain the reward that you had set out for.

In material terms, you did not achieve the goal, you didn't fulfil

17 *Ṣaḥīḥ:* Hadith narrated by Imam Muslim
18 Holy Quran; Chapter of the Women: 4:100

the objective of the project, but the intention was there in the steps you made. Allah says, "his reward has become established with Allah". Allah used the Arabic word (وقع) *waqaʿa* which means to fall, in a literal sense. It is like the reward has fallen and has become established, as opposed to something in the air.

There is a story in this regard related to one of the Companions Jundub ibn Ḍamurah ؓ (جندب بن ضمرة) who was in Makkah, and he heard the verse where Allah ﷻ was inviting people to come out and migrate, and only excusing those who had an excuse. This man said, "I don't have any excuse," even though he was an old man. He said, "I must go and migrate to Madinah to catch up with the Prophet ﷺ."

Upon leaving, he died on the outskirts of Makkah, so he did not even manage to get far. The idolators of Makkah mocked him saying, "He wanted to go, yet he didn't even make it. He didn't stay in Makkah, nor did he reach Madinah!"[19]

So, Allah ﷻ revealed that verse in this regard.

Also, Allah said:

$$﴿ رَبُّكُم أَعلَمُ بِمَا في نُفُوسِكُم ﴾$$

❲Your Lord knows best what is in your selves.❳[20]

This is another verse that adds to this whole concept and understanding of the intention. Because at the end of the day, your actions are there for people to see, but what is really inside your heart, and what is the real reason you are doing certain things: only Allah knows. Allah knows what is inside you, and He is more aware, so you cannot - in any way - attempt to trick Him.

---

19 *Ṣaḥīḥ:* Hadith narrated by Imams Abu Yaʿlā and al-Ṭabarānī
20 Holy Quran; Chapter of the Night Journey: 17:25

Allah says:

﴿لَن يَنالَ اللهَ لُحُومُها وَلَا دِماؤُها وَلَكِن يَنالُهُ التَّقوى مِنكُمْ﴾

﴿Its[21] flesh and blood do not reach Allah;
rather your *taqwa* (piety) is what reaches Him.﴾[22]

This verse was revealed in the context of the *'uḍḥiyah* or *hadī* that is presented in hajj. Allah says that neither its flesh nor its blood will reach Him, instead it is your *taqwa*, your God-fearing, your God-consciousness: that is what reaches Allah ﷻ. Allah doesn't need the actions, nor does He need the rituals and this goes for everything. It is not just about the sacrifice here, and it is not about the material things that you give, everything that you do; Allah ﷻ doesn't need it.

In the *qudsī* hadith, Allah says:

يا عِبادِي إنَّكُمْ لَنْ تَبْلُغُوا ضَرِّي فَتَضُرُّونِي وَلَنْ تَبْلُغُوا نَفْعِي، فَتَنْفَعُونِي،
يا عِبادِي لو أنَّ أوَّلَكُمْ وَآخِرَكُمْ وإنْسَكُمْ وَجِنَّكُمْ كَانُوا علَى أتْقَى قَلْبِ
رَجُلٍ وَاحِدٍ مِنكُمْ، ما زَادَ ذلكَ في مُلْكِي شيئًا،

"O My Slaves! You will not attain the ability to harm Me. Nor will you be able to attain the ability to benefit Me. O My Slaves! If the first of you and the last of you, the humankind of you and the *jinn* of you[23]; were to be the most pious, as the most pious heart of any one of you, that would not increase My Kingdom by anything."[24]

21 That of the sacrificed animal
22 Holy Quran; Chapter of Hajj: 22:37
23 meaning all the creation from the beginning of Adam ﷺ to the end, and beginning from the shayṭān from the jinn side till the end
24 *Ṣaḥīḥ:* Hadith narrated by Imam Muslim

Nothing we do will benefit Allah ﷻ. And the same goes the other way, **"If the first of you and the last of you, the humankind of you and the *jinn* of you, were as wicked and evil as the most evil heart amongst you, that would not decrease My Kingdom by anything."**[25]

So, at the end of the day, our actions and intentions are not going to affect Allah ﷻ in any way: He will not benefit from them, nor is He going to be harmed by them. Rather, it is Allah who benefits, and it is Allah who harms.

The simple reality is that you need Allah ﷻ, not the other way round.

Ibn ʿAbbās ﷺ saidas he commented on this verse: "It means that your intentions reach Him."

'Ibrāhīm said, "*Taqwa* is the means by which you desire Him."

'Ibrāhīm is saying that what Allah ﷻ is referring to by the term *taqwa* are the actions that you do seeking Him and His pleasure.

How do you know that something is *taqwa*? It's something that you intend with it the reward of Allah ﷻ.

Then, the Imam narrates the saying of al-Zajjāj: "The meaning of this is that Allah will not accept an offering of flesh and blood when it is offered without fearful awareness of Allah. He accepts that through which you show Him your fearful awareness of Him."

So again, the concept to understand is that Allah ﷻ will not accept the sacrifice unless it is engaged with that *tawqa*.

25 *Ibid.*

Here, a person should not understand the opposite meaning, which is as some people might say, "Well, therefore we don't need to perform the actions because at the end of the day what is important is just the intention." Or "as long as my intention is good, as long as I have *īmān*, it doesn't matter about the actions." This is an entirely wrong perspective. Actions are essential, and intention is vital.

The Imam says that all the above [references] indicate that no act of worship is without intention. The intention is that you want to draw nearer to Allah and carry out His command. He is reiterating an important principle concerning the acts of *'ibādah*, which is that these cannot be correct except with intention. There must be a conscious effort that there is an intention. That intention with any act of *'ibādah* must be that the person intends to come closer to Allah ﷻ by fulfilling that which Allah has ordered him to do. This includes - as he mentions later on in the book - *wuḍū'*, *ghusl*, *ṣalāh*, *zakāh* and hajj: all require a correct intention.

This is the opinion of the majority of the scholars. The *Aḥnāf*[26] – however - differ slightly from this notion. They say that the things which are considered general and basic practice do not need any intention (*niyyah*). For example, if you have something *najis* (impure) and poured water over it to clean it, it is purified and becomes clean. They say that you do not have to have the intention that I intend to clean it. Because you have cleaned it: it is clean. So, therefore they extrapolated this to *wuḍū'* by aligning the removal of a physical impurity with the removal of ritual impurity (*ḥadath*). Hence, they concluded that you don't need an intention when you are making *wuḍū'*.

To explain this further: according to the *Aḥnāf*: if you are walking on the riverbank and somebody pushes you in the river, you will have become purified, ritually. Just by falling into the river, you

26 Ḥanafīs

have got *wuḍū'* and *ghusl*. It's all done for you, even if you didn't even think about it. If you didn't have ritual purity: you have now.

Whereas, in the other *madhāhib*: when you are pushed into the river: if you don't make the intention while you are in the water such as "I'm doing *ghusl*!" or "I'm doing *wuḍū'*!" even if for a moment, then you will not achieve that purity. And as you can see, each school has its own perspective. This does not mean that the *Aḥnāf* belittle or disregard intentions, but in this specific area, that's their conclusion.

Even in the Shāfi'ī *madhhab*, the obligation of the intention is only at the beginning of the act. So, when you do the first pillar of *wuḍū'*, which is to wash the face, the intention must be there. After that, if the intention slips away, it doesn't affect the validity of the *wuḍū'*. This happens to many of us after we commence *wuḍū'*, we start to think about other things and go into autopilot mode. All of a sudden, we realise that we are washing our left foot. However, it is recommended that your intention is there throughout the *wuḍū'* and not just at the beginning. It should continue right till the end, so you get that reward as well. [Note: if you suffer from continual ritual impurity of menorrhagia, urinary incompetence or uncontrollable flatulence, then your intention must be there throughout the *wuḍū'*.]

The same with the *ṣalāh*: how many of us enter *ṣalāh*: we have the intention, we have the focus as we announce "*Allahu Akbar*" in the beginning, but shortly after that, our focus goes somewhere else, or in fact, we are everywhere, but the *ṣalāh*. And then at the end, as we are sitting for the final sitting, we realise that we are here, we don't realise how we got there, except by following all the motions. No doubt that is a problem; and obviously there is a problem with the *ṣalāh* in terms of the reward, in terms of the *'iqbāl* of turning towards Allah. In terms of it being performed: we can say it has been achieved, and you don't have to repeat it, but Allah knows best, whether you got the reward for that prayer or not.

The Imam then just goes on to mention the foundation of intention from the hadith perspective. At the outset, the Imam said that he is not going to elongate a lot when he narrates a hadith. But because this hadith is such an important one, he gives its *'isnād*.

The *'isnād* is the line of transmission, and this is something that the scholars of the past held in high status. Furthermore, the *'isnād* is unique and specific for this *'ummah*. The *'ummah* of Islam preserved things through *'isnād*, and they would use these chains to verify the authenticity of the text. That is how we know that a particular hadith or narration is correct and sound: *ṣaḥīḥ*, *ḥasan* or *ḍaʿīf*. The transmission is crucial and very significant. I won't dwell too much into that because that in itself is a whole topic. In the introduction, I mentioned a couple of sayings in regards to *'isnād*.

The Imam in his *'isnād* narrates that which goes back all the way to ʿOmar ibn al-Khaṭṭāb ﷺ who narrates from the Prophet ﷺ that he said:

إِنَّمَا الأَعْمَالُ بِالنِّيَّاتِ، وَإِنَّمَا لِكُلِّ امْرِئٍ مَا نَوَى، فَمَنْ كَانَتْ هِجْرَتُهُ إِلَى اللهِ وَرَسُولِهِ، فَهِجْرَتُهُ إِلَى اللهِ وَرَسُولِهِ، وَمَنْ كَانَتْ هِجْرَتُهُ إِلَى دُنْيَا يُصِيبُهَا، أَوْ إِلَى امْرَأَةٍ يَنْكِحُهَا، فَهِجْرَتُهُ إِلَى مَا هَاجَرَ إِلَيْهِ

"Indeed, actions are only by intentions. And every person shall only get what they intend. Thus, whoever's migration is to Allah and His Messenger, then his migration shall be to Allah and His messenger. And whoever's migration is to attain something of the *dunyā* or to marry a woman; then his migration is that for which he has migrated for."

This hadith is unanimously agreed to be *ṣaḥīḥ* (authentic). Its position is immense. It is one of the foundations of *īmān*, and it is also a unique and precious hadith. The scholars of hadith consider this hadith as what is known as *gharīb*, which is translated as strange. It is just terminology. It does not mean that there is something strange about it, but it means that its transmission is only through one chain.

That's why the Imam clarifies by conveying to us what the *Ḥuffāẓ* (the Hadith Masters) have said:

"Because the only person that narrates it from the Prophet ﷺ is ʿOmar ibn al-Khāṭṭāb.

The only person that narrates it from ʿOmar ibn al-Khaṭṭāb is ʿAlqamah ibn Waqqāṣ al-Laythī.

The only narrator who narrates it from ʿAlqamah is Muhammad ibn ʾIbrāhīm al-Taymī.

The only one that narrates it from Muhammad, is Yaḥyā ibn Saʿīd.

One can note at these four levels: there is only one person. That is why it is termed strange. However, after Yaḥyā ibn Saʿīd it disseminated; from him, more than 200 people narrated it, and most of them are imams in their own regards."

This hadith is obviously a very important narration. It is a foundational hadith. It sets the standards for a lot of things. This is why Imam al-Bukhārī narrated this hadith in seven places in his Ṣaḥīḥ with different chains. He related it at the beginning of his book and in the chapters of *īmān*, marriage, freeing slaves,[27] migration, abstaining from deceit, and in the book of oaths. It also has various wordings. One wording is "**Actions are according to intentions**". Here the Imam says that according to Abu Mūsā al-Iṣfahānī, the chain of this specific one is not sound. This is contrasted with "**Indeed, actions are only by intentions**".

27 Known as emancipation

The difference between the two is that the main narration has the word (إنما). It is a small word, but when it is used in a sentence, it implies specificity. So, the version which has the word (إنما) means actions can only be by their intentions. Whereas the other one which doesn't have the (إنما) means actions are by intentions, but it also implies that actions can be without intentions because it is not limiting the sentence that follows it.

An example from the Quran can be seen in the verse in which Allah says:

﴿ إِنَّمَا الْمُؤْمِنُونَ إِخْوَةٌ ﴾

The word (إنما) begins the verse and therefore restricts the following sentences, which is "Believers are brothers", making it read:

﴿Indeed, the believers are nothing but brothers.﴾[28]

If the verse didn't have (إنّما), then it can be read that believers are brothers, but they can also be adversaries.

What is the *Niyyah*?

Basically, intention is the resolve [to act]. It is you wanting to do something: it is your aim and objective. The Prophet ﷺ gives that simple example: if you do *hijrah*, what is your intention? Why are you doing the *hijrah*?

The Prophet ﷺ gives us a simple comparison. The *hijrah*, as an act, is the same. Two people leave their homes, leave their cities, their families and friends, and go to the same destination. They are both

28 Holy Quran; Chapter of the Apartments 49:10

outwardly doing the same action. However, internally one is going for Allah and His Messenger because he's been ordered to perform the *hijrah*; while the other has gone because he is looking for some worldly gain, such as to do business or to marry a woman, etc. The outward action is the same, but the reward will be according to that person's intention.

The Imam says that our Imam Muhammed ibn ʾIdrīs al-Shāfiʿī ﵁ has said that this hadith is a constituent of seventy chapters of fiqh. Meaning that this hadith applies to 70 chapters; and he is saying that there is an application for the intention in every aspect of the fiqh. That is when you consider all aspects of *ʿibādah*, transactions, even when you are joking, the words you say in jest: they all have to rely on the intention or the intended purpose behind it.

In this aspect, the scholars have a general principle: (الأمور بمقاصدها) which is translated as: "Matters are according to their intended purpose". I will explain.

When you say something, we refer to your intention from saying this and not merely the words. For example: *ṣalāh*. You are coming to *ṣalātul ʿIshā*ʾ; you've left your house, and in your mind, you are saying: "I'm going to perform *ʿIshā*ʾ." The time is *ʿIshā*ʾ, and everything is *ʿIshā*ʾ. As you are about to enter the prayer, you say, "I intend to pray *Maghrib*.", then you enter the *ṣalāh*.

In your mind and heart, you want to pray *ʿIshā*ʾ; but you said *Maghrib*. We say your tongue's mistake is forgiven and has no impact on the prayer's validity because your intention was correctly aligned. Hence, it doesn't affect the *ṣalāh*.

However, what does affect the correctness of your *ṣalāh*, is if you came out of the house, and your intention is "I'm coming out to pray *ʿIshā*ʾ!" You intend to pray *ʿIshā*ʾ, and that's what is in your heart and mind. However, the actual timing was *Maghrib* time: it wasn't *'Ishā'*. Then you join the prayer thinking you are praying *'Ishā'*, but actually, it's *Maghrib* prayer. Now here's the problem: your *ṣalāh* is not going to be valid because you intended something different to what it should have been. It wasn't a mere slip of the tongue.

Take another example of buying and selling. If I said to one of you: "Take my phone for £30."

And you replied, "Okay, I accept that."

Then you went ahead and gave me £30, and I gave you the phone. Later on, the following week [or whatever] I said, "Where's my phone?"

And you will say, "No, you sold me this phone for £30! You said, 'take this phone.'

I will respond, "No, I meant for you to hire it for £30 and then give it back to me. And when I said 'take it', I meant 'loan it', not 'sold it'.

So, the word "take it" can imply either meaning. But then what is your intention behind it? Here it becomes a dispute, and then you have to go back and get some arbitration if you cannot agree on the way forward.

Even when a man says some wordings to his wife which are not explicit, we would need to ask him about his intended purpose. Like if he says to her: "Go back to your family!" or "I have no further need of you!" These wordings are not clear in their objective. Did he intend to divorce her with these words, or was he merely instructing her to go away and leave him alone?

So, you can understand Imam al-Shāfi'ī's saying that this hadith enters into 70 chapters of fiqh.

Another saying which Imam al-Shāfi'ī ﷺ said: "This hadith is one-third of knowledge." A similar narration has been narrated by his student Imam Abu AbdUllah Ahmad ibn Muhammad ibn Ḥanbal ﵀.

Imam Abu Bakr al-Bayhaqī ﵀ in his book "The Summary of the Sunan" explains what al-Shāfi'ī meant when he said it is one-third of knowledge:

"What al-Shāfi'ī ﵀ meant about the fact that it is a third of knowledge is derived from the fact that the slave[29] acquires everything by means of his heart, his tongue and his limbs.[30] The 'intention' [with the heart] is one of the divisions of his acquisition, yet it is the most predominant of the three because it is an act of worship in its merit. The other two are not. Words and actions can be perverted by showing off. But this does not affect intention in any way."

Meaning that if you do an action, and you're doing it with the wrong intention, or you're showing off, then you will lose the reward of that action. If you show off your action (either what you say or what you do), you will lose the reward. Whereas, you cannot show off your intention because your intention is hidden; unless you start speaking about it. But, when you utter it, it has now changed to become words.

But if your intention is there, it's not going to be affected because nobody can look at your intention. Whereas they can hear your words, and they can see your actions, and if you are doing it for the wrong reason, you are losing that reward. And that is the summary of the saying of Imam al-Bayhaqī ﵀.

Scholars recommend that one begins all compilations with this hadith. The Imam narrates from Imam Abu Sa'īd Abdul Raḥmān

29 Slave refers to a person, as any person is the slave of Allah.
30 In the original text it reads "intentions" instead of "limbs" which doesn't seem to fit with the words. Then I found other texts which say "limbs"; and one version which reads "fingers" which in the Arabic script is closed to "intentions".

ibn Mahdī 🙵 who said, "If I had compiled a book, I would have started every chapter with this hadith." And he said: "Whoever wants to compile a book, let him begin it with this hadith."

Also, it has been narrated from Imam Abu Sulaymān Ḥamd ibn Muhammad ibn 'Ibrāhīm al-Khaṭṭābī 🙵, at the beginning of his book "al-I'lām" (the commentary on Ṣaḥīḥ al-Bukhārī) that he said, "Our foremost shaykhs recommended that we give precedence to this hadith, 'Indeed, actions are only by intentions' at the beginning of all matters of the *dīn* that are initiated or commenced; as it is generally needed in all aspects of the *dīn*."

The scholars always recommend that if you had a compilation, begin it with this hadith, and we can see Imam al-Bukhārī doing so, as aforementioned.

How al-Bukhārī Begins His Ṣaḥīḥ Compilation
————•••◆•••————

There is a beautiful thing about what Imam al-Bukhārī did when he narrated this hadith at the beginning of his book.

This hadith is made up of four phrases.

1 - Indeed, actions are but by intentions.

2 - Every person shall only get that which he intended.

3 - Whoever's migration is to Allah and His Messenger, then his migration is to Allah and His Messenger

4 - Whoever's migration is for the *dunyā* or marriage, then his migration is what he has migrated to.

When al-Bukhārī narrates the hadith at the beginning of his book, he narrates it by removing the third sentence. Why does he do this? He does this for two main reasons.

The **first** reason is to show a *madhhab* amongst the hadith scholars that the hadith does not have to be narrated in full. The hadith compiler can choose from the hadith and just relate that part of it that is relevant to the subject as long as the sentence is complete. For example, the hadith: "**All of you are from Adam, and Adam is from earth**"[31] is a very short hadith; yet it is part of a very long and powerful hadith which the Prophet ﷺ gave in his farewell *khuṭbah* at ʿArafah. So, by omitting a sentence, he demonstrates that this is permissible, according to a *madhhab* amongst the hadith scholars.

The **second** reason he is doing this is that the third sentence is saying that a person's intention can be for Allah and His Messenger. He removes that phrase to say that if you are thinking that I am inserting this hadith at the beginning of my compilation to show off, by saying that I am compiling this book for Allah and His Messenger, I am removing that. It is almost like a form of etiquette to say that I am not trying to boast that I am doing this for Allah and His Messenger ﷺ. So, he removed that phrase just to remove the potential accusation that some may make, which is that he is showing off and narrating this hadith at the beginning to boast that he is doing this for Allah.

The Imam also tells us about many more similar sayings conveyed to us from the early Predecessors ‎رضي الله عنهم which demonstrate their concern with this hadith. Of it is that the chain of transmission (*'isnād*) of this hadith is very rare and unique among the people of hadith. This is because its chain includes three Followers[32], each one relating the hadith from the other. These three Followers are: Yaḥyā ibn Saʿid al-'Anṣārī, Muhammad ibn 'Ibrāhīm al-Taymī and ʿAlqamah ibn Waqqāṣ ‎رضي الله عنهم.

Although this is marvellous, there are several *ṣaḥīḥ aḥādīth* that have three Followers relating the hadith from one another, and there are even some that include four Followers in the chain. The Hadith

31 *Ṣaḥīḥ:* Hadith narrated by Imams al-Bukhārī and Muslim.
32 Follower (*tābʿī*): someone who has met and studied with a companion of the Prophet ﷺ

Master Abdul Qādir al-Rahāwī ﷺ has gathered them in a section of his book. The Imam has transmitted it and condensed it at the beginning of his commentary on Ṣaḥīḥ al-Bukhārī, where he has also added some others which are similar, making them more than thirty *aḥādīth* of this kind.

This whole chapter, the entire concept of intentions (*niyyāt*), is a big aspect within itself. So, the Imam in this book dwells a little bit more on it, and he further wants to emphasize the whole concept of intentions and *ikhlāṣ*. We have to remember (that at the end of the day), this is the basis of being aware of Allah: The Garden of the Aware, and I am not exaggerating. These are not my words, but these are the words of scholars: "If a person manages to perfect his intention even for a short while, then he will be saved."

Because having that perfect intention, having that *ikhlāṣ*, even if it's just for a moment, is very difficult. So that's why the 'ulamā' continuously hammer it in, because if you just managed to achieve that, then you have achieved your status with Allah ﷻ.

03

The *aḥādīth* around which the sphere of Islam rotates

The Imam takes a little bit of a tangent regarding his book, although we are still in the Garden.

After he mentioned the foundational hadith regarding intentions, he went on to look at what the famous Hadith Master Ibn al-Ṣalāḥ spoke about and had compiled through his efforts. Ibn al-Ṣalāḥ had examined the *aḥādīth* corpus, and from them, he chose the ones which he considered the sphere of Islam rotates around. By this, he means those texts which are the core of most of the teachings within Islam.

The Imam mentioned in the Bustān all the *aḥādīth* chosen by Ibn al-Ṣalāḥ, which amounted to 26. Then, he added three more that he considered are also in this category, bringing them to 29.

What we can deduce from this simple fact, is that this book was compiled before the famous compilation of **40 Hadith Nawawī**, in which Imam al-Nawawī compiled 40[33] *aḥādīth*. This book became widespread amongst the *'ummah* – and has been given much attention in study circles. After mentioning 29 *aḥādīth* here, the Imam would have added a further 13 and then published that work.

33 They are actually 42 *aḥādīth*

I have chosen not to include these 29 *aḥādīth*, as one can refer back to my translation of the Bustān book, and can find them there. Also, because the mention of the *aḥādīth* here is very much a tangent, and so, for the sake of brevity, I have opted to omit them in this book.

04

Attaining *Ikhlāṣ*

After the Imam spoke about the foundational hadith, he concentrates on the section of *ikhlāṣ*. He mentions the saying of Allah ﷻ:

﴿ وَمَا أُمِرُوا إِلَّا لِيَعْبُدُوا اللَّهَ مُخْلِصِينَ لَهُ الدِّينَ ﴾

﴾And they were not commanded except to worship Allah, sincere to Him in their *dīn*.﴿[34]

We addressed this before at the beginning of the book. However, I can add the following:

The word *ḥanīfa* means "inclined". In Arabic linguistics, (ح ن ف) *ḥa-na-fa* is inclined towards something good. This is in contrast to another similar-sounding word which means inclined to something bad, or deviation towards that: and that is the word (ج ن ف) *ja-na-fa*.

The Imam further says that we have been narrated to from Hudhayfah ibn al-Yamān ؓ who said, "I asked the Messenger of Allah ﷺ about *ikhlāṣ*; what is it?

He said, "I asked Jibrīl about *ikhlāṣ*; what is it?"

34 Holy Quran; Chapter of the Clear Proofs 98:5

He said, "I asked the Lord of Might about *ikhlāṣ*; what is it?"

He said, "It is a treasure from My secrets which I safely place in the heart of whom I love among My slaves."

سَـأَلْتُ جبريلَ عَنِ الإخلاص مَا هُوَ؟ فَقَالَ: سَـأَلْتُ رَبَّ العِزَّةِ عَنِ الإِخْلاصِ مَا هُوَ؟ فَقَالَ: سِر من أسراري أودعته قلب من أحب من عبادي

This Hadith is mentioned by the Imam - at the beginning of this section, yet he doesn't comment on the *'isnād*. We know that in terms of transmission, the hadith is not authentic, as has been stated by Hadith Masters al-'Irāqī and Ibn Ḥajar ۞.

Can Weak Hadith be of Any Value?

Here we can take a brief tangent and talk about the concept of what is considered an accepted hadith and rejected hadith. Some people have the mistaken idea that any hadith which is not *ṣaḥīḥ* is of no value. It is mistaken because there's a bigger picture, and it's not as simple as that. There's a bigger concept to understand even with a hadith which is not considered of the rank of *ṣaḥīḥ*, there's still a lot of value in it.

I am not going to dwell long on this matter, as a whole chapter will be needed to discuss this topic.

To begin with, one needs to understand that weak hadith are not all the same. There are several reasons why a hadith may be classified as weak; each reason opens up a topic of discussion among the hadith scholars.

Sometimes a weak hadith is classified as such, because the narrator has poor memory; or his memory weakened with old age. Whilst his memory has weakened, it is possible that what he is narrating is correct, because in this particular instance, his memory hasn't failed him.

Or another example is a hadith narrator who used to rely on his books for narrating, then his books burnt in a house fire. What he narrates after that may easily be classified as weak, yet it may be that he is narrating it correctly.

Other reasons would include someone who is a known liar or fabricator, or a person of poor Islamic standing; or someone who contradicts more reliable narrators.

The basic inference from the general examples above is that hadith Masters were very stringent in classifying hadith narrations, as it would be a grave error to allow incorrect or fabricated words to enter into the hadith corpus which in most instances has a divine element.

However, they understood that a hadith classified as weak may actually be sound; and vice versa. That's why they said, "a fast horse may trip", meaning that even a thoroughbred horse may stumble, and so the best are not protected from erring.

Scholars have differed about the usage of a weak hadith. However, the great Hadith Masters have concluded (among the differing views) that a weak hadith can be narrated and acted upon with the following conditions:

1 - It is in the matter of virtuous actions or morals, and not rulings or *'aqīdah*

2 - That the weakness is not severe

3 - That it comes under a generally accepted category of *'ibādah*

4 - That the weakness is conveyed, and not hidden

5 - That one does not necessarily believe that the Prophet ﷺ said it

With these conditions in mind, one can see the benefit of narrating weak narrations as supporting evidence; not as principles or pillars in the *dīn*. Furthermore, it is possible that a weak narration may become sound if it has multiple good chains.

Meaning of *Ikhlāṣ*

Despite this hadith not being authentic in its transmission, its meaning is wondrous. It is stating that *ikhlāṣ* is unlike many things, for it is essentially a gift from Allah ﷻ. It is a gift from Allah, which He bestows upon whom He chooses from His slaves. It's much like *hidāyah* (guidance). At the elementary level, *hidāyah*, which is Allah's guidance, is a gift from Him. On a higher level, we have different aspects of guidance. So, when Allah guides you to Islam, that's one level. And when He guides you to be amongst the people who do good deeds and acts of righteousness, that's another level. Then, you have the guidance of when Allah chooses you to be amongst those who (for example) pray in the night; that's another gift that Allah gives to a select few. And when you are amongst those who have *ikhlāṣ* which is the absolute sincerity, that's a further gift from Allah ﷻ, meaning that all these things are essentially gifts that Allah ﷻ will bless in accordance to what He sees and knows.

The Imam then proceeds to bring some of the sayings of the different Imams. He starts by mentioning some of the words from Imam al-Qushayrī, who said: "*Ikhlāṣ* is to single out the Truth [Allah] in obedience with resolve. It is when one intends with one's obedience to come close to Allah the Exalted, over anything beneath that from flattery for the sake of a creature; or to attain praise with people or to be awarded commendation from the creation, or any meaning other than the proximity to Allah, the Exalted."

He is defining for us what *ikhlāṣ* is all about because we all understand *ikhlāṣ* as being sincere, but what does that really mean?

The following sayings are all about how to understand it more comprehensively. Through making mention of different definitions, the concept becomes enriched. As scholars say, "With examples, the wordings become clearer."

'Ustādh al-Qushayrī said that *ikhlāṣ* is when you single out *al-Haqq* meaning Allah ﷻ with your obedience and with your intention: with your determination to go towards Him with that obedience. So, singling out Allah with obedience and firm resolution: you intend Him, and that you want - with your good deeds and obedience – to come closer to Allah ﷻ not to anyone else. You don't want to achieve anything else, whether trying to come closer to any of His creation, trying to get some sort of praise from others, or getting some sort of status, title or mention, or any of those meanings. It might be that you are not trying to get any material object or any payment; but just trying to get some sort of praise, like somebody saying, "that's well done" or "that's really good"; that is even more dangerous because it is a hidden thing, unlike money or material gain.

If somebody invited you to give a speech or teach a course, and you are paid for this, you might say, "Look, I charge this much," then it becomes clear that you are taking money in exchange for this task. It is evident. However, when you're not doing that, and you are saying, "No, actually I will do it for Allah", but what you want is that people would say something nice to you or praise you. If that is your intention in doing that, then you have lost that *ikhlāṣ*. And that goes for any action. You can measure this on any action, whether it is helping people out, even standing up for the truth, or whatever action it may be.

The Imam goes on to explain another of al-Qushayrī's saying, which is a briefer explanation of *ikhlāṣ*: "It is correct to say: *ikhlāṣ* is to beware of the observation of people."

That's as simple as *ikhlāṣ* can be: to beware of the observation of people. So you are no longer observing how others are observing you; that is how you are trying to achieve that sincerity. You're trying to do it for Allah ﷻ, so you're no longer looking at people, whether they're smiling, whether they're praising you, or whether they're angry at you. You can see the very nature of how it is; about really trying to keep away from any aspect where there is involvement in that regard.

The Imam goes on to mention another meaning of the word *ikhlāṣ*. This is from Abu 'Alī al-Daqqāq, who was the shaykh and father-in-law of al-Qushayrī رحمه الله.

'Ustādh Abu 'Alī al-Daqqāq said, "*Ikhlāṣ* is to beware of the observation of the creation. Truthfulness is the cleansing from the noticing of the self. Thus, the sincere person has no showing off; and the truthful one has no admiration for himself."

What al-Daqqāq said is similar to what al-Qushayrī said: to beware of the creation looking onto you. However, the other aspect that al-Daqqāq mentioned is the description of what *ṣidq* (truthfulness) is, which is to be purified from observing the self. In addition to not watching others, you are not observing yourself and what you are gaining from carrying out a particular action. And that means even when you're doing the action, you're not looking at what you are attaining for your self. The first part is to ignore people. The second part is to ignore what you are trying to achieve through the *nafs*. Because even with good deeds, your *nafs* will get something out of it; even that feeling of "Hey, aren't I so good!" could lead one to a path of self-admiration. That's why *ikhlāṣ* is invaluable and rare to achieve. Even when you feel you're getting satisfaction from this action, there could be an element of untruth in your *ikhlāṣ*.

For example, you prayed *qiyām al-layl*. You got up in the night; nobody's watching you, nobody's aware of you. You are doing it alone: between you and Allah. If you feel content that you're doing this *ʿībādah*, then that happiness might come from Allah ﷻ. But if you have a feeling of satisfaction that: "I've really achieved something here" and you feel on top of the world, you think that you've done something really great. That feeling of doing something great might be an element of untruth because now it's like you are gaining something else apart from the pleasure of Allah from it.

It is similar to *rīyāʾ*, although *rīyāʾ* is usually related to other people. So, it's much more nuanced than this because there is nobody here, nobody is observing you, nobody sees you, it's just between you and yourself. So, in yourself, if you feel so satisfied, you've lost the finer element of *ikhlāṣ*, because *ikhlāṣ* is about not getting something for yourself.

If you're happy and that happiness comes with the contentment that you've done something good, then that is good; a sign of *īmān*, as opposed to admiring yourself and feeling satisfied that you've actually achieved something great here. It is very delicate, and that's why it isn't easy initially for somebody to get that fine-tuning because here we're talking about *ikhlāṣ* we're trying to have the correct *niyyah.* That's why he says there is *'ujb* (feeling of pride). Because when you feel that you've achieved something for yourself and it's not for Allah, you are in danger of not being true. You have to be careful; it's very easy to say, "I'm not doing it for anybody!", but it's harder to say "I'm not even doing it for myself!". Because if you're doing it for yourself, you're not doing it for Allah. So that is the kind of thing that you have to achieve.

The Imam goes on to say that we have been narrated to from Abu Ya'qūb al-Sūsī ﵁ who said, 'Whenever they observe in their "sincerity" that they have Sincerity, then their "sincerity" is in need of Sincerity!'

It is a lovely saying which means that whenever someone finds or feels or observes that he has *ikhlāṣ:* he is noticing his *ikhlāṣ*, then his *ikhlāṣ* needs ***ikhlāṣ***! His sincerity needs to be purified. There is no sincerity because he sees himself, and he is happy with himself. This is something called *'ujb*, which is to be delighted with oneself.

Then he says that we have been narrated to from the noble master Dhu al-Nūn al-Miṣrī ﵁ who said: "Three [things] are from the signs of *ikhlāṣ*:

1 - Praise and disparage from the general people are the same.

2 - To abandon noticing the actions in the actions.

3 - Seeking the reward of the action in the Hereafter."

The **first** one is that it is equal for him whether people praise him or disgrace him: he doesn't care. And for him, it's the same whether people speak highly of him or they speak low of him. Why is it the same? Because he is not doing it for them. So, he is not seeking their praise, nor is he concerned that they think bad of him.

The **second** one is to abandon seeing the actions in the actions. That means that when a person is doing actions, he is not observing the intricacy of those actions, and therefore he is not happy with the actions, per se. Again, this goes back to what we said before that one should not be delighted by one's actions. He gets on with the work, and he does the acts of *'ibādah* without attempting to do good for the sake of the actions, and it's one of the finer points of trying to achieve that.

Thirdly: to attain or to try to look at the rewards of the action in the *Ākhirah*. So again, it's about anticipating the rewards. It is not looking at the action itself and trying to see what you are doing. Instead, it is more about the heart and where the heart is in all of this.

Another definition is from Abu 'Othmān al-Mughrabī ؛ who said: "*Ikhlāṣ* is forgetting to regard the creation by constantly regarding the Creator."

This definition addresses one's mindset. If you are continuously and continually thinking about Allah ﷻ and what pleases or displeases Him, you will ignore or abandon what people think. *Ikhlāṣ* is to reach that level when you measure matters according to Allah's standards, not the creation.

There is another saying that "the people who have reached a level of truthfulness, have not reached it because of the actions that they have done, but rather about what's inside them." That's something that we will dwell more on *in shā'* Allah.

Then, the Imam continues narrating useful insights; he mentions that of Hudhayfah al-Mar'ashī ؛ who said: "*Ikhlāṣ* is that the slave's actions outwardly and inwardly are equal."

Ikhlāṣ is when your actions - and this is something I think is easy to understand - outwardly and inwardly are equal: they are the same. Meaning that when you act alone or in front of people, it's the same: you don't adjust your actions.

You know, when you are praying in the *masjid*, you might pray with more humility. You are more focused, or at least, it appears like that. You may take a little bit longer with your *rukū'* and *sujūd* and so on. However, when you are by yourself, you are rushing the prayer. So, this disparity goes against *ikhlāṣ*; for *ikhlāṣ* is when you are doing the same, whether you are in front of people or by yourself.

The Imam narrates from the Noble Master Fuḍayl ibn 'Iyāḍ ؆ who said: "Leaving an action for the sake of people is showing off. Doing an action for the sake of humankind is *shirk* (associating with Allah). *Ikhlāṣ* is that Allah protects you from both."

When you leave actions for the sake of others, this is *rīyā'*; it's a form of showing off or a form of pride. When you do things for people, it's *shirk*, for you are not doing it for Allah; you are doing it for other than Allah. And *ikhlāṣ* is when Allah protects you from either of these two. You do things for people that is *shirk*. If you leave something for the sake of people, that's also a form of *shirk* because *rīyā'* is minor *shirk*.

How does one leave things for the sake of people? For example, you want to donate. In your mind, you are going to give charity. However, when you want to contribute, you think, "I am not going to give this charity because people might observe me giving!" So, you stopped the donation for the sake of the people. Another example is with regards to prayer. You might typically be praying at a certain length, and you are praying an extended prayer. But, then you felt that people are observing you, so you think, "I'll just shorten my *ṣalāh*, as others are watching me". So, when you abandon an act because of the people, this also contradicts *ikhlāṣ* because you should not be doing it for the people in the first place. Here, I mention an amusing narration to demonstrate this. It is narrated that once, a shaykh was in the rear of the *masjid* teaching his students about *ṣalāh*. Whilst he was doing that, a man entered and started praying near the front end. The shaykh observed this man's prayer, and it was beautiful and demonstrated what he was trying to explain to his students. So, he said to them, "Your *ṣalāh* has to be good outwardly and inwardly. It has to have focus: much like that man who is praying there."

The students observed him silently.

After the man finished the prayer, he turned round to the shaykh and remarked, "Not only that: but I am fasting as well!"

Quite a bemusing incident, but demonstrates how easily one can fall into the aspect of showing off.

I remember a friend of mine, who came to visit me in my home, one Thursday. After a short while, I offered him some refreshments: "Tea or Coffee?"

He looked at me, almost offended, saying: "It's Thursday, today!"

I nodded my head, understanding what he implied, which is that "I fast every Thursday: how could you not know that!"

A sentence of three or four words, but look at the potential it has to destroy the hidden act of fasting that day, and probably some others. I say "potential" because only Allah knows the consequence of such words. Especially, when you consider one of the righteous people who used to fast every day, and not even his family would know about it. As he left for work, he would take with him two loaves of bread to give his family the impression that he is having lunch. He would then donate those loaves to some poor person as an act of charity. At work, if they asked him about eating, he would tell them that he will eat when he gets home. And so, for years, he would conceal his fasting even from his family.

And that's why it is good practice not to ask someone whether they are fasting or not. It may be hard on occasions, but one should avoid asking to prevent a hidden act from becoming outward.

The Noble Master Abu Muhammad Sahl ibn AbdUllah al-Tustarī ﵀ was asked: "What is the most difficult thing on the *nafs*?"

He said: "*Ikhlāṣ*; as in it, there is no share for it."

The concept of the *nafs* is essential for a person who seeks to be aware in the Garden of the Aware. Aware people are aware of their *nafs*; how to look after it and how to deal with it. The *nafs* is something that Allah ﷻ has mentioned many times in the Quran. It can be translated as one's alter ego: it is another person who is you, but it's not you. It is like you are two entities; there's you who's trying to control your other you: your *nafs*. The *nafs* is usually trying to come out of control. It wants to take charge and satisfy itself in achieving its needs. It is eager to follow desires and realise certain prestigious things. It wants people to acknowledge it. It wants to feed its fill. It wants, it wants, it wants. And you, as an individual, have to tame your *nafs*. So, there's a lot of discussion about the *nafs* within the understanding of *ikhlāṣ* and that's why Allah ﷻ said:

﴿ وَأَمَّا مَنْ خَافَ مَقَامَ رَبِّهِ وَنَهَى النَّفْسَ عَنِ الْهَوَى
فَإِنَّ الْجَنَّةَ هِيَ الْمَأْوَى ﴾

﴿As for the one who fears the standing in front of his Lord, and he forbids the *nafs* from the desire. Then *al-Jannah* will be the place of abode.﴾[35]

You can see here, Allah ﷻ is clearly showing the contrast between two entities. The first entity is the one who fears standing in front of Allah (meaning on the Day of Judgement). The second entity is the *nafs* which the first entity has to deny it from what it lusts.

35 Holy Quran; Chapter of Those who Extract 79:40-41

The *nafs* is inside you, so how do you control that *nafs*? Felicity is founded in understanding and mastering this concept; we will talk about that *in shā'* Allah in due course.

So, al-Tustarī was asked what is the hardest thing on the *nafs*? What is the most challenging thing for the *nafs*?

He responded: "*Ikhlāṣ*."

Why? Because the *nafs* has nothing to gain from *ikhlāṣ*. Because the *nafs* has no share with *ikhlāṣ*. Remember how we defined *ikhlāṣ*: there can be no self-admiration. Even to be happy and satisfied with the action, means that the *nafs* is attaining something. So, *ikhlāṣ* is when even that is not happening.

The Imam narrated from Yūsuf ibn al-Ḥusayn ﵀ who said: "The most magnificent thing in this life is *ikhlāṣ*."

From Abu 'Othmān al-Mughrabī ﵀ who said, "The *ikhlāṣ* of the common people is that which the *nafs* has no share in. The *ikhlāṣ* of the elite is what is bestowed on them, not [what happens] by them. Acts of obedience appear from them while they are disconnected from them. They do not 'look' at them, nor do they reckon them."

What Abu 'Othmān is saying is that the basic, general public kind of *ikhlāṣ* is the one which we are talking about: which is that the *nafs* has no share in it. But then there is an *ikhlāṣ* of the elite. These are the people who are special; they are the ones who are chosen. They are people who have a higher class of *'ibādah* and a higher grade of *ikhlāṣ*. Their higher grade of *ikhlāṣ* is that even when they are doing the actions, it is like they are not even thinking about the whole concept of the *ikhlāṣ* and it's not even on their mind.

Remember that when you are looking at your *ikhlāṣ*, and you are happy with your *ikhlāṣ*, then your *ikhlāṣ* is in need of *ikhlāṣ*. So, these people are not even thinking about *ikhlāṣ*. They are doing the actions, and in their mind is that this is already for Allah ﷻ. It is like they are entirely in a different world, for they are completely segregated from the whole concept of action. They are not looking at the actions. They are not scrutinizing their actions, rather it's just happening for them. It has become natural to them. And these are the elite: a special category of people. All the good deeds that occur from them; it's like they are completely segregated from these good deeds. It's a high level, and I think we shouldn't dwell too much on it because we're trying to concern ourselves with the general public *ikhlāṣ*, which in itself is already a task to achieve.

But why does it seem that sincerity is hard? The answer is because *ikhlāṣ* is rare. It is not easy to achieve, and it is something that a person tries to acquire or wants to achieve. But it becomes difficult because you have to leave everything and everyone at the door. Nothing for the people, nothing for yourself, even the basics. So, it becomes a struggle. That struggle - like anything - with dedication, patience and practice, will slowly, but surely, come to the individual if he were to persevere.

He said that one of the rarest things and one of the most precious things to find in this life is *ikhlāṣ*; as aforementioned, it is not very easy to achieve. It needs that dedication and all the narrations that we have spoken about before, show how hard it is.

Sayings about *Ikhlāṣ*

Now, the Imam narrates some of the scholars' opinions about what kind of things would a person attain, if he manages to have *ikhlāṣ*? We have to understand that this is not formulated by a hadith or confirmed by a saying of the Prophet ﷺ. Instead, the opinions narrated are based on experience over time. All these are prescriptions by *'Ulamā'* who would have experienced certain things, and they would have assessed certain matters, and that is where they would make these suggestions.

For example, let us consider the concept of medicine and *ruqyah*. Allah ﷻ has told us that the Quran is *shifāʾ*, for it is one of the modes of medicine. He said:

﴿ وَنُنَزِّلُ مِنَ ٱلْقُرْءَانِ مَا هُوَ شِفَآءٌ وَرَحْمَةٌ لِّلْمُؤْمِنِينَ ﴾

﴾And We send down of the Quran that which is healing and mercy for the believers.﴿[36]

We know that the Quran is *shifāʾ*, but how does the healing of the Quran work? What are the verses that will remedy specific illnesses? How is it to be read? All these things are down to a particular element, and those certain elements are related to trial. That is because the Prophet ﷺ only mentioned to us some aspects of it, and the majority he did not. An example of which is the hadith relating to the Chapter of al-Fātiḥah (Chapter 1).

Abu Saʿīd al-Khudrī ؓ said: "A group of the Prophet's ﷺ Companions went on a journey until they ended up at one of the Arab tribes. The Companions sought hospitality, but they were denied. The chief of that tribe was bitten, so his people sought all types of cures for him, but these didn't benefit him. Some of them said, 'Why don't you go to those people who have come. It may be that they have something.'

So, they approached them and said, 'Our chief has been bitten, and we sought for him all things, but nothing benefitted him. So, do you have anything that may help him?'

One of them said, 'Yes. I have some cure. But, by Allah, we sought your hospitality, and you didn't host us. So, I will not heal him for you until you appoint for us a payment.' So, they agreed to

36 Holy Quran; Chapter of The Night Journey 17:82

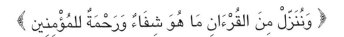

be given a flock of sheep. The Companion went to him and started to spit on his wound and recite *surat al-Fātiḥah*[37]. So, it was like he was released from being tied down; he got up walking, free from any symptoms.

So, they gave them their payment. Some of the Companions said, 'Divide it!'

The healer said, 'Let's not do anything until we return to the Prophet ﷺ and ask him, and he can look into what we did.'

So, they came back to the Messenger of Allah ﷺ and related to him what happened.

So, he ﷺ said, **"And how did you know it is a *ruqyah*!"**

Then he said as he laughed, **"You have done right. Divide it, and give me a share with you!"**[38]

Meaning that how did you know that this chapter can be used in that way? So that was like an *ijtihād* (an opinion) from the Companion; and the Prophet ﷺ affirmed it.

Similarly, one can extend that to a broader perspective. We know, for example, that the Prophet ﷺ said:

فِي الحَبَّةِ السَّوْداءِ شِفاءٌ مِن كُلِّ داءٍ، إلَّا السَّامَ

"The black seed is a medicine for all illnesses except death."[39]

But how does that work? It is open to trial and error, investigation and research, because it doesn't mean that you just eat the black seed, and it will cure any disease. Rather, it must be taken or used in a certain way. Similarly, with the Quran, you will have that same thing. Certain verses read in a certain way is related to how people have experienced their effect.

37 Holy Quran; Chapter of The Opening 1
38 *Ṣaḥīḥ:* Hadith narrated by Imams al-Bukhārī and Muslim
39 *Ṣaḥīḥ:* Hadith narrated by Imam al-Bukhārī

You can also see another example from Shaykh Ibn Taymiyyah, who is quite a literalist in his Islamic and academic approach, and he'd probably be one of the people who would be very explicitly saying: "Where are the hadith and the evidence?"

Yet he recommended that when a woman is giving birth to recite Surah al-Zalzalah[40], as that would make the delivery easy. His student Ibn al-Qayyim also adopted this view. However, if you were to ask them where is the evidence from the Quran or Sunna, then there is no authentic narration; you may get the reply: "It has been tried and tested!"

So, it is more about the experience of how certain verses may be used in a certain way and obviously, with the permission of Allah ﷻ, the cure would happen. That's why it is vital to understand this because some Muslims (especially the literalists among them) are always looking for a specific hadith; and it must be *ṣaḥīḥ*; and if there isn't one, then it's all cancelled. And this is not how the *'ulamā'* of the past practised. For they considered things and indeed, there were elements of trial, research, etc. Whether it is related to medicine or related to other aspects. I gave that as an introduction to what we are going to read now.

This is what the Imam related from Makḥūl, a student of AbdUllah ibn 'Abbās, ؓ who said: "A person who has *ikhlāṣ* or practises *ikhlāṣ* absolutely for 40 days, then the springs of wisdom will sprout from his heart and his tongue."

Meaning that the fruit of *ikhlāṣ* is that he will have these kinds of things. He will be able to say things that are wise and insightful. This is not something to be astonished by because we know that the source of *'ilm* and *hikmah* is Allah, and not all knowledge can be attained through learning. It is true that a vast vault of knowledge

40 Holy Quran; Chapter of the Quake 99

can only be accessed through education, but not all knowledge can be attained through learning. That is why Allah ﷻ said:

﴿ وَاتَّقُوا اللَّهَ، وَيُعَلِّمُكُمُ اللَّهُ ﴾

﴾Fear Allah, and Allah will teach you.﴿[41]

Sometimes, somebody might have an individual connection with Allah ﷻ, which is a gift from Him the Almighty; which can be a key to an aspect of knowledge that nobody else has been given before. That is why you will see that in every generation throughout Islamic history, there have been people who produced *tafsīr* of the Quran (as an example). Starting from the time of the Companions ﷺ till this day, there are people who write *tafsīr*. There are people who publish their understanding and their comprehension of the Quran. If *tafsīr* was a restricted, limited science, meaning that the verses could only have one meaning, then the *tafsīr* would have been finalised maybe after the third or fourth generation of Muslims, because everybody would have known the *tafsīr*, nothing new to add. However, you will find that throughout time, there might be someone who finds some specific aspect and sees something in a verse, which nobody else has observed before. That person may understand the verse in a certain way, and this is the whole instruction of reflection:

﴿ أَفَلَا يَتَدَبَّرُونَ الْقُرْءَانَ، وَلَوْ كَانَ مِنْ عِندِ غَيرِ اللَّهِ
لَوَجَدُوا فِيهِ اخْتِلَافًا كَثِيرًا ﴾

﴾Do they not reflect upon the Quran? And had been from other than Allah, they would have found in it much disparity.﴿[42]

41 Holy Quran; Chapter of the Cow 2:282
42 Holy Quran; Chapter of the Women 4:82

This is a clear instruction to continue to reflect upon the Quran. And if Allah ﷻ chooses; it could be that somebody who lives in this era and this society can understand the Quran in a particular context that has never been understood before. And that understanding could be valid, because the Quran's wonders never cease, as was conveyed by ʿAlī ibn Abi Ṭālib ؓ from the Prophet ﷺ who said:

ولا تنقضي عجائبُه

"…its bewilderments will never cease…"[43]

Meaning that it will continue to bewilder people with the things that emanate from it.

Here I wanted to mention some verses[44] which I was reflecting on. It is the saying of Allah:

﴿ وَالسَّمَاءِ وَمَا بَنَـٰهَا ، وَالْأَرْضِ وَمَا طَحَـٰهَا ﴾

It has been translated as an oath by Allah, swearing by the Sky and by Himself who built it; and by the Earth and by Himself (again) who spread it. However, upon my reflection, I came to the conclusion that whilst the pronoun (مَا) in Arabic can be used to refer to Allah, it isn't the pronoun of choice. Rather the pronoun (مَن) is more related to persons, as opposed to inanimate things. And so, it appeared to me that the pronoun (مَا) was indeed referring to the process in which the Sky and the Earth have been created. So, Allah is swearing by the Sky and by the magnificent process which has brought it and the Earth into being. I mention this here, as I am not aware of anyone else[45] who has come to this understanding. This understanding is indicative of the greatness of the process of the creation, as much as the items which are created.

43 *Ḍaʿīf*: Hadith narrated by Imams Ahmad and al-Dārimī
44 Holy Quran; Chapter of the Sun 91:5-6
45 Not being aware does not mean that there isn't someone who may have said that

On this note, we can understand how Makḥūl has derived his saying.

Furthermore, Sahl al-Tustarī ﷺ said: "Whoever abstains from the *dunyā* for forty days, truthful and sincere from his heart, then the gifts[46] will appear for him. And for whomever they don't appear, then he has been denied truthfulness in his abstinence."

It was said to Sahl at-Tustarī, "How do the noble gifts appear for a person?"

He said, "He takes what he wants, as he wants and from wherever he wants."

These people are honoured by certain honourable gifts. These gifts are known as *karāmāt*. The *'aqīdah* of Ahl al-Sunnah regarding these gifts is that *karāmāt* are like miracles that Allah can give to any one of His special people. But they are given not for the reason of challenging people. This is in contrast to the Prophets, who are given *karāmāt* and are given *mu'jizāt*. A *mu'jizah* is a miracle that is meant to challenge others, and linguistically, it is about disabling or incapacitating the opponent from rejecting this miracle.

We will dwell more on that towards the end of this book, as there is a whole chapter dedicated to this topic.

Carrying on with Sahl al-Tustarī said, in which he summarises for us the whole concept of *ikhlāṣ*: "The intellectuals looked into the meaning of *ikhlāṣ*, and they did not find anything[47] other than this: 'That one's movement and stillness in private and in public is for Allah, The Exalted, alone. The self, nor the desire, nor the world are mingled with it."

According to Newton's first law of motion, a body can either be static or moving, as you can't be anything else. So, his motion, or his stillness, in secret or in public, they are all for Allah ﷻ. It is

46 The actual word is "*karāmāt*" which we will explain later on
47 Meaning anything more succinct

not mixed, disturbed, polluted or impurified by anything; neither the desire or the *nafs*; or anything related to *dunyā*. So, basically, everything that you are doing, whether you are moving or you are still, in secret or in public, everything is for our Allah ﷻ and not mixed with anything.

Lastly in this section of *ikhlāṣ*, he mentions another phrase from another one of the righteous people: al-Sarī al-Saqaṭī ؓ who said: "Don't do anything for [the sake of] people, nor leave anything for their sake, nor give anything for their sake and don't reveal anything for their sake."

Now somebody might say this is a very mean attitude: not to do anything for people. Obviously, it does not mean that you should not help people or serve them. But what he means is don't do anything for the sake of people, as aforementioned. Don't let people be the reason for your actions. So, don't do anything for the sake of people, and don't leave anything for their sake. Basically, if you're going to do something, do it for Allah ﷻ; if you're not going to do something, don't do it for Allah ﷻ. As for not leaving anything for people and not giving them anything, it means that, within the same context, you shouldn't be doing something for their sake. If you're going to give them for their sake then you're going to lose out on the reward that could be anticipated with Allah ﷻ.

Allah says:

﴿ وَيُطْعِمُونَ الطَّعَامَ عَلَى حُبِّهِ ﴾

⟪They give the food out of love for Him.⟫[48]

One of the *tafsīr* of the word "*ḥubih*" is for the love of Allah; they feed food to others.

---

48 Holy Quran; Chapter of the Human 76:8

﴿ إِنَّمَا نُطْعِمُكُمْ لِوَجْهِ اللَّهِ لَا نُرِيدُ مِنكُمْ جَزَاءً وَلَا شُكُورًا ﴾

﴿We are feeding you for the sake of Allah. We do not desire from you any compensation or gratitude.﴾[49]

Therefore, when you give, don't give anything to people for the sake of people; if you provide to others, seeking their reward, then if they do reward you, that will be your payment. If they say, "thank you!" or they do something good in return, then that will be your payment. You will not get anything from Allah ﷻ. If you do it for Allah ﷻ, Allah will reward you, and perhaps, the people will be grateful to you, also.

Again, within the same meaning, you need to keep your actions to yourself; don't reveal your actions to others. You don't need to tell them what you are doing and how good of a Muslim you are, and how great you are, because by doing that, you are potentially going to lose the reward from Allah ﷻ because you have allowed the *nafs* to get a share. This share may be in the form of applause or congratulations, or gratitude. So it's a very fine rope to walk upon.

Shaytān's role in voiding the human's sincerity

Imam al-Nawawī says that Ahmad ibn Abi al-Ḥawārī said in the Book of "al-Zuhd": I heard some of our companions, I think it was Abu Sulaymān – referring to al-Dārānī - ؓ who said: "'Iblīs has a devil named 'Mutaqāḍ': he pursues the son of Adam for [up to] twenty years trying to make him expose his secret actions and to bring them out in public, so that he loses the reward difference between doing it in secret and in public."

The different *shayāṭīn* have different roles to play in their enmity

49 Holy Quran; Chapter of the Human 76:9

to the humans. This *shaytān* has a specific role, which is to get you, the son of Adam to announce your actions. So, what he does is he removes the barrier of what is private and public; and when that happens there is more of a likelihood that you will lose the benefit of that secret act, as the reward that is done in secret is usually greater than the one done in public, although both of them can be good.

Allah ﷻ talks about giving:

﴿ إِنْ تُبْدُوا الصَّدَقَاتِ فَنِعِمَّا هِيَ وَإِنْ تُخْفُوهَا وَتُؤْتُوهَا الْفُقَرَاءَ فَهُوَ خَيْرٌ لَكُمْ وَيُكَفِّرُ عَنْكُمْ مِنْ سَيِّئَاتِكُمْ ﴾

﴾If you reveal your charities, then it is good thing. However, if you make it secret and give it to the paupers, then it is better for you.﴿[50]

There are people who will give money in private and public; and both have their own times. There is an encouragement there; but usually that which is done in secret is better, as it is less likely to attract the self. If you think about the hadith:

يَعجَبُ ربُّك مِن راعي غَنَم في رأسِ الشَّظِيَّة للجبلِ يؤَذِّنُ بالصلاةِ ويُصلِّي، فيقولُ اللهُ: انظُروا إلى عَبْدي هذا يؤَذِّنُ ويُقيمُ، يَخافُ مني قد غفَرْتُ له، وأَدخَلْتُه الجَنَّةَ

"Your Lord is delighted to see a shepherd on the top of a mountain. He calls the *ʾadhān* and establishes prayer. So Allah says, "Look at My slave here: He makes the *ʾadhān* and establishes the *ṣalāh*. He fears Me. I have forgiven him and admitted him al *al-Jannah*."[51]

50 Holy Quran; Chapter of the Cow 2:271
51 *Ṣaḥīḥ:* Hadith narrated by Imam Ahmad and al-Nasāʾī

And this is one further example of the importance of keeping action secret.

Because the Shayṭān wants the human to lose out on any matter; he tries to make him lose the reward of the good action, by trying to corrupt his internal.

05

Ṣidq - Truthfulness

Now we will talk about another aspect of *ikhlāṣ*, which is not usually something that many are formally acquainted with in terms of terminology, and that is *al-ṣidq*: truthfulness. Often, we associate the word *al-ṣidq* with a person's honesty with their tongue. You say somebody *ṣadaqa* (صدق) when they speak the truth. But here the definitions that the Imam mentioned in *Bustan al-ʿĀrifīn* is more about a broader and deeper meaning of *ṣidq* which is the truthfulness in terms of your attitude, your character, your heart and your sincerity. So, it's the wider perspective of *ṣidq*.

The Imam says, quoting the Quran:

﴿ يَـٰٓأَيُّهَا ٱلَّذِينَ ءَامَنُوا۟ ٱتَّقُوا۟ ٱللَّهَ وَكُونُوا۟ مَعَ ٱلصَّـٰدِقِينَ ﴾

﴾O You who believe fear Allah and be with those who are truthful.﴿[52]

As we will explain now that this truthfulness has that broader meaning.

The Imam says that we have been narrated to from the authority of 'Ustādh al-Qushayrī ﷺ who said: "Truth is the pillar of the matter; and with it: lies its completeness; and in it: is its order."

52 Holy Quran; Chapter of Repentance 9:119

The word "matter" here refers to Islam, and this is similar to what the Prophet ﷺ said:

رَأسُ الأَمرِ الإِسلام

"The head of all matters is Islam."[53]

So *ṣidq* is that pillar of Islam, and with *ṣidq*, you will get that completion. With *ṣidq*, you will have the correct organisation and order that comes with it.

And then he said that he [also] said: "The least [level of] honesty is the equality of the private and the public."

And that means that part of being truthful is that you do not show something other than this. And you can see what kind of character this would be. If a person shows something outwardly, but his reality is something else, the term for this kind of person is a *munāfiq* (hypocrite). Hypocrisy is different kinds. There is *nifāq* of *īmān*: which is when you have disbelief inside your heart, yet you display Islam outwardly. There is the *nifāq* of *'amal*, and that is when you carry actions are contrary to your belief. You might be a sloppy Muslim, but you are showing something else. There is *nifāq* of practice: which is when you are full of contradictions: when you speak, you lie; you make empty promises and so on. So, the least form of *ṣidq* is that a person has equality in their outward and what they are doing secretly.

And he said that we have been narrated to from Sahl (may Allah Almighty have mercy on him) who said: "The fragrance of honesty will not be smelt by a slave who has flattered himself or others."

Meaning the one who is distant from *ṣidq* (because to smell something, you have to be in close proximity to it) is someone who has flattered himself or others, indicative of someone who

53 *Ṣaḥīḥ:* Hadith narrated by Imams al-Tirmidhi, ibn Mājah and al-Nasā'ī

has compromised his state; and we will understand later on what that means.

The Imam says that we have been narrated to from Dhu al-Nūn ﵀ that he said: "Truth is the sword of Allah: it is not placed on anything, without cutting it."

Meaning that *ṣidq* is a form of a reality check. It really puts things into perspective. When a person wants to be truthful, he will show and expose things as they indeed are.

Then the Imam said that we have been narrated to from the Glorious Master, the knowledgeable Imam al-Ḥārith al-Muḥāsabī ﵀ who said: "The truthful is the one who does not care if all of his reputation goes out of the hearts of the creation for the sake of the goodness of his own heart.

This person does not like to inform people about [even] an ant's eggs' weight of his good deeds. In addition, he doesn't dislike that people notice the bad aspects of his actions, for his dislike is evidence that he loves his eminence with them; and this is not the sincerity of those who are truthful."

That truthful person does not care or is not bothered even if all respect and all honour that people hold for him go out of their hearts for the sake that he corrects his own heart.

People have status in front of others. People look at others, and they'll say, "*Ma shā' Allah*", "this guy is an imam", "this guy is a shaykh!" "this guy is this, that guy is that!". The person who is truthful - this goes back to what we talked about before about being equal in the eyes of people whether they praise him or not - is not concerned if he loses all the regards from people, as long as it is for his own benefit. And that's also the more significant meaning of *ikhlāṣ*, because we said that you don't do things for the sake of people. You are not concerned about the regard people have for you, rather you're concerned about the regards Allah ﷻ has for you.

And then al-Ḥārith ؓ goes on to say that he will not love or he does not love, does not care, does not want that people look at – even – a small aspect of his good works. Again, part of that is he doesn't care about whether people see his good works or not: this is showing sincerity, because at the end of the day, why is he doing this good work? It is only for Allah ﷻ. And if you are doing the good work, and at the same time, you want other people to see what you've done, and to praise you, then there is an aspect of untruthfulness with yourself.

Al-Ḥārith goes on to say that at the same time that he does not want people to look at the good deeds, he also does not dislike or is not worried that they look at his bad deeds. Because if he dislikes that people see his bad deeds, then this is an indicator that he desires to have higher regards by them. Because obviously, if they see him doing something bad, or maybe they do not quite see when he does of good deeds, he may lose that respect in their eyes. And therefore, he is now thinking about the people, not about Allah ﷻ; this is not from the *ikhlāṣ* of the *Ṣiddīqīn* (truthful).

Now there is a finer point here as well (which is an aside) because a person who does something bad should not be happy that people see him doing something bad. Let's say if a believer's practice is that he is unhappy if he does something bad and is aware of it; he's not proud to have committed a wrongdoing. And so, he wouldn't be glad that other people witness his wrongdoing. There is a fine line between people who are unhappy and those who do not care about doing sin. The people who commit sin, they do something wrong and they do not care about doing them. This kind of people don't care about the sin itself, so they are not ashamed to sin in front of others and do not care.

What al-Ḥārith is talking about here is that if somebody does something which is bad and he despises that act, he knows it is *ḥarām* and it is wrong; yet he does not want people to see it for the sake that they do not think less of him. So, he does not fall into the other category. It is a fine line.

At the same time, he should not think that while he still feels reservation and feels shame from doing the sins, what are people going to say about him? Instead, when he does fall into sin, then he should repent to Allah ﷻ immediately.

That's why we have references from the actions of the righteous people of the past that they used to take into account what people viewed and how they looked at things not for the sake of the people, but for a bigger picture. The bigger picture is that they don't want people to get the wrong end of the stick when it comes to the *dīn*.

Take the case of Maryam عليها السلام when she wished for death:

﴿ قَالَتْ يَٰلَيْتَنِي مِتُّ قَبْلَ هَٰذَا وَكُنتُ نَسْيًا مَّنسِيًّا ﴾

﴿She said, 'I wish I had died before this; and I was unknown, forgotten.﴾[54]

Some people wrongly think that she said that because she was going through the pains of labour. The reality was that she was saying this because she was worried that people would grossly misunderstand things by assuming that she has become pregnant and is having a child out of wedlock. And the fact that she was a person who was dedicated to the *masjid*, she was from a pious family: that of ʿImrān عليه السلام and related to Zakariyā عليه السلام, and his son Yaḥyā عليه السلام: that people will think "look at Maryam what she's done, she's brought disgrace to us!"; and so, the *dīn* will then be attacked. So that's why she said I would rather have died before this, than allow the *dīn* to be attacked because of me. She knows she hasn't

54 Holy Quran; Chapter of Maryam 19:23

done anything wrong, but she was looking at the perspective of not wanting people to think bad of the *dīn*. And probably, knowing how righteous she was, she would have not wanted others to get bad deeds for thinking evil of her. And this falls into the category of "distancing yourself from suspicion".

The is how the Prophet ﷺ dealt with the situation involving two men who saw him walking with an unidentified woman at night. To prevent them from thinking ill of him, and thence getting grave sin for doing so, he shouted to them, as they diverted their path:

على رسلكما ، إنها صفية بنت حيي

"Wait, it is Ṣafiyyah bint Ḥuyay!"[55]

Because Ṣafiyyah was his wife.

A nice story that also demonstrates this is that once two great scholars were walking together. One was Imam 'Ibrāhīm al-Nakhaʿī and the other his student Sulaymān ibn Mahrān al-'Aʿmash. The former was either blind or one-eyed, and the other had weak eyesight.

As they were walking, 'Ibrāhīm suggested to his student that they should walk down a particular path to avoid others, as they may mock them for two partially sighted people walking together.

Sulaymān said, "So what? We walk together. If they speak about us, they will get the evil deed."

'Ibrāhīm said, "Rather, we should walk a different path, and prevent them from getting any bad deed."

This basic story further demonstrates the importance of looking out for others to avoid them getting sins, by avoiding certain behaviour. On a different level altogether, we see scholars like Imam al-Shāfiʿī

55 *Ṣaḥīḥ:* Hadith narrated by Imam Abu Dāwūd

– as an example – who used to pray the *sunnah* prayer in the *masjid* even though he knew that the best *sunnah* as the Prophet ﷺ said is that which is prayed in one's house.

The Prophet ﷺ said:

اجعَلُوا مِن صَلاتكم في بُيوتِكم، ولا تتخذُوها قُبورا

"Make of your prayers in your homes, and do not make them as graves."[56]

Because people don't pray in the graves, or the inhabitants of the graves cannot pray.

And he said:

صَلُّوا أيُّها النَّاس في بيوتِكم
فإنَّ أَفضَلَ الصَّلاةِ صلاةُ المَرءِ في بيتِه، إلاَّ المكتُوبة.

"O Mankind, pray in your homes, for the best prayer is the prayer of a person in his home, except the obligatory."[57]

However, Imam al-Shāfiʿī رضي الله عنه - now and again - would pray the *sunnah* in the *masjid* because he didn't want some people to think - out of misunderstanding or bad suspicion - that the *ʿulamā'* do not pray the *sunnah* at all and they are just leaving the *masjid* without prayer.

Sometimes, there is an element of education, not for the sake of getting any position or status with the people, but rather to clarify things, so that people don't misunderstand things.

56 *Ṣaḥīḥ:* Hadith narrated by Imams al-Bukhārī and Muslim
57 *Ṣaḥīḥ:* Hadith narrated by Imams al-Bukhārī and Muslim

There is another story that amusingly demonstrates this. Once the great Imam Ibn Abi Dhi'b ﷺ entered the *masjid* and sat down, awaiting his students to give them a class. He sat down without praying the two *rakʿah* salutation for the *masjid*. These two units are highly recommended, but they are not obligatory. We don't know the reason why he didn't pray them. Imams may do this on occasions to demonstrate that they are recommended and not obligatory. Nonetheless, after he sat down, a man by the name of al-Ghāzī ibn Qays came to him and said in a harsh tone: "Get up and pray two *rakʿah*, for your sitting without saluting the *masjid* is ignorance!"

Ibn Abi Dhi'b got up and prayed them. A short while after, he sat down and leaned his back to the wall, and the *masjid* started filling up with his students who circled him, waiting to learn from him.

When al-Ghāzī saw this, he was embarrassed and felt sorry. He asked about him, and was told this is Ibn Abi Dhi'b, one of the jurists of al-Madinah, and among their nobles. Al-Ghāzī got up and apologised to Ibn Abi Dhi'b. The latter replied, "My brother, don't worry. You commanded us to do good, and we listened to you."

The Imam used the words "it is said" which means he hasn't ascribed this narration to a chain, and this format weakens the narration because he is not saying who said it or where it is made.

He said, "If you ask Allah (Exalted be He) for honesty, He will award you a mirror in which you can see everything from the wonders of the *dunyā* and the Hereafter."

I think the most bewildering thing is your own self. The mirror allows you to look at yourself and see in truth who you are and what you are about. You can see when you are true because Allah shows you this is the reality: this is who you are. Obviously, that is closer to attaining *ikhlāṣ* and righteousness.

Then he said: "We have also narrated to from the Noble Master Abu al-Qāsim al-Junayd 🕮 who said: "The truthful one fluctuates forty times a day, and the hypocrite (show-off) is static in one state for forty years."

[Later on, I will speak more about al-Junayd *in shā' Allah*.]

Whereas the one showing off will remain in one status, or one condition, or one appearance for 40 years, the truthful one is continuously changing. Here, the Imam chose to explain this because maybe this is something that people need to understand a little more.

The truthful person: his heart is with the truth. So, wherever the truth is, he doesn't have a problem changing to that. So, he might be doing something, and then he finds out that there is something closer to the sharia, so he leaves that first thing which might be his custom, and he performs the alternative which is closer to the sharia. And if something more important, or apparent presents itself to him and he is unable to do both, then he performs the one that which is better. So, he doesn't have a problem changing in accordance to what is correct and what is shown to him to be correct because he is with the truth. Therefore, he will continue to change. He might even change a hundred times, a thousand times because he does not have a problem with change. He will just change according to where he sees the benefit is because that's where his heart is.

As for the person who shows off, he will always stay in the same situation because people have known him as that. So, he will continue with that behaviour for the sake of people not misidentifying him and saying, "He is not doing this anymore or he has changed, and so on". Thus, even though something has come to him, he always adopts one situation and even when somebody says to him, "Look, the truth is this! Do this!" he will not change his way. He will continue in that state that he is, even if it means staying most of his life doing the same; because he is showing off with his *'ibādah*. He wants people to be aware of him. And if he changes that situation, people might think, why has this guy changed?

Today we have some *'ulamā'*, who – after research and study – may conclude on matters in a way which contradicts their previous stances. However, they are afraid if they do change their opinion (usually to a more lenient position) that people will judge them according to this new stance.

Unfortunately, some people may have read a hadith or studied a book; they believe that they can pass judgment on scholars. Because of this, they force scholars to adopt certain opinions, and not "allow" them to change, by way of propaganda, or continual hammering that, "this is the way, this is the correct opinion!"; so they think that alas, that is the accepted opinion.

Therefore, when they see a fatwa that goes against their established way of thinking, they might question that and try to "bully" the scholars to adopt a certain line. So, the risk for the scholar there, is that he might not want to say the truth or not speak out because he's afraid that people will judge him or they will "downgrade" him, or they will abandon him or whatever.

Levels of *Ṣidq*

Imam al-Ghazālī in this chapter, explained some matters, and he has some sayings with regards to *ṣidq*. He says, "*Al-ṣidq* (truthfulness) is essentially on many levels.

The **first** level is the truthfulness of the tongue. And this is what we understand, generally, when we say *ṣidq*. We are thinking about honesty of the tongue: somebody that doesn't lie, and without a doubt every person should guard what they say to make sure that he only speaks that which is true and does not speak anything false. And even Imam al-Ghazālī says, "You have to be careful from *al-maʿārīḍ*". *Al-maʿārīḍ* is when somebody says something which is true, but he says it in a way to give a different impression in the other person's mind because he does not want to provide him with the full story. So it's not lying, but it is almost like it.

He said *maʿārīḍ* (or *tawriyah*) is almost like drawing a picture that some people might imagine or perceive differently from the original object. It is more like giving a different aspect, and it's like misleading somebody to think something else. Even though in itself, it is not lying. Sometimes it can be used for causes like, if you wanted to bring people together. Two people who are arguing over an issue and you want to bring them together, so you might mention his name to the other person in a way which he thinks or understands that guy's asking about him. So, it's like giving him a different impression. And if this delivery has a purpose, it is not disliked therein. This is similar to why lying with a valid reason is not *ḥarām*, as explained by the Prophet ﷺ:

ليسَ الكَذَّابُ الذي يُصْلِحُ بيْنَ النَّاسِ، فَيَنْمِي خَيْرًا، أوْ يقولُ خَيْرًا

"He is not a liar: the one who reconciles between people, and thus he nurtures good or says good things."[58]

This is what happened with ʾIbrāhīm عليه السلام with Nimrod and with the king of Egypt. He said something to get him to think the opposite way. He wasn't lying. Rather, he was merely trying to give a different impression for another reason.

58 *Ṣaḥīḥ:* Hadith Narrated by Imam al-Bukhārī

As for Nimrod, he said, "I am sick!" giving the impression that he was ill, but he meant that I am sick of your idolatry.

And as for the king of Egypt, when he and his wife Sara went to Egypt, the ruler arrested and brought them to his court. He then asked 'Ibrāhīm, "Who is this with you?"

'Ibrāhīm ﷺ replied, "She is my sister!". He intended that this is my sister in faith. He did this because if he had said this was my wife and that ruler had wanted her, then he would have had to kill 'Ibrāhīm because he is her husband. So, saying "she is my sister" prevented him from being killed. 'Ibrāhīm ﷺ didn't lie: it's still the truth. But he said it in a way for the other person to understand something different. Obviously, in this case, 'Ibrāhīm ﷺ did this because there was a reason, which is to preserve his life. The same explanations can be given to the third incident relating to 'Ibrāhīm ﷺ with regards to the big idol smashing the small ones.

Indeed, our Prophet ﷺ also did this on one occasion when he wanted to give some people a different impression, so that they wouldn't know who he was. He and Abu Bakr went on a secret mission to find out about the Quraysh caravan. They found someone whom they asked. They didn't want him to know who they were, so as not to give away their location. That person asked the Prophet ﷺ and Abu Bakr ؓ about where they were from. So, the Prophet ﷺ said: "من ماء" "From water". People would have understood that the water refers to the water of Iraq, implying that they are from Iraq. However, the Prophet ﷺ was saying *min mā'*, meaning that we are from water; i.e., we are created from water. So, it's not a lie, and Allah forbid that any of His Prophets would lie, but it was to detract him so he doesn't think that the Prophet ﷺ was coming from Madinah; and that would have given away the military tactic.

The Prophet ﷺ also did this out of jest with his companions, but clarifying his statements later on. He demonstrated that this is permissible on the one hand; and on the other hand, showing that a true leader is one who relates to his people, and may joke with them on some occasions.

One example that I mention here is when a man came to him ﷺ asking for a ride. The Prophet ﷺ replied, "**We shall carry you on the child of a she-camel!**"

The man said, "The child will not be able to carry me, and I do not want that!"

The Prophet ﷺ insisted, "**Rather, we will.**"

Then he explained, "**And who gives birth to the [grown] camels except she-camels!**"[59]

However, Imam al-Ghazālī said that we should keep away from this when the intent is to deceive people. As for when there is a reason to do so, then each person will assess the need accordingly. So that's the first level.

In relation to the truthfulness of the tongue, the Imam narrates in regards to Rabʿī ibn Ḥirāsh.

Rabʿī was a trustworthy *tābiʿī* and he was known for his honesty. He had two boys who were revolting against al-Ḥajjāj[60] and these people were rebelling against him because he was a tyrant.

It was said to al-Ḥajjāj: "Their father has never lied, send for him and ask him about them."

He sent for him and asked: "Where are your sons?"

He said: "They are at home!"

59 *Ṣaḥīḥ:* Hadith narrated by Imam al-Tirmidhī
60 An 'Umayyid Governor/ General, who was renowned for being one of the most brutal tyrants in the history of Islam

It is true that al-Ḥajjāj was a tyrant, but he had some dignity and he recognised good behaviour. So, he said: "We have pardoned them because of your honesty!"

Rabīʿ Ibn Ḥirāsh[61] was a man who was very serious in his attitude to life and very much aware of it. That's why he made an oath and had sworn that he would never laugh until he knows his fate: i.e., if he is heading towards *Jannah* or to the Fire. Al-Ḥārith al-Ghazzī said, "So, he only laughed after his death!"

And his brother, Rabʿī - after him – [also] swore an oath that he would not laugh until he knows whether he is in *al-Jannah* or in the Fire!

Al-Ḥārith said: His washer[62] told me that he continued to smile on his bed, whilst we were washing him until we finished!

Allah ﷻ blessed them with this.

The **second** level of *al-ṣidq* is the truthfulness in the *niyyah* and the intention, and the want. And that is obviously related to *ikhlāṣ*. We have already spoken a lot about *ikhlāṣ*; it is about being truthful in your intention.

The **third** level is the truthfulness in one's resolve to do things: *al-ʿazm*. This is about trying to be truthful in wanting to achieve things which are good, and to have a strong resolution which has no weakness, no deviation, no inclination, no second guessing, no doubt, but to go full steam ahead in its regard. That is another meaning of truthfulness; that when you say something you are truthful and you proceed to do it.

The **fourth** level is to be truthful in fulfilling one's promise. So, when you make a promise you fulfil it in the best way, even though

61 Rabīʿ and Rabʿī were brothers
62 Meaning the one who washes the dead person.

it might go against your wishes or your desires. And he said, that is what Allah ﷻ said about some men:

﴿ مِنَ الْمُؤْمِنِينَ رِجَالٌ صَدَقُوا مَا عَاهَدُوا اللهَ عليه ﴾

﴾Of the believers: are men who were truthful in what they promised Allah.﴿[63]

The **fifth** level is truthfulness in actions. That is a person who takes appropriate work, struggle and effort in his external actions. The truthfulness is that his external actions do not convey something which is different from his internal. That is the kind of truthfulness that we have been saying and hearing about with the different qualities. An example given here by Imam al-Ghazālī, is that when one is standing in *ṣalāh*: one is performing it as best as possible with *khushu*ʿ and humility; such that anyone observing thinks that this guy is concentrating in his *ṣalāh*. He has the focus and the concentration. Although internally, he is elsewhere: thinking about other things.

So, these are the five levels of *ṣidq* that Imam al-Ghazālī mentioned.

Basically; to summarise: truthfulness and being true is to make things equal between the external and the internal. More than this is the person making his internal better than his external. So, what he actually does privately is better than what he does in public, because he does not want the people to judge his external and they think of him better than what he is internally.

63 Holy Quran: The Chapter of the Confederates 33:23

Good Companionship

Allah ﷻ said:

﴿ اتَّقُوا اللَّهَ وَكُونُوا مَعَ الصَّـٰدِقِينَ ﴾

﴾Fear Allah and be amongst those who are truthful﴿[64]

Because no doubt, when you sit with others, or associate with them: you will learn from them and you will pick up qualities from them. And even if you do not learn it: the nature of attitudes and behaviours is that they imprint on each other. So even if you sit with people who are badly behaved: people who are of certain characters, you will find that you will start to behave that way. And if when you sit with people who are people of truthfulness, people who are tranquil, people who are calm, people who remember Allah, then you will be affected by that.

The Arabs have a saying which is a clever play on words: (الصاحب ساحب), which translates as "the companion pulls".

A beautiful saying of 'Omar ibn al-Khattāb ﷺ:

لولا ثلاث: لولا أن أسير في سبيل ﷻ أو يغبر جبيني في السجود،
أو أقاعد قوما ينتقون طيب الكلام كما يُنتقى طيب الثمر
لأحببت أن أكون قد لحقت با لله ﷻ

"Had it not been for three [things]: Had it not been that I can proceed in the Path of Allah ﷻ, or that I can dust my forehead in prostration; or that I can sit with people who chose the best of words, like the best of fruits are picked; I would have preferred to have gone back to Allah ﷻ."[65]

64 Holy Quran: The Chapter of Repentance 9:119
65 Narrated by Imam AbdUllah ibn al-Mubarāk in the "Book of Jihād"

The point here is the last one which is the superiority of sitting with those who pick the best words to speak; and they are the company worth having.

Also, on the authority of Imam al-Shāfiʿī ﵀ who said: It was said to 'Ubay Ibn Kaʿab ﵁ (a Companion): "O Aba Mundhir! Advise me." He said: "Befriend your brothers in accordance with their piety. And do not make your tongue an initiator for those who do not want it. And do not envy the living except how you envy the dead."

This reiterates the importance of befriending people according to their *taqwa*. And don't use your tongue unnecessarily, be that to give ad hoc advice or to reply without need. There are people who have to say something in all matters, even if they are irrelevant. Your tongue has to be guarded with great scrutiny.

The other piece of advice is to not envy the living, and if you must, then envy them as much as you would envy the dead, which is almost nothing. We will look at a further perspective of that when we examine the words of Abu Yazīd.

06

Recalling One's Intention at all Times

There are two general aspects of *'amal*. There is the *'amal* of the *qalb* (heart) and the action of the limbs: the internal and external actions, respectively. Sincere intentions (heart) are more important than outward actions, as we have read previously. However, the Muslim is required to attain betterment in both aspects: purification of the heart and performance of righteous deeds. And that is in tune to what the Prophet ﷺ has taught. The internal aspect is more important and that's why there has to be more focus on the heart, because the actions of the limbs will follow. This is derived from the Prophet's ﷺ saying:

أَلَا وإِنَّ في الجَسَدِ مُضْغَةً: إذَا صَلَحَتْ صَلَحَ الجَسَدُ كُلُّهُ،
وإذَا فَسَدَتْ فَسَدَ الجَسَدُ كُلُّهُ، أَلَا وهي القَلْبُ

"Truly in the body, there is an organ the size of a morsel: if it is sound, the whole of the body is sound. And if it is corrupt, the whole of the body is corrupt. Truly, it is the heart."[66]

In this section, the Imam is going to talk about recalling the intention. To have *ikhlāṣ* is the ultimate aim. Prior to that, one has to learn to have an intention in which he can be sincere in. It's about

66 *Ṣaḥīḥ:* Hadith narrated by Imams al-Bukhārī and Muslim

thinking and focusing on how to have an intention and how to be conscious in the different aspects of one's life and actions.

And so he says that you have to know that whoever wants to do any aspect of obedience, any good deed - even if it is small – then he must try to make his intention present. He must recount or recall his intention. And on the very basic level, he needs to recall what is that intention that he intends with the action.

He seeks Allah ﷻ. He seeks the pleasure of Allah for that work. That intention has to be present during the action. Then, he says that the intention has to be in all aspects of *'ibādah*; whether it's *ṣalāh*, *ṣawm* (fasting) *wuḍū'*, *tayammum*, *'i'tikāf*, hajj, *zakāh*, *ṣadaqah* (charity); and then the wider aspects as well.

The Imam chooses to list a wide range of actions for the reader to get the picture. He includes: fulfilling others' needs, visiting the sick, following the funerals, initiating *salām* and replying to it, blessing the one who has sneezed, denying evil and commanding the good. He includes answering the invitation when somebody invites you to dinner or to a cup of tea or coffee, attending the gatherings of knowledge and *dhikr* (remembrance); visiting those who are righteous, spending on the family as well as the guest, honouring the people of affection, and relatives; the study of knowledge, glancing through it, revising, teaching, reading, writing and compiling it; and fatwas, as well as what is similar to these acts.

Even if he should eat, drink, or sleep; to intend the strength for the act of obedience to Allah, or to rest the body to give it energy for obedience. Here we can read the matter of Abdul Raḥmān ibn al-'Aswad.

Ahmad ibn Abi al-Ḥawārī said- it was narrated that Abdul Raḥmān ibn al-'Aswad ؓ never used to eat bread except with intention. It's as specific as that. They used to question, "How was eating the bread with intention?" So, he would reply that when he felt weak, and a bit lethargic, lacking energy, he would eat bread with the intention of having energy; it was like an energy food. Then, he would get his energy, and he could carry on with his day-to-day life, his *'ibadah*, his *ṣalāh*. And when he feels that he's eaten too much and starting to feel a bit heavy, he would stop eating the bread. So, eating and fasting was all linked to an intention. Therefore, even, his food and all that was being rewarded.

The Imam narrates the saying Bishr al-Ḥāfī ﷺ who said: "The people of the past who were close to Allah ﷻ, they didn't use to eat out of delicacy and they didn't used to wear for luxury."

They were not people who ate to feed their palate or their taste buds. They were people who used to eat with a purpose which was coupled with an intention. The intention was to gain the strength and the energy to worship Allah and continue their duties. They were not looking for the luxury of tasting the food in the palate. Unlike today, you have a category of people called "foodies". There are people who are looking for food and looking for the best restaurants and the best meals and the best spices and the new best way to cook this recipe or consume this spice. It should be clear that I am not saying this is *ḥarām*, because food is from the *tayyibāt* and from *al-rizq*. If you want to eat nice food, it's not against Islam, but here we are talking about those people who really were concerned with coming closer to Allah ﷻ. The food was just a means for them: a kind of fuel. It doesn't matter what they put inside as long as it was fuelling their body and they can carry on.

Once 'Omar ibn al-Khaṭṭāb ﷺ entered on his son 'Āṣim, who was eating some meat. He asked him, "What is this?"

'Āṣim said, "Something that we desired!"

So, 'Omar said, "Is it so that whenever you desire something, you eat it? It is enough extravagance that whenever someone desires something, he eats it!"

Bishr ibn al-Ḥārith al-Ḥāfī is one of the righteous people who was an *'ālim* and an imam. He was someone to be followed in terms of his obedience to Allah ﷻ. And he was amongst the companions of scholars, the likes of AbdUllah ibn al-Mubārak and others. 'Ibrāhīm al-Ḥarbī said, "Baghdad has not produced someone with a sounder mind, and most guarding of his tongue than Bishr al-Ḥāfī."

The story of Bishr is quite a strange one as well. He is known as Bishr al-Ḥāfī, which is translated as the barefooted Bishr. It is narrated that the reason behind this was that he was initially someone who was distant from Allah: he wasn't really into the *dīn*. He was very much wasting his life; and on occasions, he would have parties at his house, alcohol, dancing, music and things like that. On one occasion, a man passed by his house and could hear the music and noises coming from the house. The man knocked on the door; and Bishr's daughter answered. The man asked: "Is the owner of this house someone who is *ḥūr* (free from slavery) or an *'abd* (slave)?"

She said, "Rather, he is a free man!"

So, the man replied, "Yes, I thought so, because a slave would not behave like this!" and the man walked on.

Bishr had his ear on the conversation, so he went running after him, because he was startled by what he had heard; so much so that he left his house without putting his sandals on. Barefooted, he chased the man, and asked him to repeat what he had just said.

And so the man repeated to him what he said.

And that was like his wake-up call and he realised that an *'abd* wouldn't behave like this. Now the man had used a play on words, because his question was about the status of the owner, as to whether he was a free man or a slave, but what he meant that a slave of Allah: 'abd Ullah would not behave like this: being ungrateful to Allah ﷻ to an extent of being distracted and following his lusts and desires; and engaging in prohibited acts. So, Bishr understood this, and realised he was far away from his purpose; so that was his repentance.

He went back and chucked everybody out, saying, "party's over!" and Allah ﷻ guided him. Later, he became one of the leaders and an Imam in knowledge and Sufism.

Avenues of Good Deeds

Then he adds another aspect which the Prophet ﷺ mentioned when he addressed the different avenues of *ṣadaqah*. He ﷺ said:

وفي بِضعِ أحدِكُم صدقة

"...and even in one of you having intercourse with his wife there is reward."

The Companions were surprised saying, "Will anyone of us satisfy his desire and still get reward for it?"

The Prophet ﷺ replied, "**Consider if he had done the same act in a *ḥarām* avenue would he not be punished for that?**" They said, "Yes."

He said, "**Likewise, if he does it in a halal way, he will be rewarded in that.**"[67]

And this is a great blessing of Allah, as you are satisfying your desire you are getting rewarded for that. Such a great gift. This is similar to what Imam Ibn al-Qayyim رحمه الله mentioned when he said, "One of the greatest help or aids is that Allah ﷻ gives somebody happiness and contentment in something which he is obliged to do."

67 *Ṣaḥīḥ:* Hadith narrated by Imam Muslim

Think about that. One is obliged to do things and carry out certain acts, but not only is he obliged to do them, he also feels happy in doing them. This is like the highest level of help that Allah gives, because the person is doing something he enjoys and is rewarded for it as well. It is like employment: many of us go to our jobs, and after a while, we feel that we hate our jobs. But we have to do the job, because at the end of the day we need the money and we need to earn our livelihood. But, if Allah ﷻ gave you a job in which you are actually happy, you really enjoy the job; you want to get up in the morning and just go to work. Then you would have attained double achievement, because on the one hand you are earning money, and at the same time you are happy and delighted for the work you are doing.

This is the same for anybody's *'ibādah*. If you think about *ṣalāh*: many of us pray, and we feel that the prayer is a chore, like we have to do it. Sometimes you feel a bit tired and so on; and in some cases, you just want to pray to "get it out of the way!" But imagine those few people who actually feel that *ṣalāh* is a nourishment for them. They feel the delight and they feel the happiness when they are in *ṣalāh*. So, not only is that they are doing the act of *'ibādah*, but they really feel that they want to perform it. They are content in doing that act of worship, as the example of the Prophets and their likes. Indeed, in the *ṣaḥīḥ* hadith, the Prophet ﷺ would ask Bilāl to make the *'iqāmah* by saying:

يا بلال، أقم الصَّلاة، أرحنا بها

"O Bilāl! Make the call to pray. Give us rest in it!"[68]

[Aside: one narration records that the incident of this narration, was a man from the tribe of Khuzā'ah saying, "I wish I could pray, so I would find rest." And those who heard him faulted him for saying that. Then he said, I heard the Prophet ﷺ say the above words."

68 *Ṣaḥīḥ:* Hadith narrated by Imams Ahmad and Abu Dāwūd

This demonstrates that even during the second generation some people missed the point of *ṣalāh*.]

When you look at it in this regard, even with a good act which you are feeling satisfied and you are achieving your desire: if you have that right intention, you will get the reward. And here he says that when the person does that act of intimacy, he should intend that he is giving his wife her right. Maybe he is also intending a righteous child who worships Allah, he is intending to protect himself, to keep it away from doing anything *ḥarām*. And this also teaches the importance of having a multi-layered intention.

Then the Imam tells us that whoever has been denied the *niyyah*; meaning whoever has been denied the ability to make an intention, then he has been deprived of a lot of great things. And whoever has been given the ability to make that intention, then he has clearly been given good sizeable rewards. We therefore, ask Allah – Most Generous to help us with that, as well as He directs us towards all facets of good.

The evidence of this rule is what has been aforementioned of his saying ﷺ: "**Actions are but by intentions; and every person shall only get what he intended.**"

So, the core message of this chapter is that making that intention and thinking about every aspect, because we are trying to achieve so many basic things in our lives to reach Allah ﷻ. And it will be a such a great bonus if every step of our lives, every action that we do is rewarded by Allah ﷻ. It is almost like the meter is continuously running, getting that reward from Allah ﷻ. Even when we are sleeping the meter is running. Even when we are eating, drinking, doing any acts, we are just continuously getting *ḥasanāt*. And that can only happen with having an intention and recalling the intention at the commencement of the action. And like many other things, it comes with practice. And that's why we are discussing it; that's why the Imam has focused a large point of this concept of being aware of Allah ﷻ on having the intention and having the *ikhlāṣ*, and being aware of that.

For me, as the author of this book, it has been very beneficial because just by me reminding myself and others with these lessons; it has really helped me to focus more on the intention. And so, a person should try to be more focused on every aspect of his life. Whenever one is doing even small acts in life, one should think "Why am I doing this? And how can I make the intention to make this for Allah ﷻ." Be it as basic as putting your head on the pillow before you go to sleep, making that intention there, or whether it's when you're eating and even if it's checking your messages on your phone or whatever. If you think about the intention and try to make the intention good, then you will be rewarded by Allah ﷻ and I think this is an important practice.

I have a great tip, which I suggested to my students. You would have read earlier about some of the scholar recommended beginning their compilations with the hadith, "Actions are but by intentions…" and how they considered it a praiseworthy act. In the same way, one can consider each day as a new record, a new book. My tip, is as you wake up in the morning, begin your day by reading this hadith out loud. If you can read it in Arabic, then do so, as well as a language that you understand. This will set the precedent for the day, and will *in shā' Allah*, help you to focus and think about intention during the day.

Now he just gives us a few examples. The Imam said that we have been narrated to from the Noble Imam - whose status as an Imam, his nobility, majesty and mastery is agreed upon: Abu Yaḥyā Ḥabīb ibn Abi Thābit the Follower, and the reliable amongst them[69] رحمهم الله.

69 i.e., the Followers, who are the students of the Companions of the Prophet ﷺ. A Follower is someone who has met and studied with at least one companion.

Abu Yaḥyā was a *faqīh*, one of the *fuqahā'* of Kūfah and he was one of the Followers. It was said that during his time the fatwa was only with three people in Kūfah. There was three people who were the most knowledgeable and learned, and they were the ones whom people would go to for fatwas. Abu Yaḥyā Ḥabīb was one of them.

It was said to him: "Tell us about the most difficult thing?"

He said: "Until the intention comes." or "The coming of the intention."

He meant for the attention to be present, to recall the intention, that is the hardest of things to achieve.

Sufyān al-Thawrī ﵀ was also one of the great *fuqahā'*; and one of the early ones who unfortunately, didn't sustain a school. He didn't establish a school or the school didn't establish him, because obviously it depends on how people follow him. Nonetheless, he was one of the great *'ulamā'*. He said, "I haven't dealt with anything more intense than my intention." Which is understandable, taking into consideration what we have mentioned.

Yazīd ibn Hārūn ﵀ said: "The intention has not become precious [or rare] in the hadith, except for its nobility."

Because of its nobility and its honourable status, its status is precious.

Ibn 'Abbās ﵄ said: "A person is preserved in accordance to the value of his intention."

This means that a person will be protected or guarded depending on how much of his intention is present and how magnificent it is. This means that if he has the intention, then that will be a source of his protection. Allah ﷻ will guard him, and look after him. And you should recall that Ibn 'Abbās ﵄ is the narrator of the famous hadith, which begins by the Prophet ﷺ saying:

احفَظِ اللهَ يَحفَظْكَ، احفَظِ اللَّهَ تَجِدْهُ تُجاهَكَ

He said, "I was behind the Prophet ﷺ one day when he said, **"O Young boy, I will teach you some words: Guard Allah, He will guard you! Guard Allah, you will find Him before you!"**[70]

What does guard Allah mean? It means guard Allah in the limitations that He has placed, which are what He has prohibited. You guard those limitations; Allah will guard you and He will look after you. Ibn ʿAbbās ﷺ is further explaining this aspect that depending on how your intention is, and how lofty it is, the same will be the guarding that comes from Allah ﷻ.

The Imam continues telling us that others have said: "People are given in accordance to their intentions." Meaning in the Next Life, their rewards will be according to their intention. Now consider: how many people, how many actions, which were great and big, but were despised because of the intention, meaning the underlying intention was not good. And so, even though they did big actions, big works, but what kind of intention was behind it? If the intention was for showing off and display, then their reward may be in this life. Look at some of the big *masājid* built today, in the Muslim lands: how much money is spent on them and how much decorations and how many ornaments and things like that were spent on these mosques. But what kind of value did that bring? Obviously, we can't talk specifically about people's intentions because we don't know their intentions, but imagine a big action like this was done for the wrong reason. It would be lost. Or consider those people establishing schools, or charities or whatever. And we all know in the hadith, which is the key aspect of intention and doing things for Allah. Of those people who will be the first

70 *Ṣaḥīḥ:* Hadith narrated by Imams Ahmad and al-Tirmidhī

who will be furnaced in the hell fire, would be somebody who learnt Islam just so that he will be called *ʿālim* or *qārī* or that he was brave, or generous or whatever, so that people will give him a good mention. He might have achieved so much, but his intention was wrong; and so he lost a lot. [We had mentioned the hadith in the introduction.]

Similarly, how many small actions would be magnified greatly because of the great intention. The intention can make the difference between two extremes in that regard. And he then goes on to say a few quotations from Imam al-Shāfiʿī ﵁ and then one quotation from Abu Yūsuf ﵀.

I am sure the reader is aware of who Imam al-Shāfiʿī ﵁ was, as he is not someone who is unfamiliar for the lay Muslim. He was someone who was very learned and extremely eloquent. He was very eloquent in his arguments and debates. During his time, essentially, there were two big schools, the school of *ahl al-Ḥadīth* (the people of hadith) and *ahl al-Raʾī* (the people of opinion). They were basically, debating each other intensely about the different aspects of how to derive rulings and opinions.

Ahl al-Raʾī, especially in Iraq, had the upper hand, as they were better equipped at arguments; they were advanced in debating. *Ahl al-Ḥadīth* on the other hand, because their reliance was mainly on the sayings of the Prophet ﷺ and the later scholars, they were more rigid in their conceptual thinking. Obviously, the sayings of the Prophet ﷺ without due understanding can be problematic. His sayings need comprehension of the applications of the hadith and how it is used, and which hadith is relevant to what scenario; whether the hadith has been misunderstood and so on. Without this appropriate knowledge, the hadith can be rendered of no benefit for the person who learnt it. And this is a very technical point. That's why the Prophet ﷺ himself said:

رُبَّ حامل فقه ليس بفقيه، ورُبَّ حامل فقهٍ إلى مَن هُو أفقهَ منه

"It might be that somebody carries the fiqh, but he is not one of comprehension. And it might be that somebody carries fiqh to one who has more understanding than him."[71]

He may have a good memory (as did most early Arabs did), but that doesn't mean he understands the knowledge to derive the rulings from them.

The people of *Ahl al-Ra'ī* were mostly the followers of the *'Aḥnāf*. Imam Mālik was the leader or the iconic head of *Ahl al-Ḥadīth*.

There is a tradition that Imam Abu Ḥanīfah met with Imam Mālik and they had a debate. According to that narration Imam Malik was sweating, and he was sweating from the intensity of the arguments of Abu Ḥanīfah ﷺ. Such that when Imam Mālik was asked did you meet Abu Ḥanīfah and debate with him? He said, "Yes. I met a man who could argue that a pillar made of rock, is made of gold, and he would establish his argument."

However, it is important to note that the people of opinion did not reject hadith but it was more about the application of hadith. The people of hadith said "We used to be grounded and hounded by the people of *ra'ī* in Iraq until Imam al-Shāfi'ī came along". So, Imam al-Shāfi'ī, if you like, put the balance back for *ahl al-Ḥadīth* because he now collated the hadith with the application or with the understanding of the hadith, so he hammered them.

Once, the followers of Abu Ḥanīfah were debating with Imam al-Shāfi'ī about who is more knowledgeable: their teacher (Abu Ḥanīfah) or his teacher (Mālik). So, al-Shāfi'ī said to them: "I ask you by Allah, who is more knowledgeable in Quran? My shaykh or your shaykh?"

71 *Ṣaḥīḥ:* Hadith narrated by Imam Ahmad and others

They said, "Yours."

He then asked, "I ask you by Allah, who is more knowledgeable in hadith? My shaykh or your shaykh?"

They said, "Yours."

He then said, "I ask you by Allah, who is more knowledgeable in the sayings of the companions and their followers? My shaykh or your shaykh?"

They said, "Yours."

He said, "All that remains is the *qiyās* (analogy); and that revolves around the previous three."

A simple debate, which rendered the opposition speechless.

Despite mentioning all of the above, people of the past – in the main – understood that differences in matters of jurisprudence should not be allowed to cause division, contention, or hatred among them. They knew that every seeker of knowledge is rewarded. And when disagreement arose, they did that in an atmosphere of love (for the sake of Allah) and co-operation with the aim of realising the truth, as we will read from the sayings of al-Shāfiʿī ﷺ.

Going back to what Imam al-Shāfiʿī was saying: "I wish that the people would have learnt this knowledge even though they do not attribute a single letter to me."

Meaning that even if none of the attributions are made to Imam al-Shāfiʿī, the main thing is that people learnt it and apply the knowledge within it. Again, showing the importance of clarity in the intention when compiling knowledge.

And then he said: "I never debated with anyone to try and just defeat them for the sake of just defeating them but rather, whenever I debated with somebody, whenever I argue with somebody, I always had the intention or wish, that the truth would come from their tongue, or their hands because I don't want to be looking like I'm the one who is achieving that truth."

This shows that aspect of having the right intention in that regard even in the matter of debates where it is intense, and people always want to win a debate, as they want their opinion to standout.

Also, he said, "Whenever I spoke to somebody, [meaning debated with him] I always loved that this person would have been given the guidance to say the right things, to be given support, to be aided, and guided, and provided for by Allah ﷻ."

So those three quotations all within that same perspective of having the correct intention, that even with arguments which are the pinnacle of people wanting to satisfy their *nafs* in defeating the opponent; Imam al-Shāfiʿī was saying that it wasn't his intention in any of those to just defeat people; which again shows the importance of having that clarity.

Then, the Imam mentioned the quotation of Imam Abu Yūsuf who is one of the most prominent students of Abu Ḥanīfah ﵀. He said: "Intend Allah with your knowledge. Because never have I sat in a gathering in which I intended to be humble, except that I would have left that gathering being the highest of the people there. And never have I sat in a gathering where I intended to be the highest, or maybe wanted to overwhelm people with arguments, except that I would not get up without having been ashamed, and I have made ridiculed there."

Imam Abu Yusuf's saying demonstrates that one should not assume that he has much knowledge, because he may be sitting there and somebody can come with a question or an argument, which one may not know the answer, and he is made to look like he has no knowledge. So again, an emphasis from Imam Abu Yūsuf in this regard.

Going back to what Ibn ʿAbbās ﷺ said "that the person will be given according to his intention," is the reality when you look today at those people of knowledge and how they were preserved.

If you think about all the people throughout history from the time of the companions till today: there are hundreds of thousands of ʿ*ulamā*ʾ who have passed by through the ʾ*ummah*. From those hundreds of thousands of scholars, if we wanted – at this moment amongst us- to name them, maybe we will struggle to name a hundred, even.

So, from those hundreds of thousands you can see that only a few of those have their names preserved throughout time. For example, it is a credit that we're sitting here today, seven to eight hundred years after the passing away of Imam al-Nawawī, and we are reading his book and explaining it in English, a language which he didn't even speak. And he's getting all that reward and all that virtue while he is in his grave, which shows that this is the blessing that Allah ﷻ gives. There are people who are chosen to get that blessing. Truly, it's a virtue and blessing from Allah ﷻ. We can even say it is a gift (*karāmah*).

We know the hadith when the *Ṣahabah* - the poor amongst the *Muhājirūn* - came and complained to the Prophet ﷺ. They said those people who are rich they have taken all the rewards, because they pray like we pray, they fast like we fast, but they give charity. So, the Prophet ﷺ taught the paupers how to make their own *ṣadaqah*; he said, "**Should I not tell you about all the avenues of how you can get charity?**"

"To say ʾ*subḥāna Allah*ʾ is a charity, to say ʾ*Allah Akbar*ʾ is a charity, ʾ*alḥamdulillāh*ʾ is a charity, to remove a harm from the path is a charity, enjoining good is charity, forbidding evil is charity." [72]

72 *Ṣaḥīḥ:* Hadith narrated by Imams al-Bukhārī and Muslim

It doesn't have to be that you have money. They went away feeling content with this. They went away, but after a few days they came back complaining again, saying that those rich folk had learnt all these things, and now they're doing those things as well.

So, then the Prophet ﷺ said, "**That is the virtue from Allah, He awards to whom He wants.**" Allah has given them that gift. We can't question Him. He gives to whomsoever He wants and He denies whomever He wants.

Similarly, within the same aspect of the action; the reality is that it's all according to the intention. So, people with their intentions Allah ﷻ will give them, will bless them such that their awards, and their rewards will be continuous, despite them having stopped thinking about the matter, Allah ﷻ continues to preserve them.

Imam Mālik was one of the early people to compile a book of hadith. And his book was called "al-Muwaṭṭa'" meaning "that which has been well-trodden", "that which has been established". It's a strange name, and actually it's the only one with that name – now - when you look at the hadith books. Other books have titles like al-Ṣaḥīḥ, al-Jāmiʿ, al-Sunan, al-Musnad; and so on. And what you will be surprised to know is, actually, during the time of Imam Mālik there were tens of books called "al-Muwaṭṭa'"; other people also wrote books which they named al-muwaṭṭa' as well but these were not preserved with due time.

People used to compile their books and increase the size of their books, because what used to happen is they would find a shaykh or a *muḥaddith* (hadith narrator) they would go and sit with him and just start to write hadith, so the more a person compiled the hadith, if you like, will add hadith to their status. To a certain extent, there was an aspect of the intention being a little bit out of tune.

They used to increase the volume of their book, whilst Imam Mālik, was refining and abridging his book. He was removing some of the hadith, rechecking them; and omitting certain narrations. So famously, somebody said to him, "Everyone is adding to their books, yet you are reducing your book and you're removing narrations."

So, he said, again his famous statement which has been preserved for time:

"Whatever is for Allah will remain and will be connected. And whatever is not for Allah will be disconnected and it will end."

And so it came to pass that the book of Imam Mālik was the only one that remained from these books named "al-Muwaṭṭa'". The rest, time has almost forgot them; they were overtaken and engulfed in other narrations.

One could say something similar about the other books of hadith. Again, people who compiled hadith: tens of thousands of people, but what has remained is what Allah ﷻ has chosen for people. Even the *madhāhib* today, when we had many of *al-Sunnah*, only four schools (*madhāhib*) remained, because they were the people who kept on going. The students served the school and contributed in preserving it. One example is that of Imam al-Bayhaqī ؆ who served the Shāfiʿī School extensively to the extent that the Imam of the Two Sacred Masjids al-Juwaynī ؆ commented: "There is no shāfiʿī *faqīh* (jurist) except al-Shāfiʿī has a favour upon him, except Abu Bakr al-Bayhaqī, for he has a favour over al-Shāfiʿī for his many compilations in supporting his school."

In reality, there were hundreds of *madhāhib*, like that of Sufyān al-Thawrī, Sufyān ibn ʿUyaynah, al-ʾAwzāʿi and al-Layth ibn Saʿad, to mention a few. These were teachers and scholars who had their own opinions and they had their own understandings, but they didn't have their own school. Their students didn't preserve their teachers' knowledge. So, with time they ended up losing the school and therefore it no longer existed. Imam al-Shāfiʿī commented, "Al-Layth is more knowledgeable than Mālik; but his students didn't preserve him."

Allah preserved of the *madhāhib* for reasons that He knows best. However - and Allah knows best – it is due to the intention of those people and the way that they were, as a lot of the good deeds go back to them. For whenever somebody follows a certain practice or reads a certain hadith compiled by someone, or learns, then that person gets the reward that Allah ﷻ wants for him. And that's why it is important for any Muslim who has not reached that level to understand the different branches of Islamic jurisprudence and to deduce the reasoning behind the rulings, to follow one of the four great Imams of this religion: Abu Ḥanīfah, Mālik, al-Shāfiʿī and Ahmad ibn Ḥanbal. And in following one of them, he should try his best in getting to grips with the evidence they have put forward to support their positions, as well as continue to exert themselves to acquire higher levels of understanding and comprehension.

So that was the chapter about recalling the *niyyah*. It is, once again, a short chapter as the Imam explained that his intention was not to elongate the sections and the points that he has mentioned here. He will go back to it again in the next section; to understand the principle and then it's for us, to go away and to put that into practice as much as possible. So, every time we do an action and that is basically every moment of the day, we need to make that intention, to think about it, to recall it so that the clock continues to tick in our favour, *in shā' Allah*.

Further Dimensions of Intention

In this chapter, the Imam deals with further aspects of intention. Firstly, he discusses the recording of good deeds and bad deeds. And as you will see from the following hadith, he illustrates a whole important concept in how we try to reap the rewards from Allah ﷻ.

It has been established in the *ṣaḥīḥ* hadith that the Messenger of Allah ﷺ said:

إِنَّ اللَّهَ كَتَبَ الْحَسَنَاتِ وَالسَّيِّئَاتِ ، فَمَن هَمَّ بِحَسَنَةٍ فَلَمْ يَعْمَلْهَا كَتَبَها اللَّهُ لَه عِنْدَهُ حَسَنَةً كَامِلَةً، وإِنْ هَمَّ بِها فَعَمِلَها كَتَبَها اللَّهُ لَه عِنْدَهُ عَشْرَ حَسَنَاتٍ إِلَى سَبْعِ مِئَةِ ضِعْفٍ إِلَى أَضْعافٍ كَثِيرَةٍ

"Truly, Allah has recorded the good deeds and the bad deeds. Such that whoever is concerned with a good deed, but does not do it, Allah will record it with Him as a complete good deed. And if one is concerned with it; and enacts it, Allah will record it as [anything from] ten good deeds up to seven hundred times to manifold multiples." [73]

Why is this hadith fundamental in this chapter? Because by just reading this hadith at a basic level, one can see the power of intention. Even without doing anything: just having a good intention is enough for you to get the reward from Allah ﷻ. So, when you change that intention into actual actions, then your potential for the reward is much greater.

Now, one can ask about what differentiates a person getting 10 and 700 good deeds? It's much more than this, and what is going to differentiate this (which is probably why the Imam mentioned

73 *Ṣaḥīḥ:* Hadith narrated by Imams al-Bukhārī and Muslim

this here) is the intention, how pure it is, how varied and how much effort you have put into it. Because the more your intention is varied, the more innovative and aspects you bring into it, then the more reward you will get from that good deed rather than just something basic.

For example, when you come to the *masjid*, you could be on a very basic level intending to come and pray *ṣalāt al-jamāʿah* (congregational prayer); that could be an intention. However, if you left your dwelling and you intended not just that you are coming to the congregational prayer, but you are coming to one of the houses of Allah; which is one of the greatest and beloved places to Allah; you intend with going to the house of Allah to also meet the good people. And you intend with that to give *salām*, and you intend do that to do *'iʿtikāf* as long as you are in the *masjid*. And you intend to learn something and you intend to get the rewards of walking to the *masjid* and towards knowledge. And you can almost variably multiply your intentions just by doing simple acts. Therefore, you can note the difference between somebody, doing the same thing, but getting a whole different set of reward. It is very much similar to the initial hadith: "**Whoever's *hijrah* is to Allah and His Messenger…**".

It's the same act, but the intention is what is going to change the reward.

The Imam further emphasizes the point about intention, by narrating another hadith, which is also sound, in which the Prophet ﷺ said in regards to the army that intends the *Kaʿbah* to destroy it:

يُخسَفُ بأَولِّهم وَآخِرِهم

"They will be quaked: from their first till their last."

ʿĀ'ishah ﵂ asked: "O Messenger of Allah! How will their first till their last be quaked, and amongst them are the nobles and those who are not of them?"

He ﷺ said:

يُخسَفُ بأَولِّهم وَآخِرِهم، ثُمَّ يُبْعَثُونَ على نِيَّاتِهِمْ

"They will be quaked: from their first till their last, then they will be resurrected according to their intentions."[74]

Her question was relating to how will they *all* be destroyed? How will the earth swallow *all* of them? And amongst them there will be people who are obviously the leaders, and there'll be people who are not amongst them, meaning that they didn't have the intention of attacking the *Kaʿbah*: they were forced to come along. And in another narration, he ﷺ was asked if there were true believers among them. So, the Prophet ﷺ clarified that they will all be destroyed, but then they will be resurrected according to their intentions. Again, this further emphasizing the importance of intention in this regard, and demonstrating that good intentions can save one in the Next Life, even if they are in dubious situations.

Then the Imam mentions another hadith. He mentioned that it has been established in the two *Ṣaḥīḥ* books from Ibn ʿAbbās ﵄ that the Messenger of Allah ﷺ said:

لا هِجْرَةَ بَعْدَ الفَتْحِ، ولَكِنْ جِهادٌ ونِيَّةٌ

**"There is no migration after the conquest.
Rather it is *jihād* with intention."**[75]

There is no more *hijrah* after the *Fatḥ*, meaning after the conquest of Makkah, but there will continue to be *jihād* with intention. So,

74 *Ṣaḥīḥ:* Hadith narrated by Imam al-Bukhārī
75 *Ṣaḥīḥ:* Hadith narrated by Imams al-Bukhārī and Muslim

the *'ulamā'* differed about what it does mean?

The Imam said: "Our companions and others have differed regarding the meaning of 'No *hijrah* after the conquest'. It was said that it means no migration from Makkah, as it has become an abode of Islam. It was also said that there is no migration – complete in virtue – after the conquest, as it was before the conquest. And as for the migration from the abode of the disbelievers today, then it is an emphasised obligation for whoever has the ability to do so, as one will not be able to manifest the *dīn* of Islam there. However, if one can manifest his *dīn* in these places, then it is recommended and not obligatory; and Allah – the Most Exalted – knows best."

So, some of them said, there is no *hijrah* from Makkah because initially the *hijrah* was leaving Makkah to go to Madinah and it was an order to do so. But now that Makkah has become one of the lands of Islam, there is no need to leave it. So there is no *hijrah* because it is part of the abode of Islam. And others said that it means that there is no *hijrah*; in terms of the full reward. So, the *hijrah* can still be done but the reward is not the same, because we know that they are not equal: those who have spent their money before the conquest of Makkah and those who have spent their money after the Conquest.[76]

And if you look even at the Companions, their levels have been ordained by the writers of biographies. The determination is that the Companions are categorised into different levels. And those who became Muslims in Makkah, they are essentially the *Muhājirūn*, and then you have the *Anṣār*, who are the ones who received, hosted and supported the Prophet ﷺ and the new emigrants. However, there is a changing point which made a difference, and that is the actual *Fatḥ* (conquest), which is not the Conquest of

Makkah, but the Treaty of Hudaybiyyah, which Allah named it a *Fatḥ*.

76 Holy Quran; Chapter of Iron 57:10

Allah ﷻ revealed:

﴿ إِنَّا فَتَحْنَا لَكَ فَتْحًا مُّبِينًا ﴾

﴾Truly, We have opened for you a great opening / victory.﴿[77]

So they considered this treaty as a *Fatḥ*. It was an opening and a victory because it changed things. And that is why it was considered an important change because after that, no longer was Islam and the Muslims on the back foot. This was now an opportunity for them to go outward, going forth to bring the good news to the other Arabs, by giving *da'wah*. There was no fear of having the enmity of Quraysh as a barrier.

Khālid ibn al-Walīd ﷺ was one of the prominent *Ṣaḥābah*; however he embraced Islam after the conquest. So even though he is one of the great Companions, but in terms of his level, he is considered of the later ones. And so, his status is not like those who were before him in entering Islam.

As an aside, the Imam talks about *hijrah* from a fiqh aspect. So, at this junction, he asks what is the actual ruling about somebody who has to do *hijrah* from a land which is ruled by disbelievers? Is that something that he has to do? Is it the same as Makkah or not? And he answers this question by saying that it basically becomes compulsory on someone to do the *hijrah* if he cannot practise his *dīn*. If he cannot practise his *dīn* in that land, then he has the obligation to go to a place where he can practise. And this is in line with what Allah ﷻ said when He spoke about "those who when the angels come to take their souls and they have wronged themselves, will be questioned, 'What did you think you were doing?' they will say, 'We were oppressed in the land.' So, the angels will respond, 'Was Allah's Earth not spacious enough for you to emigrate?'."[78] Implying why didn't you go to a land which allowed you the freedom to worship Allah and for you to practice your *dīn*."

77 Holy Quran; Chapter of the Conquest 48:1.
78 Holy Quran; Chapter of Women 4:97

Conviction in Allah

The Imam narrates a short story relating to one's conviction and belief in Allah. So he says that we have been narrated to from the Noble Master Abu Maysarah 'Omar ibn Sharḥabīl the Kufan Follower al-Hamdānī - that if he took his wage, he would give of it in charity. When he would return to his family, and they would count his wages, they would find it the same.[79]

He said to his nephew: "Why don't you also do like this?"

They said: "If we knew that it would not decrease, we would have done so!"

Abu Maysarah said: "I am not stipulating this for my Lord – Honoured and Graced."

If you are given a bag of money and you know that wherever you spend from it is going to be replaced, there's almost like a lack of conviction. The test of *īmān* is not there. If you are expecting that whatever you give is going to be replaced, it defeats the purpose. Here is a righteous man Abu Maysarah who was giving, and he wasn't expecting it to be replaced, but without doubt, he had the belief in Allah ﷻ and the *īmān* that Allah will replace for whomever He wishes.

We know that is important in terms of what is known as *tawakkul*, which is to trust in Allah. When you trust in Allah, then no doubt Allah ﷻ owns everything. And He is the one who provides. He is the one who will replace, as He promised:

﴿ وَمَا أَنفَقْتُم مِّن شَيْءٍ فَهُوَ يُخْلِفُهُ ﴾

﴾And whatever you spend, He will replace it.﴿[80]

[79] Meaning it hasn't decreased from the charity given.
[80] Holy Quran; Chapter of Saba' 34:39

We know the famous narration of Abu Hurayrah who brought some dates to the Prophet ﷺ and asked him to bless him in his food. The Prophet ﷺ held the dates together and he made *du'ā'* for Abu Hurayrah that Allah will bless him in his food. He told him to take these dates and put them in a pouch. When you want some dates, put your hand in the pouch and do not take all the dates out spreading them. And do not count the dates. This incident was towards the end of the life of the Prophet ﷺ because Abu Hurayrah only became a Muslim after the Battle of Khaybar[81]. So in effect, he was only with the Prophet ﷺ for three years. He said, "I continued to eat through the lifetime of Prophet ﷺ until he passed away, and then through the lifetime of Abu Bakr, and then the lifetime of 'Omar and then 'Othmān. It wouldn't leave my shoulder. But then it discontinued on the day 'Othmān was killed."[82] So, for more than 25 years, he was eating from those dates: an obvious *karāmah*. It might also be an indicator that when people become unjust and rebel against a righteous leader, that the blessings will be lifted up from them.

Having that *tawakkul*; that trust in Allah that He will replace what we have spent is vital. But you can't do this to "try it out", you cannot be testing Allah ﷻ. Because some people try to test Allah, saying that "Okay, I'll give, and I'll see if it is really replaced or not?" That's not how it works. And this is what Abu Maysarah meant by his statement: "We don't make this condition on Allah."

A similar reference can be demonstrated by the words of the Prophet 'Īsā عليه السلام who was tempted by the Devil. In the New Testament it says that the Devil came to Jesus عليه السلام and tried to tempt him. He carried him up to the pinnacle of the temple, and then said, "If You are the Son of God, throw Yourself down. For it is written: 'He will command His angels concerning You, and they will lift You up in their hands, so that You will not strike Your foot against a stone'."

81 In the year 7 AH
82 *Ḥasan:* Hadith narrated by Imams al-Tirmidhī and Ibn Ḥibbān

Jesus replied, "It is also written: 'Do not put the Lord your God to the test'."[83]

I don't want to discuss the false attribution of "the Son of God" as this isn't the scope of this book, but I draw attention, to 'Isā's reply in that he is not going to test Allah, by throwing himself from a high place, and expecting Allah to save him. Because it is not our position to test Allah, as we do not know how Allah will deal with us.

Another narration which is a more amusing story is that of a shaykh in a village. The shaykh had young pupils who would come to the *masjid* to learn Islam. On one occasion, it rained heavily, and there were puddles of water everywhere, as well as mud. The shaykh didn't expect anyone to come.

Despite this, a young boy appeared with dry and clean clothes. The shaykh was surprised to see him and questioned, "How did you get here without getting wet or muddy?"

The boy replied, "As you had taught us about *tawakkul*; I put my trust in Allah and I walked on the water."

The shaykh was now shocked to hear this. It is true that he may have been teaching this, but for it to actually happen – in real life – was not something he expected.

So he said, "I must try this, myself!"

Indeed, he stood in front of a large puddle. He stopped for a short while, psyching himself for the moment and thinking, "*tawakkul, tawakkul*." Then as he put his foot forward, he instinctively reached out to his dress and pulled it up.

And obviously, this small act meant that he was expecting his feet to get wet, and thus lacked true dependence on Allah. Of course, he ended up falling face down into the puddle!

83 Bible; Matthew 4:6-7

Best of the *Dunyā* and Hereafter

Then, the Imam says that our Imam Abu Abdullah Muhammad ibn 'Idrīs al-Shāfi'ī ﷺ said: "The best of the *dunyā* and the Hereafter are in [practising] five qualities:

1 - The enrichment of the soul,

2 - averting harm,

3 - earning halal,

4 - the dress of piety; and

5 - trust in Allah ﷻ in all situations.

This means that if you have these five qualities you will attain the goodness of this life and the next.

The **first** one is *ghina al-nafs* which is to be rich within yourself, the richness of the self. And this is what the Prophet ﷺ said when he defined richness. He ﷺ said:

لیسَ الغِنَى عن كَثْرَةِ العَرَضِ، ولَكِنَّ الغِنَى غِنَى النَّفْسِ

"Richness is not how much property or material you own. Rather, richness is the satisfaction of the *nafs*."[84]

Meaning to be content.

84 *Ṣaḥīḥ:* Hadith narrated by Imams al-Bukhārī and Muslim

The Fourth *Khalīfah* 'Alī ibn Abī Ṫālib ﷺ said in prose:

النَّفسُ تَجزَعُ أَن تَكُونَ فَقيرة   والفَقرُ خيرٌ مِن غِنى يُطغيها

والغنى هُوَ الكَفَافُ فإن أبت   فجميع ما في الأرض لا يغنيها

The *nafs* despairs to be impoverished.

However, poverty is better than wealth that causes it to transgress.

True richness is satisfaction, but if it refuses...

Then all what is on Earth will not enrich it.

The *nafs* doesn't want to be poor, it always wants more. The real richness – thus - is to be satisfied. When you are truly satisfied, that is when you really become rich, because if you are not satisfied, you will always want more. And that is why the Prophet ﷺ said:

لَوْ كانَ لابْنِ آدَمَ واديانِ مِن مالٍ لابْتَغَى ثالِثًا،
ولا يَمْلأُ جَوْفَ ابْنِ آدَمَ إلَّا التُّرابُ

"If the son of Adam had two valleys full of wealth, he would have wanted a third. And nothing will fill the interns of the son of Adam except earth."[85]

Meaning he will not have his full, until he is put in the ground, dead and buried. Only then, he would stop his endeavour for more. So *ghina al-nafs* is the satisfaction.

Secondly: *Kaf al-'Adhā*, which is to keep away from harming others and to push away harm from one's self. Today, this has become trickier, especially when you are mixing with lots of

85 *Ṣaḥīḥ:* Hadith narrated by Imams al-Bukhārī and Muslim

people, in person and online. The more you mix with people, the more you are prone to being harmed by them: by their words, by their looks, by their actions. You cannot escape unless you go and live segregated, like the life of a monk. For if you don't leave, then you will never escape.

This is why the Prophet ﷺ said:

المؤمِنُ الَّذي يخالطُ النَّاسَ ويصبِرُ على أذاهُم ، خيرٌ مِن الَّذي لا يخالِطُ النَّاسَ ولا يصبِرُ على أذاهُمْ

"The believer who mixes with people and is patient on their harm is better than the one who doesn't mix with people and is not patient on their harm."[86]

Because that is part of life you have to learn to be patient in. The biggest challenge is when you are keeping your harm away from people. You don't harm others: not with your words, your looks, or unnecessary actions.

Similar to richness, where it is about the satisfaction; *kaf al-'adhā* is also about satisfaction, because it gives you that emotional and psychological ease. Today two of the main things that put a lot of people under the pressure are grudges and arguments, especially with their neighbours. If you have problems with your neighbour, it can sometimes become a feud. They are always harming you, and you are retaliating; or even with other people that you might deal with. When you have an argument, you are always trying to get the better out of them. So, they say something. Then you say something that you will try to attack them in some way. And so on. So, preventing harm gives you that tranquillity by avoiding this situation.

86 *Ṣaḥīḥ:* Hadith narrated by Imams Ibn Mājah and Ahmad

I know of a person who had an argument with his neighbour which quickly developed into a feud. This feud led them going to court, and it ended up costing him tens of thousands of pounds, and ultimately it ended with him having to sell his house.

Thirdly; *kasb al-ḥalāl* to earn that which is halal. That in itself is a great *barakah* and blessing when your food and your consumption is all halal and you're not mixing anything with *ḥarām*. The way you are earning, the method, the actual stuff you are earning as well has to be halal, and Allah ﷻ will bless you. This is what the Prophet ﷺ advised Saʿad ibn Abī Waqqāṣ, when the latter asked the Prophet ﷺ "O Messenger of Allah, make *duʿā'* for me that Allah answers my *duʿā'*."

He wanted to be someone who Allah responds to his requests. In a way, he is asking what are the modes to make someone's invocations answered. The Prophet ﷺ said, and note his wisdom; he didn't just say "okay I'll just make *duʿā'* for you", but he gave him the key. What is the key to having your *duʿā'* answered? *Kasb al-ḥalāl*, which is what we were talking about. It's all about halal earning. He ﷺ said:

يا سعدُ أطِبْ مَطْعمَك تكنْ مستجابَ الدَّعوةِ

"O Saʿad! Make your intake *ṭayyib*, your *duʿā'* will be answered."[87]

And this is in reference to the hadith;

"Allah is good and He only accepts that which is good…"[88]

87 *Ḍaʿīf:* Hadith narrated by Imam al-Ṭabarānī
88 *Ṣaḥīḥ:* Hadith narrated by Imam Muslim

"And then he mentioned the story of the man [who makes the *du'ā'*]**, who was on a long journey, he is dusty, dishevelled. He lifts his hands to the sky "Ya Rabb! Ya Rabb!"** [making *du'ā'*]**. But his food is *ḥarām*; his clothing is *ḥarām*; his drink is *ḥarām*; he is nourished by *ḥarām*. So, how will he be answered?"**

There is a link between earning halal and between your *du'ā'* being answered. And obviously Sa'ad was amongst those people who Allah ﷻ blessed him and he became amongst those who had their *du'ā'* answered.

There was a worrying incident in relation to this. Sa'ad ؓ was the governor of al-Kūfah during the time of 'Omar ibn al-Khaṭṭāb ؓ. The people under his authority were generally happy with him. However, one man sent a complaint to the Caliph 'Omar. So, 'Omar went to visit, to ask about him and to check the matter. He gathered the people and asked about Sa'ad; whilst he was present. One of these troublemakers said, "Well, Sa'ad does not go out with us on expeditions. He doesn't deal with us fairly. And he does not divide wealth equally between us."

Basically, he was complaining about Sa'ad. Sa'ad said, "O Allah, if this man has got up out of arrogance and showing-off; then let him live a long life, and increase his poverty and let him be affected by trials and afflictions."

He basically countered the 3 accusations with 3 *du'ā's*. He asked Allah if this man is lying about me and is seeking to show off, then let him reach old age, let him be poor; and let be affected by difficulties. So, as a result Sa'ad was relieved of his post, and he didn't carry on his role because it was almost like a public scandal. Anyway, this man was seen many years later. He was seen as an old man who lost his eyebrows due to old age. He was very poor, begging on the streets. And whenever young women would pass by, he would harass them, which is kind of the *fitnah* that he was exposed to. And he would say about himself: "The *du'ā'* of Sa'ad has affected me!" Meaning that he was a liar when he accused Sa'ad wrongly.

The Imam narrates from Khalaf ibn Tamīm that he said: I saw Ibn 'Ad-ham in al-Shām[89], so I asked him: "What has brought you here?"

He said: "As for me, I did not come here for *jihād* nor for army stationing, but I came so I can eat my fill of halal bread."

This statement re-emphasises the need to search for halal, which may even mean that you have to relocate. We know from the biography of the Imam that he was wary of eating fruits in Damascus, as he was suspicious of its source.

Fourthly; he said *libās al-taqwa* – which is literally translated as the clothing of piety. Allah ﷻ said:

﴿ وَلِباسُ التَّقوَى، ذَلكَ خَير ﴾

﴿The clothing with piety: that is best.﴾[90]

He said this after he sent down clothes to our parents Adam and Ḥawā (on them both be peace). The meaning of which is that your clothes are the things which are closely linked to you, that's your closest item. They guard you, they veil you, as well as protect you. So let *taqwa* be your clothes, let the *taqwa* be what guards you and veils you. Let *taqwa* be your identity. In doing that, it will enable you to guard yourself against a lot of things, because *taqwa* essentially is about having that consciousness to avoid *ḥarām*. The more *taqwa* you have, the more you are going to keep away from the prohibited matters.

89 Translated as the Levant, it includes present day Syria, Jordan, Palestine and Lebanon.
90 Holy Quran; Chapter of the Heights 7:26

And **lastly**; he said "to have trust in Allah" at all times. We have already spoken about *tawakkul* briefly.

Honour of the Scholar

Then the Imam says that we been narrated to from the Noble Master Ḥammād Ibn Salamah ﵀; and he was considered amongst *al-'Abdāl* [which we will talk about later on]. He said that Ḥammād said, "Whoever has sought hadith for other than Allah, then he will be plotted against."

"Hadith" here refers to knowledge, as was a common usage for the word. And so, Imam Ḥammād is saying that whoever seeks knowledge for other than Allah, and thus his intention is not sincere, then he will be shown up and exposed, and he will therefore lose out.

This was also an explanation or a reflection about the importance of having the right intention and the right reason to do the right thing.

It is something that has and will continue to happen; and that is why people would seek knowledge for different reasons. We know that some people will seek knowledge for fame; others for status; some in order to come close to the rulers. Others would do so that they would be able to argue with others: they just seek knowledge for the sake of arguments. Others seek knowledge for money. So many different reasons for people seeking knowledge. Whoever was doing that for the wrong reasons then he will be exposed one way or another.

Today, you will see that there are people who have exposed themselves. They have put on the turbans and they have these nice clothes and long beards and things like that. One way or another, their acts, their sayings for a long time might have been very bewildering and baffling, and impressive to the masses. But then, with time you would have seen these same people applauding and cheering for the tyrannical rulers. They associate themselves with killers. They were associating with people who would commit *ḥarām* and lots of things. They were basically signing cheques, blank cheques for the ruler in the form of fatwas, whatever the ruler wants of them, they would give. To be in such a situation is to despise oneself.

Allah ﷻ says:

﴿ لَا تَرْكَنُوا إِلَى الَّذِينَ ظَلَمُوا فَتَمَسَّكُمُ النَّارُ ﴾

﴿And do not be inclined to those who have wronged themselves, lest the Fire will touch you.﴾[91]

I was told a narration which I don't believe to be fabricated. I say this because I trust those who told me, but (for obvious reasons) I could not verify it. Some Saudis told me that a certain Saudi king wanted to expand the *al-Ḥaram* (the sacred area). This has been their ongoing ventures, to expand and add their names to the expansion. So much so that the Gate of Abdul ʿAzīz and that of Fahad are bigger gates compared to the Gate of the Prophet ﷺ. If these kings venerated the Holy Sanctuary and the Prophet ﷺ, they would not do such a despicable act of making the gates carrying their names bigger than the Prophet ﷺ. More so, if they had any shame, they would not use the title "king" at the Holiest Mosque of the King of kings.

Anyhow, this king wanted to expand, and that meant pushing back the mounts of *Ṣafā* and *Marwah*, which are the two hills that pilgrims walk between, as part of the pillars of Ḥajj and ʿUmrah. Effectively it was going to be shifted out from between the two

91 Holy Quran; Chapter of Hūd 11:113

Hills such that the *Ṣafā* was not going to be where it has been for 1400 years, in an attempt to expand everything. This king formed a board of shaykhs to study this matter; is it acceptable from an Islamic and fiqh perspective?

The board accepted this appointment and they said that they will study it and will look into it, considering the different texts and opinions on the matter. While they were deliberating, construction work had already started on the expansion. So the work had already started, and the board of shaykhs hadn't delivered their verdict yet.

They reported back to the king saying, "We thought you were waiting for our verdict?"

And so, the reply came, "I knew that you would reach this verdict, anyway."

This demonstrates to you that sometimes people are used and abused and sometimes people allow themselves to be abused. And it is a hard situation. It is a difficult situation to be. And you need only see how many of the Saudi shaykhs changed their *ʿaqīdah* and thus their fatwas in the Gulf War, to support the desire and whims of the tyrant.

There is a saying attributed to Bishr al-Ḥāfī, and some say to al-Fuḍayl ibn 'Iyāḍ in which he said, "For me to seek the *dunyā* with playing a flute is better than for me to seek the *dunyā* with *dīn*."

This means that it is so despicable to use *dīn* to attain the *dunyā*, that he'd rather go and earn money playing a flute or any musical instrument. You see in the saying how despicable it is for someone to use their knowledge as a source of income, because when you do that, you are going to be guided and guarded by what to say, because obviously now what's bringing in the money is your fatwa and your "*ʿilm*". For if your money is going to come from somewhere which says to you "don't make this fatwa," you are not going to make this fatwa because that is your source of income. It is one of those things related to intention and also related to how a person acts in that regard.

I remember my opposition to the policies of the kings of Saudi Arabia. Yet, in the year 2011; AbdUllah – the Saudi monarch of the time invited many western dignitaries and Muslim Community leaders to come and perform hajj on the expense of the Kingdom. As the President of the Muslim Association of Britain, I received such an invite. Many of us went. After all, who wants to refuse an opportunity for a free hajj. [Unlike that brother who won a competition we had organised by the Muslim Association of Britain, and the top prize was an all-expenses-paid hajj, sponsored by a travel agency. But, because he disagreed with my views regarding apostasy, he refused to accept the prize, out of protest. Something, he later regretted and begged to have back; but it was too late.]

Anyhow, I couldn't refuse a free hajj, even though it was close to a large convention (MAB Creating Hope) we were organising. The strange thing was that when I was in receipt of this gesture of a gift, I felt that inside me I had to be grateful to the king for his gift; and that it would not be appropriate for me to criticize the monarchs anymore, because of this. This demonstrated to me the effect of a simple gift on the feelings that one has. What about someone who is on the payroll of a monarch or president or government?

Excuse from Taking Office

Because of what I mentioned above, you would find those scholars who sought to escape from certain positions. In the past, some of the scholars were afraid and cautious of being associated with the kings, princes and rulers. They didn't want to be associated with them, even though they were "*khulafā*"; meaning they were ruling by the laws of Islam. Even then, they didn't want to be associated with those in authority because they knew that being associated with them meant there will be some sort of compromise in their *dīn*.

This is the way of the creation. It is the reality of people: when someone does good to us, then our attitude to them will notably change: very few of us will not. For example, if I were to invite you out to dinner, every night. And after dinner, I will give you £20 to go and buy some ice cream or just to pocket it. Every day, without fail, I say, "Let's go!" and I buy you some dinner and give you some money. After a month or less, if someone else speaks bad about me, you are going to come to my defence. You might even hit that person because I have won you over with my hospitality and money. Similarly, if you work in a place and you are under somebody's payroll, then by virtue of the position you are going to find it difficult to speak against that person. So, it becomes something that you have to be aware of and that's why the scholars didn't want to do that. They don't want to take any position of being a judge, or a *mufti*, or whatever in the state because they know that will put them in that situation.

'Ibrāhīm Pasha son of Mohammad Ali Pasha was the governor over Egypt in the Eighteen Century. He was known for his tyranny. On one occasion, he entered the 'Umayyad Masjid in Damascus, with his soldiers and entourage. Shaykh Sa'īd al-Ḥalabī was sitting with his students, teaching them. He was relaxed in his position, his legs extended forward. When 'Ibrāhīm Pasha entered, the soldiers commanded everyone to get up. The Shaykh didn't get up, and continued to extend his legs.

'Ibrāhīm was infuriated by this, but didn't want to worsen matters by executing or harming the Shaykh. After leaving, he sent someone with a pouch with 1000 golden liras to give it to the Shaykh, in a format to ridicule the Shaykh in front of his students, by making him seem that he is willing to take bribes.

When the messenger came with the pouch, Shaykh Saʿīd refused to take the money and said a famous line which remains engraved in the pages of time: (الذي يمد رجله، لا يمد يده) "The one who extends his legs, does not extend his hand!"

This line is an eloquent summary of how the early scholars viewed this whole matter. If you want to remain free, having the freedom to extend your legs, then don't extend your arm out to take handouts.

One of the people was called Ibn Abi Mirthad. The Imam says Ibn Abi Mirthad was found in the market; in his hand was some bread and a bone with little meat on it, and he was eating of it. Prior to this, he was called to the judiciary; and he did so until he escaped (being appointed as a judge).

Someone might say what was wrong with that? In the past, society used to consider that as one of the behaviours which injured one's credibility. Eating in the markets was considered poor manners, and especially for those who had a raised status in the community. Doing this openly would be a stain on one's character. If you ate in the market, you would be viewed as someone who was deficient in character; it was a practice of somebody who had no nobility or honour. It would be something that will be frowned upon. And he was doing that to give the impression that something was wrong with him and he wasn't a stable person, mentally; and therefore he wouldn't be ask to be a judge by the caliph, so he will escape from this.

And the Imam said this is similar to what was narrated from Imam al-Shāfiʿī to what Sufyān al-Thawrī also did. Sufyān ⚶ entered onto the Commander of the Faithful[92], making himself appear insane. He would stroke the rug and say: 'How excellent is this! What did you pay for it?'

And he would say, 'Urine! Urine!'

92 The Caliph

Until he was expelled; meaning that he fooled them to get away from the Ruler and be free from their affairs.

Something similar is narrated in regards to the Great Imam al-'A'ẓam Abu Ḥanīfah (may Allah bestow His mercy on him) who was also asked by the ruler to be a judge. Abu Ḥanīfah said that he is not fit for being a judge. The ruler responded, "You are lying!"

Wittingly, Abu Ḥanīfah responded, "Well, if I'm lying, then I'm not fit to be a judge, because the judge has to be somebody who is honest. And if I am not lying, then I am NOT fit to be a judge." Whichever way it goes, either I'm lying or not lying, I'm not be fit to be a judge."

This was the practice of some of the scholars. However, on the other side, there were noble scholars who did work with the rulers but they didn't allow that to cause them any compromise.

It really depends on an individual. It's the individual person's reality that will determine which way he can proceed. However, in the majority of cases people would have to compromise something, but if you are in a position where you think that "I can say something, I can do something" then, if you feel that you will do more good than harm, then that's a good thing to do because at least that way you will able to do the right thing, to say the right *aḥkām*, so that people will benefit. And sometimes it is not befitting for someone who has knowledge or has correct information to stand back, and allow others who are ill qualified to come forward.

I recall that I was at Istanbul Airport (Turkey) in the airport mescit and the *ṣalāh* was about to commence. All of a sudden, this guy just stepped forward and became the imam, appointing himself as the leader of the *ṣalāh*. When he started to read, his recitation was one of the worst recitations. I think in all schools, his recitation would have nullified the *ṣalāh*. Nonetheless, he pushed himself forward and he just imposed himself on others. He couldn't pronounce the words properly; he couldn't pronounce the letters properly. This was a strange scenario, as he didn't allow anyone else to come forward.

So, if you are in a position like that; and you don't put yourself forward, then someone else less equipped and perhaps ill equipped will take your place, and that can be tragic.

Ḥammād and Muhammad ibn Sulaymān

Now we will mention a short story which shows how the scholars commanded respect, and it is related to the aforementioned Imam Ḥammād ibn Salamah.

The Imam says that we have been narrated to with multiple chains, from Muqātil ibn Ṣāliḥ al-Khurāsānī, who said: I entered onto Ḥammād ibn Salamah ﵀. I found there was nothing in the house except a straw mat on which he was sitting, and a *muṣ-ḥaf*[93] he reads from, a folder containing his knowledge and a jug from which he makes *wuḍū'*.

So, whilst I was sitting in his presence, someone knocked on the door.

He said: "Oh girl, go out and look who is that!"

She said, "This is the messenger of Muhammad ibn Sulaymān!"

He said: "Tell him that he enters alone."

So he entered, gave salutation and passed him a letter.

He said: "Read it!" So in it was: *In the name of Allah, Most Gracious, Most Merciful: From Muhammad ibn Sulaymān to Ḥammād ibn Salamah. As for then, may Allah allow you to enter into the morning with the same with what He has given His 'awliyā'*

93 The term for the Quran Book or papers.

and the people of His obedience. A question has occurred and we wish to ask you about it.

He said: "Oh girl, come and get me the inkwell!"

Then he said: "Write on the back of this letter: *'Likewise, may Allah allow you to enter into the morning with the same with what He has given His 'awliyā' and the people of His obedience. We observed the scholars, and they do not come to anyone. If a matter has befallen, then come to us and ask us about what concerns you. If you come to me, do not come to me except by yourself. Do not bring your horsemen and infantry, for then I will not advise you, nor will I advise myself and salām!'*

So, whilst I was sitting with him, someone knocked on the door.

He said: "Oh girl, go out and look who is it?"

She said: "Muhammad ibn Sulaymān."

He said: "Tell him to enter, alone."

Muhammad ibn Sulaymān entered and greeted, then he sat in front of Ḥammād.

Muhammad said, "Why is it when I look at you, I am filled with terror?!"

Ḥammād said: "I heard Thābit - meaning al-Bunānī - say: I heard Anas ibn Mālik ﷺ say: I heard the Messenger of Allah ﷺ say: "**If the scholar seeks Allah with his knowledge, everything will be in awe of him. Yet, if he seeks to increase his treasures, he will be in awe of everything.**"

Muhammad said: "What do you say - may Allah have mercy on you – with regards to a man who has two sons, and he is more pleased with one of them; such that he wants to make two thirds of his money for him while still alive?"

Ḥammād said: "No! And may Allah have mercy on you. For I have heard Thābit al-Bunānī saying: I heard Anas ibn Mālik say: I heard the Messenger of Allah ﷺ say: "**Surely, if Allah ﷻ wants to**

punish a slave with his [own] money, He will enable him -as he is dying – to write an unfair will."

Muhammad said: "Any need?"

He said: "Tell me! Unless it is a calamity in the *dīn*!"

Muhammad said: "Forty thousand dirhams[94]! You can use them to seek help in the state you are."

Ḥammād said: "Return it to those whom you have wronged it from!"

Muhammad said: "By Allah, I only give you from what I have inherited!"

Hammad said: "I do not need it. Fold it away from me, may Allah fold away your burdens."

Muhammad said: "Something else?"

Hammad said: "Tell me! Unless it is a calamity in the *dīn*!"

Muhammad said: "Take it and divide (distribute)[95] it!"

Hammad said: "It might be that if I am just in its distribution, some of those who did not get a share, would say that he was not fair in its distribution, so he would be sinning! Fold it away from me, may Allah fold away your burdens."

Ḥammād ibn Salamah ﷺ was an imam from Baṣrah, which was a minaret of Islamic knowledge. He lived during the latter time of the *Ṣaḥābah*. A very righteous man, he was a person of hadith and fiqh, and he was well known.

Ḥammād Ibn Salamah was considered amongst *'abdāl*: a title which is famous amongst people who talk about the knowledge of Allah ﷻ. Translated, the word *'abdāl* means either replaceables or substitutes. Although there are a few *aḥādīth* which are not

94 Traditionally, a dirham is a silver coin. It was used extensively in the past, mentioned in the Quran. Today, a few countries still use the dirham.
95 Meaning give it to others

sound in terms of their narrations, there is a mixture of *aḥādīth* which talk about a group of people who are very close to Allah ﷻ. They are very close such that their *duʿāʾ* is always answered by Allah ﷻ. They are people who are at this high level of spirituality. And this is also going back to the hadith of the Prophet ﷺ, which is a sound one:

رُبَّ أَشْعَثَ، مَدْفُوعٍ بِالْأَبْوَابِ لَو أَقْسَمَ عَلَى اللهِ لَأَبَرَّهُ

"It might be that somebody is dusty, unkempt and is pushed away at the doors; were he to ask of Allah, swearing an oath; Allah would fulfil his oath."[96]

When he asks people, they repel him and they don't give him anything. So, outwardly he seems like somebody who is a *faqīr*, somebody was in need. However, they have that direct connection with Allah ﷻ. They are called replaceables or substitutes, because every time, one of them passes away, they are replaced or substituted with another. So, these are like the special people chosen by Allah ﷻ. And they used to consider that Ḥammād ibn Salamah as being one of them.

Muhammed ibn Sulaymān was the son of Sulaymān, the grandson of AbdUllah ibn ʿAbbās – the famous Companion. He was the cousin of the first two ʿAbbāssid Caliphs, and served as provincial governor of al-Kūfah and al-Baṣrah and its dependencies for most of his life.

The Imam comments saying how beautiful this story is. It's has so many beneficial things and that's why he has narrated it, as within it, there are many treasures and great lessons to be learnt. Although, he adds that they are so obvious that he doesn't need to really identify them.

---

96 *Ṣaḥīḥ:* Hadith narrated by Imam Muslim

The Imam tells us that this story has so many obvious benefits; and because at the beginning of the book he did say that he is not going to go into too much detail into matters by extending the explanation. And this story falls within what the Imam narrated of the hadith of the Prophet ﷺ where he said that if the scholar intends with his knowledge Allah ﷻ then everything will fear him. But if he wants with his knowledge to get the treasures and money, then he will be afraid of everything because obviously his intention now is totally different.

Although the Imam has chosen not to dwell on the many benefits, I have chosen the contrary. So, here are the benefits that I have deduced.

First of all; you see Ḥammād Ibn Salamah was a man who practised *zuhd* (abstinence) as he didn't have a lot in his house, only a few items: a *muṣ-ḥaf*, straw mat, bowl to make *wuḍū'* and so that's all the kind of thing that he had. And this is showing how little their attachment to the *dunyā*. In the tradition that when Salmān al-Fārisī رضي الله عنه was about to die, he started to cry. And they said why are you crying? He said "The Prophet ﷺ took an oath with us and we abandoned that pledge, which is that our provisions in this life should only be the provisions of somebody who is on journey."[97]

Our provisions, the luggage that we have should only be of that of a person who is on a journey. Think about when you go on a journey; you have one bag with you which weighs less than 23 kilograms, and one hand luggage, it shouldn't be more than that. And when they looked at the house of Salmān, it was very much like that of Ḥammād's. The narrator said "When we looked at what he had left, and the value of which was twenty-something or thirty-something dirhams"; but even then, he thought that he had accumulated too much of the *dunyā*, and that he had broken the pledge he made with the Prophet ﷺ.

97 *Ṣaḥīḥ:* Hadith narrated by Imam Ahmad

Secondly; look at the honour of the *'ulamā'* and the scholars. The *'ulamā'* and the scholars had honour and pride, but not in an arrogant way. They kept the honour in a way to preserve the knowledge so that scholars and knowledge were respected by others and not be allowed to be abused by the rulers.

If the scholars knocked on the doors of the kings and governors, the governors might ignore them, and push them away. That's not how the *'ilm* should be preserved. Scholars should not knock on the doors of the rulers, but the other way round. I already narrated an incident relating to that in regards to the expansion of the Holy Sanctuary in Makkah.

There are many similar stories to that of Ḥammād. We have the story of al-'Awzā'ī with al-Saffāḥ. Abu AbdUllah al-Saffāḥ was the first of the 'Abbāssian *Khulafā'* and the cousin of Muhammad ibn Sulaymān. He was called al-Saffāḥ which means the massacrer. He killed so many of the 'Umayyids, because he was the guy who overthrew them. We have a similar story with Sa'īd ibn Jubayr with al-Ḥajjāj. There are also stories where these people had kept their dignity and so on. Sālim Ibn AbdUllah ibn 'Omar ibn al-Khaṭṭāb with Hishām ibn 'Abdul Malik; and son on.

Thirdly; we can see the various points of knowledge that he gave on how to be fair, and more so how to be just to your heirs and so on.

Fourthly; look at how Ḥammād was narrating with a chain, he wasn't just giving from his own opinion. He was giving that chain back to the Prophet ﷺ; which further demonstrates their attention to the chains of transmission, as our *dīn* is based on *'isnād*.

Fifthly; when he had the opportunity to take the money, he rejected the money because he knew that would be more burden on him than it would be of help. Because it might be that he can't distribute to all those in need, and they would then abuse him.

I remember when we went to my town of origin: Mosul in Iraq. Part of our reason was to do charitable work and help those who had been affected by the battle to remove ISIS. No doubt, it was a heavy battle, with much destruction and enormous casualties. We had an opportunity to give people some charity. The UK charity that took us there, arranged to distribute 100 food bags in preparation for Ramadan. They had prepared the bags; as they knew how chaotic things can get, they handed tickets to people in advance, in order to make things orderly. However, more people came who didn't have tickets. Some families sent several members of the same household in hope of getting a food parcel each. So, it ended up leaving more people upset than happy, because everybody wanted more. Everybody wanted us to give them saying that you haven't given us and so on. So even when you are distributing and you're trying to be charitable, you'll end up upsetting more people than actually making them happy. Thence, one says it is better that I don't want that money so that I don't have the burden of having to distribute it.

Not only that, but I remember a comment by one man who was almost like a knife in my heart. The charity supervisors said that its best to abort the mission, due to the chaos. They had another food distribution in a few days. I convinced them to give me some of those tickets, so that we can, at least, give tickets to those who didn't get a parcel. He obliged me with 50 or so tickets. Now to distribute them, I got them to line up in two lines, men and women: 25 for each gender. After I distributed to the men, I came to give the women. Now, not all the men got a ticket, as I only had 25. One man commented to his friend in a tone loud enough for me to hear: "Look how he is choosing to give tickets to the beautiful women."

I felt very hurt by this comment in which he was accusing me of using this charity for some absurd flirting vantage. And this was one example of how even giving charity can be a burden on a person;

something which Ḥammād had already recognised.

Sixthly; see how Imam Ḥammād wanted to prevent others from sinning by wrongly accusing him of unfairly distributing the money. He was also looking out for others' own welfare by not taking the money.

The same person Abu Abdullah says that he narrated from his father who said that he saw Ḥammād Ibn Salamah in a dream, after he passed away. So, he said to him, "How has Allah treated you?"

He said, "Good!"

I said, "What did He say?"

He said, "He said to me: 'For a long time you tired yourself. Today, I shall elongate your rest, and the rest of those who tire themselves for My sake. *Bakhin Bakhin*[98], what I have prepared for them!'."

I do understand that the opinion of a ruler (be he caliph, king or president) or his deputy should be followed, especially in matters which are of proven benefit to the public, and provided that his opinion does not conflict with any established principle of Islam. However, one should avoid degrading himself by running after the ruler seeking their approval and closeness.

Dealing with Allah

Ahmad ibn Abi al-Ḥawārī said: "I heard Abu Sulaymān [al-Dārānī] ﵀ say, 'Deal with Allah through your hearts'."

The Imam, as is the usual aspect of the people of hadith, wants to clarify certain things which might need to be clarified in terms of names and so on. Here he just points out that Ahmad ibn Abi

98 Words said to display astonishment or delight

al-Ḥawārī: is either pronounced **al-Hawara** or **al-Ḥawārī**; the latter of which is more famous. However, he said that I have heard al-Hawara several times from our Shaykh the Hadith Master Abi al-Baqā' who narrates it from the people of precision or some of them; and Allah Almighty knows best.

The Imam comments on Abu Sulaymān's words telling us that this means cleanse your heart, purify and tame it; and don't interweave it with any of the outward actions.

So, Abu Sulaymān is saying that - in line with the whole theme of the topic, which is about how a person should deal with his heart - one should look at his heart, purify it, as it is the place where the intention and also the *ikhlāṣ* will be.

He is saying when you deal with Allah ﷻ, deal with your hearts and that should be the ultimate goal. You should always be clear. Your intention should be pure when you are dealing with Allah. Think about how your heart is because that is what you need to purify. That is what you need to correct. And so purify it, make sure that it is correct. And not only that, but try to tame it as well because the heart like any other limb may try to stray off here and there.

Then he mentioned the general theme; which we have been speaking about before is that a person who is more aware of Allah ﷻ, he is not going to be worried about others, meaning that he is not concerned about what others think or what their attitude is. That is why he said that when you are doing something apparent you don't need to hide it from people because at the end of the day, your intention should be that you're doing it for Allah ﷻ so it shouldn't make a difference in your perspective whether people see it or not. Or whether people are aware of it or not because you are doing it for Allah ﷻ. It's not like trying to hide away from people, so you don't want people to see it because if you do that there is an aspect of where you are almost taking people into consideration. You're thinking about people in your actions, and that could be a problem in itself.

The Imam tells us a little bit about Abu Sulaymān. Beginning with his title al-Dārānī. He clarifies that the name is either al-Dārānī (الداراني) or al-Dārā'ī (الدارائي). Both are linked to the vicinity of Dāriyā, a city or a village near Damascus. And so that's where Abu Sulaymān is from.

The Imam informs us that Abu Sulaymān was one of the highly ranked people who are aware of Allah ﷻ. He has many gifts from Allah, which were outwardly observed. Abu Sulaymān was one of the outstanding gnostics, who had astonishing states and apparent wisdom. His name is Abdul Raḥmān ibn Ahmad ibn ʿAtiyah. He is one of the later [notables] of our country: Damascus, and its surrounding areas: رضي الله عنه.

And he was one of the people who were from Imam al-Nawawī's city. He says he is from our city Damascus and that which is around it. Now, you will find some of the '*ulama*' who have this kind of affinity to their cities or regions. When they are associated with a certain city, they usually try to mention a lot of the people related to their city. Here the Imam is from that area of al-Shām, so obviously any of the '*ulama*' that are from that area he would try to promote them more, but not out of specificity to that person but more in favour of showing that this area is good. It's full of scholars and righteous people.

Pure Breast Towards Others

The Imam tells us that we have been narrated to from the Noble Master Abu ʿAlī al-Fuḍayl ibn 'Iyāḍ who said: "Those whom we recognise didn't realise what they realised[99] with abundant prayers,

99 Meaning they didn't reach the state they attained

or fasting; rather due to a generous soul, sound pure breast[100] and sincerity towards the *'Ummah*."

These are very important few words which sometimes may solve many problems for us. And that is he is saying that the people who have reached the stations or the levels that they have reached, didn't reach this with extensive amount of *ṣalāh*, fasting or these *'ibādah* which people do and practise. Rather it is more to do with the inner self. It is about how generous their self is and how their hearts are pure towards others. They were not people who held grudges, they were not people who had enmity towards others, and they had al-*nuṣuḥ* to the *'ummah*; which is derived from the word: *naṣiḥah*: meaning that they were sincere to other people. They wanted the good for others. Whenever they saw an aspect where they can help others, they would help them if they could. If they knew that there was an issue that needed resolving, they would give their advice; without being nosy or interfering, but they would help as much as they can. This is a form of *naṣiḥah*. You see somebody struggling with something, you go and offer your support or your help. You see somebody who might be in some sort of need, again, you offer your help. That's the kind of *naṣiḥah*. It doesn't mean that you just go around throwing orders at people and just saying "fear Allah," "do this, stop praying like this," "stop doing that" and so on.

And we know from *salāmat al-ṣadr* about the Companion whom the Prophet ﷺ said, "**A man will enter on to you who is from the people of *al-Jannah*.**" We all know that hadith[101] and when one of the Companions: AbdUllah ibn 'Amr ibn al-'Āṣ رضي الله عنه went to stay with him to find out what kind of acts of worship he does which has allowed him to attain such a status. He found that he wasn't doing much. The only thing that he was doing was what he mentioned to AbdUllah that "I do not have any grudges or bad wishes in my self for any Muslim; nor do I envy anyone for what Allah has given them." And you see that in itself was why the Prophet ﷺ said this is a man from *al-Jannah*.

100 This denotes a clean heart free from any grudges to others.
101 *Ṣaḥīḥ:* Hadith narrated by Imam Ahmad

When Zayd ibn 'Aslam visited Abu Dujānah ☙ who was ill, he found his face bright. He asked him, "How come your face is bright and happy?"

He said, "There is no action which I have firm faith in more than two. The first is that I didn't use to speak in that which doesn't concern me. And the other is that my heart is peaceful to other Muslims."

So further on, you can understand that it's the inner self. It is the *qalb*, it's the inside that is important to purify, clean, and tame. If you do that you will reach high levels. It's about having *yaqīn*, which is a higher form or *īmān*, and that is what makes people reach high status.

He goes on to say that Imam al-Shāfiʿī ☙ said, "Whoever wants that Allah prescribes goodness for him, then let him have good suspicion in regards to people."

The meaning of this is to have a pure clean heart towards others. Don't always suspect ill of others. Don't injure others. Don't always think that people are in the wrong. Don't think negatively of others. Do not repeatedly look for the faults of people. Do not always interpret actions in a negative way: why is that person looking at me like this? Why is his hand in his pocket? Why did he smile? Why is he talking to this guy? They must be talking about me and things like that: that is a kind of a bad intention towards others. So, having that is also a problem in your heart. Imam al-Shāfiʿī is saying that if you want Allah ﷻ to deal with you well, then you should start to cleanse yourself from bad suspicion and always think good of people.

And we have in this regard the saying of 'Isā ﷺ when he saw a man stealing and he said to him, "Are you stealing?"

The guy was taking something. So the guy replied, "No, by Allah who there is no God except Him."

So the Messiah 'Īsā ﵇ said, "I believe in Allah, and I denounce my sight."[102]

He says that I am going to say my sight is lying because he swore by Allah ﷻ and I believe in Allah. So that's an example of good suspicion in regards to people. That's why when you look at some of the *aḥkām* of Islam in terms of some of the punishments and the penal codes, there is a large consideration to refute away any doubt or misconceptions.

There is a saying attributed to some of the Companions, which is (ادرءوا الحدود بالشبهات), translated as "Explain away the penal punishments with doubt."

If there is any doubt about an issue, if there's no clear evidence, then punishments/penalties are not imposed on people. There must be no doubt, it has to be clear cut. And that is one example there, if somebody denies something you can't force him to say otherwise.

Longing Heart

The Imam narrates his *'isnād* with regards to the following narration. It can be noticed that the Imam mentions his full chain when potentially there is a query in regards to the narration, or it might seem like a strange one, as is the case here.

He narrates that Abu Ḥātim Muhammad ibn 'Idrīs said: I heard Abu Qubaysah say:

102 *Ṣaḥīḥ:* Hadith narrated by Imams al-Bukhārī and Muslim

I saw Sufyān al-Thawrī in a dream, so I said, 'What has Allah the Exalted done with you?'

He said:

نظرتُ إلى ربي كِفاحاً فقال لي   هنيئاً رضائي عنك يا ابنَ سعيد

لقد كُنْتَ قوَّاماً إذا أظلمَ الدُجا   بعَبْرَة مُشتاقٍ وقلبِ عميد

فدونَك فاخترْ أيَّ قَصْرٍ أردتَه   وزُرْني فإني منكَ غيرُ بَعيد

"I looked unto my Lord openly so He said to me,

'Congratulations for My pleasure on you O Son of Sa'īd.

You indeed used to be excessive in standing when the night darkened,

Having the tear of a longing one and a determined heart.

So, in front of you; choose whichever palace you want

And visit Me, for I am not far from you'."

The narrator says that he saw Sufyān al-Thawrī in a dream, so he obviously meant after he passed away. For us, we believe that dreams are a source of good tidings and good hope, as was mentioned by the Prophet ﷺ. However, we do not consider dreams or visions as references for Islamic Law. Meaning that one cannot claim to innovate something in the religion based on a dream he had, because the *dīn* was sealed with the Prophet ﷺ and no new modes of worship can be introduced by those who come after him, no matter what their level of righteousness may be.

Now, we need to know a little bit about who Sufyān al-Thawrī is, because that will give us a little bit more understanding of why he would say such a thing or why he would be treated in such a thing. This great man - Sufyān al-Thawrī - was from Banī Thawr; an Arab tribe which goes back to Muḍar. He is someone who was present during the second century. He was born in the year 97AH in al-Kūfah - Iraq, and he lived most of his life there. He left it when the ʿAbbāsīs took control. Abu Jaʿfar al-Manṣūr wanted to force him to become a judge.

With this regards, Imam al-Shāfiʿī narrates what Sufyān al-Thawrī did. He ﷺ entered on to the Commander of the Faithful[103], making himself appear insane. He would stroke the rug and say: 'How excellent is this! What did you pay for it?'

And he would say, 'Urine! Urine!'

Until he was expelled; meaning that he fooled them to get away from the Ruler and be free from their affairs. Then, he decided to leave and he began to alternate between Madinah and Makkah.

His mother was very righteous. Being a righteous woman, she said to him, "My son, you go and seek knowledge, and I will look after your income. I will knit and I will sell, and I will pay for your expenses. You just go, learn and dedicate yourself to the knowledge."

It is also narrated that she said to him: "My son! when you write 10 letters, or so, look at yourself and reassess yourself, have you changed in any way? Do you feel more arrogant? Or do you feel closer to Allah? How do you see yourself? And if you feel that you're not changing in any way, then that you should know that this is not going to harm you nor benefit you."

Sufyān was one of those people who was not only very pious and righteous, but he was also very knowledgeable and one of the people who really should have had a school: like the Mālikīs and Ḥanafīs. Al-Thawrī was a school in himself, but he didn't have any

103 The Caliph

students who really preserved his *madhhab*, so his opinions and understanding got dispersed amongst others.

Imam al-Ṭabarī said, "He was a *faqīh*, scholar, worshipper, devout, extensive narrator of hadith, trustworthy and honest."

Imam Mālik praised Sufyān. He said, "Iraq used to flood us [in Madinah] with money: gold, and silver; until Sufyān came along; and it started to flood us with knowledge." May Allah be pleased with them both.

And he has many sayings, mainly in aspects of fiqh which we can go back to. So, when he died this is what he was reported to have said that Allah ﷻ spoke to him directly. And He congratulated him on attaining His pleasure. But the point why Imam al-Nawawī narrates it here is the point to say to him that his heart was a longing heart. It was a pure heart. He wanted to meet Allah. He was anticipating the link with the Allah ﷻ.

Seekers of Forgiveness

After this, the Imam mentions a narration from Yaḥyā ibn Muʿādh al-Rāzī ؒ. Yaḥyā said: "How many seekers of forgiveness are despised; and [how many] silent ones who are shown mercy. This one says: "I seek forgiveness of Allah" yet his heart is wicked. And the other is silent, yet his heart is in remembrance."

This means that how many of a people who make *ʾistighfār*, but they are rejected and despised. And how many of people who are silent, meaning they're not making *ʾistighfār*, but they are shown mercy. What does this mean? It's explained by the fact that a person might be saying "*Astaghfir Ullah*" on his tongue, but his heart is corrupt. And somebody might not be saying "*Astaghfir Ullah*";

but his heart is in remembrance of Allah. So, it is the action of the tongue and speaking that cannot be opposite to what in the heart and that's why when we spoke about *ṣidq* before, we said truthfulness is when your actions are internally and externally aligned. So, you have to be careful in that you might be doing acts which might seem that they are good, but if your heart is opposite or in contrast to this, then actually it might a burden on you rather than something which you will be rewarded for?

Imam al-Ghazālī has a same similar saying in this regard. He said that how many a person might be prostrating himself before Allah but he is committing a sin which if it were to be distributed among the people of a village, it would have destroyed them. He is praying and he is in *sujūd*, but he's also in a state of sin that if he were to be punished for the sin it will destroy many a people. The scholars explain what he meant here was that sometimes the person is in *ṣalāh* and the default position of a person in *ṣalāh* should be that they are focused on Allah, that they are worshiping Allah, that they are attending to Allah. They are prostrating, and that's the closest that they are to Allah ﷻ. But this person, when he is in *sujūd* rather than being focused on the prayer and the situation which he is in, he is thinking about something else. He is probably in admiration of something else. So, he is completely inattentive to Allah ﷻ. In a way, what Imam al-Ghazālī is saying is that it is a form of mockery that a person is mocking with his *ṣalāh* because not only is his attention not directed to Allah, but it is directed elsewhere. It's almost like *ʿibādah* of something else.

Devoutness

The Imam then narrated to us in relation to someone named al-Jūʿī. The Imam says he has gifts that Allah ﷻ has given him. And they said maybe it's related to him being hungry. He might remain hungry for a long time so they called him al-Jūʿī which means the hungry one. He said: "The foundation of the *dīn* is *waraʿ*."

Waraʿ is to abstain from permissible matters out of fear that you will fall into doubt or into *ḥarām*; and it is a form of devoutness. This occurs at its peak level by leaving halal things in fear that you might fall into *ḥarām*. So, one is putting a barrier between oneself and *ḥarām*. This includes anything that might have any aspect of doubt or suspicion.

So, he said, "The foundation of the *dīn* is devoutness."[104] That means your basis of your *dīn* is how do you distance yourself from anything that potentially could harm you, and that goes back to the heart because it's a practice of the heart, and not the actions. And this is the whole point of what the Imam is trying to say to you: focus has to be on the heart.

Then he says: "The best *ʿibādah* is to struggle during the night," meaning to get up and pray, struggling with your self.

"And the best path to *al-Jannah* is a sound pure breast." Meaning to clear your heart and your chest free from all the grudges, from the hatred and all badness. That is the best way to get to *al-Jannah*. No action is involved here. No physical actions, no hunger, no nothing. It's about here working on inside here. And we have spoken about this before.

So as you can see from these few narrations the focus of the Imam is to remind us is that the path of those who are aware, *al-ʿĀrifīn*, those who are going to Allah ﷻ is focused on them being concerned with their inner, with their heart, correcting their heart, cleaning their heart, purifying their heart, taming their *nafs*, and getting rid of all those negative aspects. Because if you think about it, it's a very

104 *Waraʿ* is one of those words that can't be translated without explanation. It is not merely devoutness. Rather it is the aspect of one being God conscious and aware of Allah, that you become cautious of not doing the wrong thing, even if this means leaving permissible acts.

simple equation. The equation is if you want the light of the Quran, the light of Islam, the light of the understanding that comes with knowing Allah, how are you going to get this light, if your heart is contaminated and sealed? As Allah says:

﴿ أَفَلا يَتَدَبَّرُونَ القُرءَانَ، أَمْ عَلَى قُلُوبٍ أقفالها ﴾

﴾Do they not reflect upon the Quran, or is it that the hearts are locked?﴿[105]

﴿ إنّا جعلنا على قلوبهم أَكِنَّةً أن يفقهوه ﴾

﴾Indeed, We placed covers over their hearts, preventing them from comprehending it.﴿[106]

And if your heart is dark, nothing is going to get in.

So, you have to get rid of these covers that are holding you back. You have to clean the heart from all darknesses. Once cleaned, it can see the light of the Quran, and the Quran can be understood. The meanings can be reflected upon; your personality, your practice, all that will change if the heart is good.

The Imam mentions a man called al-Zaqqāq. He is given this kind of title because it is related to his occupation. Some people throughout history will get a title of their surname, which is related to the kind of work that they do, or it might be descended from ancestors. This is quite common amongst cultures. I recall in my town of origin: Mosul – may Allah preserve it and honour it – we have many families who carry names linked to an occupation that they had. These include families which are named: the Tailor (al-Khayyāt), the Tanners (al-Dabbāgh), the Butcher (al-Qaṣṣāb), the Author/Registrar (al-Kātib), the Ironsmith (al-Ḥaddād), and so on. In fact, one family is called "Chaqmaqchī", and if broken down:

105 Holy Quran; Chapter of the Women 4:82
106 Holy Quran; Chapter of the Cave 18:57

"Chaq-maq-chī" which is derived from those who used to load guns, due to the sound it makes when loading the gun!

This man was named al-Zaqqāq, as he related to *al-zaqq*, which is the skin of an animal made into pouches for carrying water. So, he would make it and sell it; and that's how he got that name.

Al-Zaqqāq said, "This affair of ours is built on four:

1 - We do not eat except from need.

2 - We do not sleep except from being overcome.

3 - We are not silent except from fear.

4 - And we do not speak except for a purpose."

By "this affair of ours" he means the kind of practices that we have.

The **first** one is that we do not eat except out of hunger or out of need. The word *fāqah* means we are in need. So, the only time we eat is if there is a need. This goes back to what the Prophet ﷺ was teaching in regards to reducing food in general. There is a tradition which some attribute to the Prophet ﷺ, but it has no foundation in the books of hadith. The tradition is that the Prophet ﷺ sent a messenger with a letter to the Ruler of Egypt. The Ruler accepted the letter and returned the messenger with a physician or somebody who had knowledge of medicine, and with two slaves. It is reported that when the physician was presented to the Prophet ﷺ, he said "We are not in need of a doctor, because we are people who only eat when we are hungry. And when we eat, we do not fill our stomachs."

Whilst, this report is not of the authenticated words Prophet ﷺ, it remains as a basic principle in the essence of medicine and good health. Today the physicians tell us that the key to good health is having a healthy gut. And there is a need to examine what you eat, and not only the food, but also a spiritual metaphysical kind of relationship here because when you are eating you are introducing a lot of toxins into your body which potentially need to be removed. These toxins might get assimilated into the body and they can cause problems. And therefore, the more you eat, the more likely you will have problems.

Secondly; "And we do not sleep except when we have been overtaken" means we don't just go to bed just for the sake of it, but there is a need to go to bed. And that itself shows that they were concerned with time and the precious nature of how they viewed time. They would not sleep unless there was a need. Unless they really felt tired, they would not go to sleep. Today, a lot of people don't go to sleep because they are watching television or on the telephone, or chatting, or playing games, or something like that. Whereas these people wouldn't go to sleep, because they would be engaged in other things like *'ibādah*, *ṣalāh*, *dhikr* (remembering of Allah ﷻ), or recitation of the Quran or studying and revision of knowledge.

I was researching online, and I found an online article by Bakr al-Buʿdāni who mentioned 18 people from the past who used to pray *fajr* with the *wuḍū'* of *'ishā'*. These included people like Abu Ḥanīfah, Saʿīd ibn al-Musayyib, Mālik, Manṣūr ibn Zādhān and others. Which demonstrates that these great people would sleep very little.

Thirdly; "And we only are silent if we fear something". Some people might think that this means that if they're scared, they will not speak. What it really means is that if we are afraid that we might cause harm to the person whom we are speaking to, or maybe it might not get the intended purpose, then we would refrain from speaking. Because, you can speak the truth and say what you can, but if you feel that the person in front of you with your dialogue, your speech, or admonishment is actually going to be more misguided, then it is better to refrain from saying anything.

I remember giving a reminder a while back about brothers who are harsh in how they admonish people. We have the classical telephone ringing in the *ṣalāh*: it always angers people and some people make a real fuss about it, as if the person who has accidentally forgotten to switch off his phone has committed a major sin. I remember once somebody shouted "*Astaghfir Ullah*, I seek refuge of Allah.... etc." The guy made a mistake and he forgot to switch off his phone: no more, no less. But it was made so major, that one or two of the attendees were willing to go to war on the issue, and that's not an exaggeration.

Once, when I was leading the prayer at the Muslim Welfare House of Sheffield; and a man didn't switch his phone off, despite the reminder being issued before the commencement of the prayer. It rang and rang, and the guy – too embarrassed to be identified – chose not to make any movement. Some people starting huffing and puffing. I sensed there was going to be an all-out assault after the prayer. Indeed, someone did get up and started a rant, but I quickly interrupted him. I said, "Brothers, I do understand your frustration when someone forgets to switch his phone off, but consider this: a man *urinated* in the mosque during the time of the Prophet ﷺ; and you all know how he responded! Now tell me this: Which is worse: urinating in the mosque or a mobile phoning ringing?"

It was a rhetorical question; and thus, the tension was diffused. However, after people had dispersed, one of my friends approached me smirking, and said, "I like what you did there. Yes. You calmed the situation down, but you didn't let the guy off the hook, as you subtly compared him to urinating in the *masjid*!"

He was right. That was my purpose, because despite being warned the guy still fell into the error; and it was annoying!

So, imagine that kind of dialogue might push a person from not coming to the *masjid* again. He might say "That's it. I'm not going to come again if that's the kind of treatment I have been given."

I remember a sister was telling us her actual story. She had an autistic son. One day, she brought him to the *masjid* to get used to the *masjid*. The *masjid* is a community space and this incident took place in America. She said on one occasion one of the sisters turned to her and said, "You know sister, you don't have to come to the *masjid*." She wanted to say to her that you do not need to come to the *masjid*, but the way it sounded was like: "Don't come, if you can't control your child."

This woman with the autistic son said, "For 10 years, I didn't go to the *masjid* after that!"

Do you see how one phrase, one word out of place can be very hurtful, and can have long lasting damaging effects. So, he was saying this, meaning that we are afraid that what we say might lead to unwanted consequences.

Indeed, the other aspect of fear is that you might be afraid for yourself. So, sometimes you might be very proud of yourself, you feel that "I'm really good. Everybody's listening to me." So, then there's a fear here about yourself that you might be showing off. And probably this is why the Imam has narrated it in this context, because it's all about having the right intention and so on. So that's what he meant here.

The **last one** is that we only speak if there is a need; and the need is associated with the fact that we know what we are saying, and we are confirmed in what we're saying. So, we're not just saying anything without any reading; or without referencing what we're saying. And again, this is also the hadith of the Prophet ﷺ:

ومَن كان يُؤمِنُ با للهِ واليَومِ الآخِرِ؛ فليَقُلْ خَيرًا أو ليَسكُتْ

"Whoever believes in the Allah and the Final Day, let him say something good, or let him be quiet."[107]

This was the saying of Abu Bakr al-Zaqqāq; and the Imam said that he was from the noble Sufis. The people who had *karāmāt* and apparent features.

Impoverishment

The Imam said that we have been narrated to from Abu Bakr al-Zaqqāq that he said, "Everyone is attributed to a lineage, except the poor: for they are attributed to Allah ﷻ. Every lineage or parentage will be disconnected, except their lineage and parentage; for their lineage is truthfulness and their parentage is poverty."

"Everyone has some sorts of lineage," means that they have parents and ancestry. People will say, "This is where I'm from. I am from Quraysh, Hāshimī, and al-Ḥasani etc. So he's saying everybody has those lineages which they may boast about, but the paupers: their actual connection, or where they are associated to is Allah ﷻ.

They are not ones to boast about which family they come from or whatever. And he said, the reality is every *ḥasab* and *nasab*, every lineage, every association, family link will one day cut off, because this is the reality of the family; it's related to something mortal. It's not something that's going to exist forever. Allah ﷻ inform us:

﴿يَوَدُّ الْمُجْرِمُ لَوْ يَفْتَدِي مِنْ عَذَابِ يَوْمِئِذٍ بِبَنِيهِ، وَصَاحِبَتِهِ وَأَخِيهِ، وَفَصِيلَتِهِ الَّتِي تُؤْوِيهِ ، وَمَنْ فِي الْأَرْضِ جَمِيعًا ثُمَّ يُنْجِيهِ﴾

107 *Ṣaḥīḥ:* Hadith narrated by Imams al-Bukhārī and Muslim

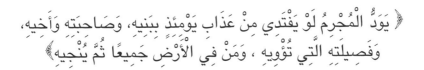

﴾The criminal would wish if he can ransom his children to escape the punishment on that day. As well as his partner and brother. And his tribe that shelters him. And indeed, all who is on the Earth, so that he may be saved.﴿[108]

Al-Zaqqāq continues to say except for the paupers, because their linkage, their heritage, is *ṣidq*, and their association is related to their poverty.

This is in a way similar to what Salmān al-Fārisī ﷺ said, when people were speaking about their lineages, he said:

أَبي الإسلامُ، لا أَبَ لي سِوَاهُ   إِنِ افتَخَرُوا بِقَيْسٍ أَو تَمِيمِ ،

My ancestry is Islam, I have no other ancestor

Should they boast about being of Qays or Tamīm

Status of the Paupers

The Imam narrates to us the saying of the Prophet's ﷺ Companion: Salmān al-Fārisī ﷺ. This saying is in line with the theme of what has been spoken about so far. It is about understanding humility, and not having improper thoughts about people who are poor or have financial problems, and not to view them as if they have no status in life or have no worth.

The Imam said that it has been related to us through three different chains, which all go back to Salmān ﷺ who said in a very short sentence but very important in this regard.

108 Holy Quran; Chapter of The Paths of Ascension 70:11-14

He said: "If people knew Allah's help for the weak, they would not have overpriced the carriage."

The term weak or weakness includes many different types of weakness be it mental, physical or financial. A profound statement which can carry many meanings. Amongst of which is that "overpricing the carriage" means that they search for material gains, when material is no relevance to the station one has with Allah. They would not in any way oppress the weak person.

The truth of the matter is it doesn't matter how strong you are or how rich; in front of Allah ﷻ that counts for nothing.

We previously mentioned a hadith which [paraphrased] means that it may be that a person who is dusty, weak poor and doesn't have much and yet, when they make *du'ā'* to Allah ﷻ it will be fulfilled.

Always think that somebody who you think is weak or useless, and has no worth in your eyes; might be higher up then you in the eyes of Allah ﷻ.

Pleasing Others

The Imam says that we heard from Imam al-Shāfi'ī ﵀ in that which was narrated by al-Bayhaqī ﵀ with his chain from Yūnus ibn AbdUllah; and it was said Ibn Abdul al-'Alā, who said that al-Shāfi'ī ﵀ said, "O Abu Musa. If you struggled your utmost in order to please all people, then there is no path to achieving this. So, if this is the case, then make your action and intention sincere for Allah ﷻ."

Al-Shāfi'ī was telling his student that if you struggle hard and did your best to make everybody happy, then there's no way to do this. You will never be able to make everybody happy. So, if that is the reality, if you understand this principle then don't waste your time with people, but make your intention sincere to Allah ﷻ, because no matter how much you try to please people they will not be pleased. They will never be happy, and they will never be fully content with you.

This is the reality, isn't it? I mean the Prophet ﷺ and he is the most truthful of all people, yet he didn't get a hundred percent people following him. He didn't get a hundred percent people happy with him, people rejected him. Today, if you asked people about Allah ﷻ, then you have lots of people who doubt Him. There are people who reject Allah, like the atheists and agnostics and so on. So, Allah ﷻ who is the ultimate truth, the absolute truth; and even then, there are people who do not believe in Him, and are not pleased with Him. There are people who reject Allah, or they make up excuses to reject Him by saying different things. So, the reality is you will never be able to please everyone. If not everyone believes and is pleased with Allah ﷻ, if the Prophet ﷺ couldn't please them, so why would you then waste your time with people. Again, going back to the fundamental point which is do not waste your time with people, make your intention for Allah.

Sufism

The Imam narrates that Abu AbdUllah al-Maghribī رحمه الله said: "A Sufi without truthfulness: the one who shovels mud is better than him[109]."

I want to dwell on some aspects of Sufism, because we have seen the word "Sufi" mentioned a number of times. We mentioned some of the sayings here as being mentioned by the Imam.

The whole concept and practice of Sufism has – unfortunately -

109 Referring to the notion that the one who shovels mud has a purpose and he has recognised it, whilst the former is without true purpose.

been distorted immensely by the attack of the extremists in the religion, and those who follow their path. Sufism has been in the *'ummah* ever since the early generations, with some attributing its beginning to the Follower al-Ḥasan al-Baṣrī ﵀. The distortion has manifest in an all-round attack on the Sufīs, Sufism and those who follow their paths. As a result, some people have misunderstood and some have misrepresented Sufism, because it has been connected with people of bad practice.

So what happens is like anything today when there is a group of people who behave badly and they carry a certain title or label; then unfortunately they give that category of people a bad name. It is like today if you take on a very large level: Muslims generally. When you have Muslims behaving badly, it gives all or most Muslims a bad name. In the UK, for example, people who behave in a bad way or say certain derogatory things, then people (often led by the media) say generalising: "Look: all the Muslims are bad", "all the Muslims are this." So there is always that potential for generalisation and therefore it's very important to remove that kind of negative understanding of how people behave and look at the essence of what it is about. So don't judge concepts or practices according to a selected sample.

Similarly, as you wouldn't ask people to judge Islam by looking at Muslims, you wouldn't ask people to judge Sufism which is the concept of purification and abstinence from the *dunyā* by looking at Sufis or the practice of a Sufi, because certainly, some of them have done things which have gone against the essence of what Sufism is about. Just because incorrect practices are common amongst people, it does not change the label it has been ascribed by Shari'a. Rather we must define the intended meaning and consider the reality, not what these names stand for.

Sufism in very basic terms is all about having less of the *dunyā* and having a path of spirituality. Sometimes, it is connected to being

with a group who are on the same path. So, it's almost like having
strength with people. It's like having a contract with certain people
to say things together, to do things together, help one another to
cleanse ourselves to purify ourselves. It is like having partners
and having friends who help you in this way. So, you would have
a group of people working together for a bigger aim. And that is
why even when you go back to the time of the *Ṣaḥābah*, sometimes
they would seek that kind of partnership. We have the saying of
AbdUllah ibn Masʿūd and Muʿādh ibn Jabal ؇ when they said to
each other, "Let us sit down and have *īmān* for an hour," meaning
let us do things which will increase our *īmān*. It is almost like
let's do things together which will help us to improve ourselves.
So sometimes, there will be a group of people who say let's sit
together, let's read Quran, let's remind each other that we've done
our work or actions. And so that's a kind of path to walk upon to
try and clarify. And that's how the *ʿulamāʾ* of the past understood
Sufism. They understood it as a process of purification; as a process
of *tazkiyah*; as a process of coming closer to Allah. No doubt,
anything, can be exploited, and Sufism was exploited by people,
who made it more into a type of cult. Some people, introduced
practices into it, wanting to make it novel. Some people started to
dance. Some people started to jump up and down. Some people
started to play with snakes. Some people started to stab themselves
with swords, swallow swords, some of them walking on glass,
things which had nothing to do with the essence of the *dīn*. And so
they brought that bad name to the *taṣawwuf* and Sufism.

What we will see in some of the narrations of the Imam who
mentions how those people who had that kind of clarity in their way
they actually were far away from all these things. And, in fact, we
will see a saying by one of the great Sufis and considered one of
the fathers of Sufism: al-Junayd (may Allah have mercy on him).
He said, "Our path is restricted by the Book and the Sunna. So,
whoever does not memorise Quran or write hadith or have fiqh,
then he is not to be followed."

So this sets the scene, anybody who comes in and brings all these messed up ideas and messed up practices, we have to go back to our reference points. The glorious Quran and the purified Sunna of the Prophet ﷺ are the reference points for every Muslim to acquaint himself with the rules of Islam. The Quran should be understood by applying the rules of the Arabic language without constraint or controversy. And the Sunna can be acquired by reference to the trustworthy transmitters of hadith and the noble scholars who dedicated their lives to learning and teaching it.

And Sahl al-Tustarī said, "Our foundations are seven:

1 - Adhering to the Book of Allah.

2 - Following the Sunna of the Messenger of Allah ﷻ.

3 - Consuming halal.

4 - Averting harm.

5 - Avoiding sins.

6 - Repentance.

7 - Fulfilling the duties."

Again, one of the many quotations which demonstrate that the essence is adhering to the foundations of Islam.

And here we know that the Imam is a scholar in hadith, he is a scholar in fiqh. And he's very much somebody who is an authenticator and verifier. And here he is choosing to open up into this aspect of purification because it's a path to knowing Allah ﷻ.

So he is quoting al-Maghribī who is saying that somebody who claims to be a Sufi and does not have truthfulness in his claim, then the one who shovels mud is better than him. So, basically, if somebody claims to have this abstinence from the *dunyā*, meaning that he is walking a path of knowing Allah ﷻ without truthfulness, then even someone who is shovelling mud is better than him. And why did he use this kind specific example? Because he said even this action of shovelling mud there is a benefit to it. Some people might think that mud is dirty, and it is not a clean job, it's not a healthy job. Today some people might talk lowly about people who collect the rubbish. Sometimes people talk negatively about road sweepers. They might see them in a negative way as a low-paid manual labour, but these people are actually serving a duty, they are doing a task, and they are benefiting people. So, there is benefit to their work in this life. And if they have the right intention, they will also get reward in the Next Life. But if you claim to be sincere and claim to have *zuhd*, but you don't, then you have no benefit. You are not worthy of time.

Collation of Īmān

The Imam starts with the saying of 'Ammār ﵁. He said that we have been narrated to with our chain up to the narration of Ṣaḥīḥ al-Bukhārī ﵀, that he narrates the saying of 'Ammār ibn Yāsir (may Allah be pleased with him and his parents) that he said - so these are the words of 'Ammār, although in another narration which is not in al-Bukhārī but in another less authenticated they say that these was actually attributed to the Prophet ﷺ, but the narration that the Imam chooses here is that which is known as *mawqūf* meaning that it stopped without attributing it to the Prophet ﷺ; as opposed to *marfū'* which is what is raised to the Prophet ﷺ, meaning that he said it.

So, what did Ammar say? He said, "There are three things, whoever manages to practise and collate them in his personality; then he has brought together *īmān*.

First of all, to be just to yourself.

Secondly to display and convey *salām* (peace) to the world.

And **thirdly**, to spend and to give despite one's poverty."

So these are the three things that he summarises in his experience as one of the great Companions.

Indeed, these are great teachings. Why? Because the **first** one which is that if you show justice to yourself - it means- that you are acknowledging and understanding your position with regards to Allah ﷻ in reference to the creation. And so, you will therefore advise yourself, you will correct yourself and you will do the best for yourself. A person who looks out for the best for himself in a pure sense, would try to protect himself from falling into *ḥarām* and sin; and he would not do something which will lead him to destruction.

Unlike the materialistic perspective which is the notion of looking after "Number One" which is you. If you love yourself you should treat yourself, enjoy life and get as much of the riches, and not be too concerned with the casualties along the way. However, Islam advocates that if you love yourself you should do what's good for yourself. And that means adhering to the teachings of Allah ﷻ and the Guidance of the Prophet ﷺ.

Secondly, to spread *salām* to as many people. Obviously, by spreading *salām* there's an important aspect here, which is humility. Because when you give *salām*, you are not considering yourself too high to greet others. Some people have that kind of attitude that "I won't give *salām*, unless somebody gives *salām* to me, then I reply"; that's almost a type of arrogance. I remember a few people like that. In fact, in Kingston Mosque, there were a few people who I would see regularly at the *masjid*, and I would greet them with a smile. After a few times, I noticed they were not smiling back, and they were not making eye contact, and it was like I offended them by giving them *salām*. I later found out, that these people had issues with my understanding of Islam, and that was their "Islamic duty" to boycott me, or at least make me feel uncomfortable. But, after a while, I decided that there is no point giving them *salām* if it "offends" them; and so I just ignored them therein on.

Another person, who was an Imam in my local *masjid* in Bradford, when I was studying A Levels. This imam was well over 65 years old. He didn't speak much, and preferred not to smile much either. And on many occasions, I would greet him with an enthusiastic "al-*Salāmu ʿalaykum*", but would barely get an "mmmh!" as a reply. Then, I started to raise my voice, naively thinking that he may be hard of hearing. But, I still got the "mmmh" as a reply. One day, I confronted him, as this bothered me. I spoke to him in Arabic as I knew he would know how to speak Arabic; and this time he smiled. However, his practice continued as before. May Allah have mercy on him, as I think he is probably under the ground by now.

So, giving *salām* to everyone without any discrimination is a form of humility. And that why we see that the Prophet ﷺ when he used to pass by children he would stop and give *salām* in a display of that reality as well.[110]

The Prophet ﷺ was asked "Which of Islam is best?"

He said, **"To give food to others; and to give *salām* to those whom you know and those who you don't.**"[111]

Lastly, which is the highest peak of generosity which is to spend despite your poverty. That is to spend when you are in need, and that is the real generosity. This is why Allah ﷻ praises the 'Ansār.

He said:

﴿ وَيُؤْثِرُونَ عَلَى أَنْفُسِهِمْ وَلَوْ كَانَ بِهِمْ خَصَاصَةٌ ﴾

110 *Ṣaḥīḥ:* Hadith narrated by Imam al-Bukhārī
111 *Ṣaḥīḥ:* Hadith narrated by Imam al-Bukhārī

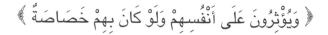

﴿They give preference over themselves even though they are in need.﴾[112]

That demonstrates that they have that quality. Because when you are in need, the priority is to feed yourself and those around you, even from a shariʿa perspective. The Prophet ﷺ said:

ابدَأْ بنفسِك فتصدَّقْ عليها ثمَّ على
أبوَيْكَ ثمَّ على قرابتِك ثمَّ هكذا ثمَّ هكذا

"Begin with yourself: spend on it; then on your parents, then on your close family and so on, so forth."[113]

But when you are saying, "No, I'm not going to start with myself; I'm going to start with others." that is generosity at its peak.

Obviously, somebody who is wealthy and has money and gives; that is also generosity, but the two cannot be equated. And that's why in another hadith the Prophet ﷺ said:

سبق دِرهَمٌ مِائَةَ ألفٍ. قالوا: يا رسولَ اللهِ كيف يَسبقُ دِرهَمٌ مِائَةَ ألفٍ؟
قال: رجلٌ كان له دِرهمانِ فأخذ أحدَهما فتصدق به، وآخَرُ له مالٌ كثيرٌ
فأخذ من عَرضِها مِائَةَ ألفٍ

"One dirham (one silver coin), has overtaken one hundred thousand."

They said, "How can one dirham overtake one hundred thousand?" He said, "**A man has lots of money, so he took 100,000 of it and gave it as charity; whilst the other had only two dirhams, so he took one of them and gave it as charity.**"[114]

112 Holy Quran; Chapter of the Exile 59:9
113 *Ṣaḥīḥ:* Hadith narrated by Imam Ibn Ḥibbān
114 *Ḥasan:* Hadith narrated by Imam Ahmad and al-Nasāʾī

It also displays *tawakkul*; dependence on Allah ﷻ because your state is saying that even though I don't have the money I'm ready to give. In addition to that, it demonstrates you are also not looking out for the *dunyā*.

07

Pursuit of Knowledge

Then, the Imam mentions a few other things relating to knowledge.

Knowledge is to Acted Upon

He narrates with his chain to Abu AbdUllah ibn ʿAtā' al-Rawdhbārī ؒ that he said: "Whoever leaves [his home going] to knowledge wanting to act upon it, then a little amount of knowledge will benefit him."

This is all within the whole concept of intention and purifying. If you go towards knowledge, seeking knowledge, and you sit in the gatherings of knowledge, you sit hearing intending to benefit from this knowledge and to transfer this knowledge into action so that you can work on it, then even small aspects of knowledge will be beneficial to you. So, there is that link to the intention of why you are sitting here. Something similar applies to those who are reading knowledge.

Another narration: Abu AbdUllah ibn ʿAtā' said, "Knowledge is suspended pending acting upon it. Actions are suspended due to *ikhlāṣ*. *Ikhlāṣ* for Allah (Exalted be He) inherits understanding from Allah – the Exalted."

This saying and the one before it further explain to us the importance of linking knowledge with actions; and that knowledge is correlated to actions, and so it is vital that one aspect of attaining knowledge is to have the intention to act upon it.

The Imam explained that what is sought should be the beneficial knowledge, as our Imam al-Shāfiʿī said, "Knowledge is not that which is memorised. Rather, knowledge is that which benefits."

And here, he mentions the saying of Imam al-Shāfiʿī that the real knowledge is that which is beneficial. When you look at the sayings of the people of the past you will see a lot of people; that was their understanding of *ʿilm*. The *ʿilm* they understood was not just information. It wasn't just things to memorise or learn. Rather, *ʿilm* was intricately part of knowledge.

In the hadith narrated by Abu al-Dardā' who said that we were with the Messenger of Allah ﷺ. He raised his sight to the sky, then said:

هذا أوانٌ يُختَلَسُ العِلمُ منَ النَّاسِ حتَّى لا يقدِروا منهُ علَى شيءٍ

"This is the time in which knowledge will be taken from people, such that they will not be able to get any of it."

Ziyād ibn Labīd al-'Anṣārī said, "How will it be taken from us, and we have read the Quran! By Allah, we will read it and teach it to our women and children."

The Prophet ﷺ said:

ثكِلَتكَ أمُّكَ يا زيادُ إن كُنتُ لأعدُّكَ مِن فُقَهاءِ أهلِ المدينة. هذهِ التَّوراةُ والإنجيلُ عندَ اليَهودِ والنَّصارَى فَماذا تُغني عَنهم

"May you mother miss you, O Ziyād. I used to consider you of the *fuqahā*[115] of Madinah. This is the Torah and the Injīl of the Jews and the Nazarenes, so what does it help them?"

Jubayr said, "I met 'Obādah ibn al-Ṣāmit and said to him, 'Have you heard what your brother Abu al-Dardā' is saying?' and I informed him."

'Obādah said, "Abu al-Dardā' has spoken rightly. If you want, I can tell you of the first of the knowledge to be raised from the people: *khushū'*. Soon you will enter a *masjid* and you will not see a tranquil man."[116]

Khushū' is the humility, tranquillity and focus in ṣalāh. In this hadith, the Prophet ﷺ named *khushū'* - which is an action of the heart - as an *'ilm* because it's a benefit that comes from that understanding. And this was the understanding of the Ṣaḥābah and later scholars. So, your knowledge isn't just something that you learn and literally: memorise. Rather it's something that extends into your work and practice. So, there is no point of merely learning words. As the saying of Anas ibn Mālik ؓ, "How many people recite the Quran and the Quran is cursing them!"

Why is the Quran cursing them? Because they read the Quran, they memorise it, but they don't practise it. And in the Quran, there are verses saying do this, don't do this and he's not paying attention to it. So, one may recite verses that carry the curse of Allah, and he may be engaging in that act, himself. So, what's the point of memorising the Quran if you're not acting on it. And that is the point here that is in need of addressing.

That's why it is the priority of every Muslim, irrespective of his language, to try to understand the Quran and to exercise his effort to learn. Why is it a priority? Because this is the word of Allah ﷻ; this

115 *pl.* of *faqīh*
116 *Ṣaḥīḥ:* Hadith narrated by Imam al-Tirmidhī

is the only remaining unaltered, unedited, unadulterated words of Allah ﷻ. All the other words have been corrupted. So, you have the literal words from Allah and you don't want to give the words Allah your utmost attention?!

Imam al-Shāfi'ī ؓ said in another saying, "Every Muslim should learn the Arabic language as much as his effort can take him." And you have to strive your utmost. You might not be able to learn fully, but put as much of your effort as you can. And similarly, if you can recite the Quran, you should put as much effort into understanding what you're reading, because it's what Allah ﷻ is addressing you. The Quran was not sent down to be only memorised in the hearts. It was sent down to be learnt, understood and to be acted upon.

Today we say *qārī* meaning that someone knows how to read the Quran. But the *'ulamā'* in the past when they used to say somebody is a *qārī*: it means he is well versed in the Quran and Islam. In the hadith[117] when the Prophet ﷺ was really upset when he sent 70 of the *qurrā*'[118] to a village to go and teach them, not just Quran, but to teach them Islam. And those tribes were treacherous, they betrayed the Prophet ﷺ and they killed all of those seventy Companions. These 70 were known as *qurrā*', not that they just knew how to read Quran. These were *fuqahā*': they understood the Quran and they knew how to practise its rulings and injunctions.

Thus, in the past, the methodology of learning the Quran was to learn it and to practise the rules and recommendations therein. There is a famous notion of the *'ulamā'* of the past, adopted from the Ṣaḥābah ؓ. They used to take 10 verses at a time. They said "We used to take 10 verses. We would learn how to read them. We would memorise them. We would then go away and practise them. Then, we would move on to the next 10. We wouldn't move on to the next 10 if we hadn't learnt, memorised and practised. So they said, "We took the *'ilm* and the *'amal* together."

117 *Ṣaḥīḥ:* Hadith narrated by Imam al-Bukhārī
118 *pl.* of *qārī*

There is a tradition as well that states ʿOmar ibn Khaṭṭāb ﷺ took nine years to memorise Surat al-Baqarah (Chapter 2). Because, taking it in a way; to understand, practise and move on, not just take it and then not practise or understand it. So it has to be, you have to put that effort in.

Knowledge Necessitates Effort

So, he said it's narrated in Ṣaḥīḥ Muslim ﷺ, that Abdullah ibn Kathīr said: "Knowledge is not attainable whilst resting the body."

Meaning if you want to rest and just go to learn at leisure, you're not going to attain knowledge because knowledge needs dedication. It needs time, energy and effort. The stories relating to this are many, which we can mention a few here. The reality is, if you want to learn you have to be ready to stay up at night, you have to be ready to wake up early. You have to be ready to give as much as you can into this.

That is the difference between the people of the past and the people of today. The people of the past understood the value of knowledge, and so they went to the extreme to attain it. They crossed the deserts, going thirsty and hungry for days and weeks; all in order to attain knowledge. Imam Ahmed, for example, on one occasion wouldn't be able to even leave his house because he only had one dress, which had to be shared. And so, he wouldn't leave his house. It was said to him why don't you borrow money? He said, "I don't want to go down that route." The reality is that scholars had sacrificed and if you want the knowledge you have to sacrifice.

The Imam says that we have been narrated to in Ṣaḥīḥ al-Bukhārī ﷺ that he said: Rabīʿah - meaning the shaykh of Mālik ibn Anas the Imam ﷺ said: "It is not befitting for anyone who has any knowledge, to place himself [down]."

Now, the Imam knows that this sentence needs a little bit of explanation. He says I'm just going to summarise it for you, even though I have extended the commentary in the "Explanation of Ṣaḥīḥ al-Bukhārī". He said that there's two essential aspects of this;

(**1**) **One** of them: it means whoever has intelligence in knowledge, and has acquired some of it; and the signs of eminence have appeared in him, he should strive for its development. He should not abandon seeking it, as he will lose his attainment and he will place himself down.

(**2**) The **second**: Its means whoever has gained knowledge, should seek to spread it, seeking Allah's pleasure, and he should spread it to people to transfer it from him, and people will benefit from it, and it benefits him in return.

He should be gentle with whomsoever takes it from him, and should facilitate the ways of acquiring it, to be more significant in the sincerity of knowledge; for *dīn* is sincerity.

The companions of al-Shāfiʿī ﷺ differed as to the one who was described in the former category: does he **have to** develop the seeking, and is it prohibited to abandon? Or does it remain in his right as a communal obligation, as it was, and he is not forbidden from abandoning it, if someone else adopts it?

The second opinion above is the view of most of them, and it is the correct chosen one, and Allah knows best.

So, the **first one** is that whoever has the intellect, meaning s/he is smart, bright, catches things quickly and understands matters, it's not befitting for someone who is of high quality to abandon studying and chasing knowledge. So, if you are a smart or intellectual, you should be studying more and more. This means putting your intellect to its best use, which is in knowledge. Thus, it is not good that you've displaced yourself by not following knowledge.

Consider practices in many Muslim countries or indeed from Muslim culture. I know definitely in Iraq, back in the days – as my father narrated to me that the students who got the highest degrees, they would go and study Medicine. If you've got something like ninety-eight (98%) in your finals, you would qualify for medicine. Anything less, then you go a step down to Dentistry. The country has already shaped the way of how people should perceive intellect. The highest would become medics. And then after that would go into Dentistry, and then Veterinary and then the different branches of Engineering. Leaving the lowest ranking students to study Humanities, like shari'a and Islamic studies.

Islamic studies were for those who got 50% or thereabouts. My father tells me that he used to know people in Baghdad who were studying *shari'a*, yet they were atheists: they didn't believe in Allah. Why? Because they didn't get the marks that would enable them to study anything else.

What the Imam is saying is the opposite should be correct. If you have the intellect, you should be guiding your intellect towards studying more and obtaining the knowledge. In fact, we know that the Imam himself wanted to study Medicine, and he purchased the book: al-Qānūn of Ibn al-Nafīs, but then he felt an internal gloom which repelled him away from it. And that's just amazing: how he was then directed towards Islamic knowledge; and look how he utilized this intellect to the best.

The **second** meaning of the saying of Rabīʿah is that whoever has attained knowledge, shouldn't displace himself or lower himself by not spreading the knowledge. So, whoever gains knowledge, he should try and spread that knowledge. Spreading that knowledge would mean that other people would benefit from this and so on. It's like a form of displacement to yourself. It is humiliation that you have knowledge, but you choose not to give it to others or make it available. And this is one of the diseases that can affect scholars. I know of several who acted this way. One of them, I displayed my eagerness to learn and to be one of his students; but he kept on putting barriers in front of me, setting for me distant tasks, until I got the message that he isn't interested in departing with his knowledge. He only showed interest when he learnt that I had intended to go to Mauritania to pursue knowledge there. Unfortunately, I didn't get to Mauritania as my father vetoed my decision; but that's another story.

On the other hand, my Shaykh Abu Tamīm who was my Shaykh in the Shāfiʿī fiqh was very eager to teach me, and to pass on his knowledge; and he did it sincerely with the most hospitable of methods. May Allah bless him.

After the Imam mentioned the two opinions, he said that our companions, the companions of Imam al-Shāfiʿī, they differed about someone who falls into the first category: meaning the one who has the intellect. They differed if somebody has that ability to study, is it obligatory on him to study and thus: *ḥarām* for him to leave the study, meaning that he has to use his ability and intellect for studying, or is it something that remains as a communal obligation, meaning that he doesn't have to do it as long as enough people are studying. They differed about this. Some say if somebody has the ability and intellect he must go and study; he shouldn't waste his time doing other things.

However, he said that the second opinion, which is that it remains a communal obligation is the view of the majority, and it is the correct chosen one, and Allah knows best. Thus, that if somebody doesn't do it, he's not going to be sinful for that.

However, I think the main aspect of the Imam mentioning the difference of opinions to show that there is already a consideration about a person who does have that; there is a portion of people who think that if you do have that intellect, you should go and study and direct your knowledge in that way.

Don't Shy Away From Knowledge

Staying with the subject of knowledge, the Imam said that we have narrated from ʿOmar ibn al-Khaṭṭāb and his son, AbdUllah ﵄ that they said, "He whose face has softened, his knowledge will be softened."

Meaning that whoever is shy to seek knowledge, his knowledge will be thin (soft); that is: little.

A person can have a fine texture, but also fine can mean in terms of amount. So, if your face is fine: meaning gentle, implying that you don't have the willingness, strength, or the enthusiasm, or you are embarrassed or shy from learning, then your knowledge will also be fine and little, and so you will not learn. If you don't go forward in terms of learning you will not learn much.

And this is further explained by the saying which the Imam narrates in Ṣaḥīḥ al-Bukhārī ﵁ that Mujāhid ibn Jabr ﵀ said: "He will not learn knowledge: someone who is shy or someone who is arrogant."

If you're shy, meaning you don't ask questions, you don't come forward, you're always reluctant, then you're not going to learn. That's why some of the people said in the past, "There should be no bashfulness in the *dīn*.", which is not the correct perspective of how to say that "No *ḥayāʾ* in the *dīn*". What it really means is that there is no bashfulness or *ḥayāʾ* in learning the *dīn*. Because *ḥayāʾ* is part of the *dīn*; and the Prophet ﷺ said:

الحياءُ شُعبةٌ من الإيمان

"Ḥayā' is a branch of īmān",[119] but you shouldn't have the *ḥayā'* in learning: meaning don't be shy from asking and coming forward.

Similarly, if you are arrogant, you're not going to learn. As you feel that maybe people will look down on you. Some people are embarrassed to ask a question because they're afraid that maybe everybody knows [or should know] the answer: "Why should I ask this question? And it might appear embarrassing for me to ask that." Or if you have pride from sitting down in front of others, again you're not going to learn.

The aspect of bashfulness is further explained by the saying of 'Ā'ishah ﷺ, in which the Imam says that we have been narrated to in Ṣaḥīḥ Muslim and others on her authority that she said: "What great women were the women of al-'Anṣār! Shyness did not prevent them from comprehendingthe *dīn*."

This meant that they weren't embarrassed from approaching the Prophet ﷺ and asking questions, because there will be questions which are very personal; and some which are gender-specific; so if they would say, "Oh! I'm too embarrassed to come and ask the Prophet ﷺ" then what will happen is they're not going to learn. So, 'Āishah ﷺ was saying that they didn't have that issue. They would come and ask the Prophet ﷺ about matters relating to *ṭahārah* related to women's bleeding, cleansing, and things like that, which were necessary to know.

An example is that Umm Sulaym ﷺ asked, "O Messenger of Allah, Allah does not shy away from the truth. Does a woman have to do *ghusl* if she has a wet dream?"

119 *Ṣaḥīḥ:* Hadith narrated by Imams al-Bukhārī and Muslim

He said, "**Yes. If she sees the fluid!**"

So, Umm Salamah[120] ﵂ laughed, saying, "And does a woman have a wet dream?!"

So, the Prophet ﷺ said, "**Then how would her child resemble her [features]**?"[121]

Another example is 'Ā'ishah ﵂ narrates that a woman asked the Prophet ﷺ about how a woman should wash following her period.

So, he taught her how and added that she should take a cloth with musk and cleanse herself with it.

She said, "How do I cleanse with it?"

He said, "**She cleanses with it. Subḥān Allah!**" then he covered [his face].

'Ā'ishah said, "So, I pulled her towards me, knowing what the Prophet ﷺ meant, and I said, 'follow the area which has blood'."[122]

Obviously, it's important as well that the person understands the importance of learning; and therefore, if one has any doubt about any matter, then he should ask. Sometimes you might have a question related to aspects of breaking *wuḍū'*, aspects of *janābah* and things like that. The person should ask, and not allow himself to continue doing something which is wrong. You may not know how to rectify it; and so, it is vital to ask in order to do it correctly rather than carrying on doing it wrongly. So that's all the sayings of 'Omar, AbdUllah, 'Ā'ishah and Mujāhid ﵃ that all pour into that fact which is do not let anything get in the way of learning, be it your embarrassment, your shyness or arrogance.

120 The Prophet's wife, not to be confused with Umm Sulaym who is asking the question.
121 *Ṣaḥīḥ:* Hadith narrated by Imam al-Bukhārī
122 *Ṣaḥīḥ:* Hadith narrated by Imam Muslim

Seek Knowledge While You Can

Another aspect of what prevents people from learning which is what ʿOmar ﷺ says, as the Imam narrated in Ṣaḥīḥ al-Bukhārī that he said: "Comprehend before you prevail."

The meaning of which is that you should learn, have the *fiqh* (understanding) before you become a master: before you become old. Because the word (تسودوا) means to become a *sayyid*. When somebody becomes a *sayyid*, he will become occupied with other things. So, get the knowledge early on while you have the ability, while you are free, don't leave it late because when you become a *sayyid*, it would be too late. And *sayyid* (master) could be like a master of your household. So maybe you set up a household: you get married, you have children; or you could be a master meaning that you become a boss in your business; or maybe you become a director, or a manager, that will prevent you from having the ability to learn, because it's going to be a barrier for you, as you are going to be busy with other things.

Its meaning: be concerned to master the knowledge, and being able to attain it whilst you are young people with no occupation, no presidency and of young age. For if you become old, and become heads who are followed, you will be denied [the opportunity] of comprehension (learning) and attainment.

Indeed, I remember when I first started University (Sheffield) back in 1993, one of the first advice that I remember receiving was from one of the ex-students who said to me "Omer! This time of being a student: this is the freest time you will have. This is the period of your life when you will have the most available time." I was surprised to hear that. I thought studying would be the opposite, as you are going to have lots of lectures, lessons and revision. Every time you have free time, you are going to be studying and revising.

However, only later on did I realise that was the reality, because once you start working and you have a 9-to-5 job, or more likely an 8-to-6 job; and you are working five days a week, at least; then you will not have that time. You will be fixed in these hours. Whereas, as a student you will get sometimes half a day off, sometimes, lectures get cancelled, lessons finish early, long vacations, semester breaks, end of term and so on: you have lots of time.

This saying conveys a similar idea; for if you leave learning to a later stage, you will become older you might not have the ability to learn.

This is approximate to what Imam al-Shāfiʿī said: "Understand before you preside. For when you preside, there will be no way for comprehending."

There's a saying which is attributed to al-Khaṭīb al-Baghdādī ﵀, in which he said that when a person - meaning a student of knowledge – gets married it's like he has been put on a boat and he's sailing, meaning that he's going away from the shore. When you are on a boat, you are busy with directing the boat, the navigation, you're busy now because it is not just like sitting on the land, you have to know where you are, you have to ensure that the boat is safe, supplies, etc. Then he said, "… and when he has children it's like a hole has been made in the boat." Now, it's no longer plain sailing, but the captain is busy with getting the water out and everything, and getting back to the shore, might be altogether near impossible.

Basically, what that means is when you get married and when you have children, you have to divert your attention towards other things. Now, you have other things to worry about as well. And if one of your children has special needs, then it becomes triple and quadruple the responsibility. My son Sulayman was born with only one ear, and later on we discovered he had severe autism. This meant that he needed extra attention and care, and all the things that were once possible with neuro typical children, were totally out of the question. May Allah cure him of this illness, and may Allah give us the patience and reward us accordingly.

The point being is that when you have a family, knowledge no longer becomes a priority, and it can't be. Especially when you consider that knowledge in the past, people had to go out and travel, they had to spend money and time and endure hardships. It wasn't something that they could just go down to the *masjid* and listen to lectures and things like that. They would leave their families; not for days and weeks, but for years and years.

Humility in Knowledge

Now, the Imam is taking another aspect of knowledge. He already spoke about *ḥayā'*, now he's talking more about the aspect of arrogance. Here, he is mentioning some of the sayings about humility and al-Junayd is one of the righteous people of the past, and is considered one of the prominent righteous of the people. He studied with somebody called Abu Thawr who was a Shāfi'ī scholar, who had studied as well with Imam al-Shāfi'ī. And he, al-Junayd, was someone who had not only studied, but aware of the whole aspects of purification and this path of walking towards awareness of Allah ﷻ.

That is why his student Ja'far in a narration said, "We never saw any of our Shaykhs who had both the knowledge and the status (concern with Allah ﷻ) other than al-Junayd". If you saw his knowledge, you would say that this guy is just like an academic. And if you saw his reality in terms of his *'ibādah* and things like that, you would have thought this guy was focusing on his station of *'ibādah*.

Many others have spoken about him; if you went to sit in his gatherings, you would have seen those who were writing and there are people who like to compile, they were just waiting to hear his words. You will see the philosophers were sitting there trying to find the specificities of his words and how he was using them. As well, you would have seen those who had aspects of studying theology they would look at what he was saying and his knowledge.

The Imam narrates through his chain to al-Junayd (may Allah Almighty have mercy on him) that he said: "I do not wish to die where I am known, for I am afraid that the earth will not accept me, and I will be exposed."

Al-Junayd was a great person who was righteous; as well as having knowledge. Yet what he was saying was that he is afraid of dying in a place where people know him, because he's afraid that when they come to bury him that the earth will reject him and throw him out, and then he'll be shamed up. Meaning that "I'm a sinner. I might be so bad that I will be shamed by the earth, as it will not want to accept me to be buried in it."[123] Obviously, he is not showing off his humility, but those are his real feelings.

And despite all this, when he died, he was seen in a dream by his student Ja'far who asked him, "What has Allah ﷻ done to you? How has Allah treated you?"

Al-Junayd replied, "All those words that we used to say, all those beautiful sayings, all those bits of knowledge and things that we mentioned, all of those have gone. And they didn't benefit us. What benefited us were the few *rak'āt* that we used to pray in the night, in secret. That's what really benefited us in the end, while people were sleeping."

By the way, this saying of "I wish to be buried somewhere…" some say that wasn't the words of al-Junayd, rather they were the

123 There are some narrations of how the bodies of some deceased were found out of their graves, despite being buried, several times.

words of his uncle al-Sarī al-Saqaṭī that he was narrating from him. There's a difference about that in narration.

With this same chain of transmission, al-Junayd said: I heard Sarī saying: "I look at my nose twice every day, out of fear that my face may have darkened!"

The Arabs consider the darkening of the face as a form of shame. It can be real or sometimes used as a figure of speech. There can be a metaphysical aspect here, as Allah ﷻ mentions in the Quran:

﴿يَوْمَ تَبْيَضُّ وُجُوهٌ وَتَسْوَدُّ وُجُوهٌ فَأَمَّا الَّذِينَ اسْوَدَّتْ وُجُوهُهُمْ أَكَفَرْتُم بَعْدَ إِيمَانِكُمْ فَذُوقُوا الْعَذَابَ بِمَا كُنْتُمْ تَكْفُرُونَ﴾

﴿On a Day when faces will be illuminated and faces will be darkened. As for those whose faces are darkened: 'Did you disbelieve after your *īmān*? So, taste punishment due to what you used to deny'.﴾[124]

There will be faces that will be bright and illuminated, and others will be dark and gloomy. And this has nothing to do with the colour of the skin. However, it will be real, it's literal, that people's faces will change on the Day of Judgment.

They also used to believe that, to a certain extent, this would also happen in the *dunyā*. Sometimes you will meet somebody irrelative of what their race is, and you will see that their faces illuminated. You can sense that there's a vibe that comes out, you might even literally see his face, quite bright and shiny. However, there will be others when you see them, they look gloomy, wretched. It's like you don't want to look at them. Al-Sarī was saying that I look at my nose every day, just to ensure that my face hasn't darkened as a punishment from Allah ﷻ.

124 Holy Quran: Chapter of the Family or 'Imrān 3:106

Abstinence and Knowledge

Al-Shāfiʿī ﷺ said: "Whoever loves for Allah to opcn his heart and to give him knowledge, then he must practise solitude, reduce his food intake; and abandon socialising with fools as well as some of those associated with knowledge who have no fairness or morals."

Because Allah ﷻ said:

﴿ وَاتَّقُوا اللَّهَ وَيُعَلِّمُكُمُ اللَّهُ ﴾

﴿ Fear Allah and Allah will teach you.﴾[125]

Excelling in Learning

In this part, there is a beautiful perspective of one of the aspects of how a person should try to achieve in being aware of Allah ﷻ.

We have been narrated to from the authority of 'Ibrāhīm ibn Saʿīd who said: I said to Abu Saʿad ibn 'Ibrāhīm: "With what did al-Zuhrī surpass you?"

He said: "He would attend the gatherings in the front, and not at the rear. And there would not remain in the gathering a young man except he would question him; nor a middle-aged[126] man except he would question him; nor a boy except he would question him; nor an old woman except he would question her. Then he would approach a house from the houses of al-Anṣār, and he would not leave a young man except he would question him; nor a middle-aged man except he would question him; nor an old woman except he would question her; nor a middle-aged woman except he would

125 Holy Quran; Chapter of the Cow 2:282
126 Middle-aged is the one who has passed the age of youth, but not reached old age. Usually between 30 and 50.

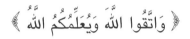

question her. He would even try with those who wear anklets[127]."

What this means is that al-Zuhrī was demonstrating his enthusiasm for learning. He didn't use to enter the circles from behind meaning he was coming early to attend the lessons. Imagine in the past, the lectures of the shaykh would be attended by hundreds and sometimes even thousands of people who would come listen. The shaykh would have some raised cushions and sit there with his books; and there would be hundreds and thousands of people writing things, so if you can imagine thousands of people sitting writing in the *masjid*, you would be sitting right at the back. So, al-Zuhrī would come early, so that he can be close. Today we have microphones that convey every utterance the speaker makes; unlike in the olden days if you are sitting right at the back how likely are you to hear exactly what is said?

In addition to this, look at Imam al-Zuhrī's humility as he didn't see himself too high up. Whether they are young or old, male or female, he would go and get that knowledge from them. You can see a very similar attitude in Ibn 'Abbās ﷺ. After the passing of the Prophet ﷺ, Ibn 'Abbās ﷺ used to go and chase the people of knowledge; and he would sometimes stay outside their houses in the early hours, sleeping on their doorsteps just so when they wake up, he would be there, and ready to take the knowledge from them and to ask them questions to clarify matters.

So this was the attitude about enthusiasm. Today, how many people have lost their enthusiasm in terms of learning and in terms of their attitude to the *'ilm*. We literally have lessons available to us at our fingertips, and we have scholars who are entering our homes via the internet and TV; yet few are those who have the eagerness to learn.

127 Referring to young women

Virtue of Intellect

Islam has given great value and weighting to the intellect. This is evident when you read the Islamic texts and note the recurring usage of the words "understand", "comprehend" and "mind". Islam liberates the mind, urges contemplation of the universe, honours science and scientists, and welcomes all that is good and beneficial to mankind. The Prophet ﷺ is reported to have said:

الكلِمةُ الحِكمةُ ضالَّةُ المؤمِنِ ، فحيثُ وجدَها فَهوَ أحقُّ بِها .

"The word of wisdom is the lost property of the believer. Wherever he finds it, he is more deserving to it."[128]

Under this section, the Imam narrates with his transmission to al-Khatīb who said that ʿAlī ibn al-Qāsim narrated to us that he said that he heard al-Ḥusayn ibn Arjak say: "Amongst the best gifts is the [intellectual] mind, and amongst the worst of calamities is ignorance."

No doubt, having a sound intellectual rational mind is a great blessing from Allah. For a sound mind is vital for attaining many things. This intellect – in essence – is from Allah as an inherent quality, but it can also be acquired.

A young boy was asked what he would rather have, "a sound intellect or lots of wealth."

He said, "A sound intellect. As having no intellect will lead me to lose all my wealth."

Imam Ibn al-Jawzī compiled a book called "Akhbār al-Ḥamqā wa al-Mughaffalīn" (The Stories of the Stupid and Fools), in which he

128 *Ḍaʿīf:* Hadith narrated by Imams al-Tirmidhī and Ibn Mājah

entertains the readers of some of those who lack basic sense.

Sometimes the way people act, the questions that they ask, or the way that they behave, attracts so much surprise and bewilderment. And so, the intellect is truly a gift from Allah; and its absence is a severe punishment.

Once I was working as a dentist in Sheffield. A young Muslim entered for his dental appointment for a filling. It so happened that this day was the first of Ramadan. He was reluctant to sit in the chair, and asked, "Is it okay to have my teeth done today, as we are in Ramadan?"

So I asked, "Why? Are you fasting?"

He said, "No!"

So, I virtually slapped my forehead and said to him, "Well, sit down, then!"

In the 2020 coronavirus pandemic, when face masks became mandatory; many people would come to the dental surgery, sit in my dental chair, with their masks on; and not thinking about taking their masks off, for me to examine their mouths!

Highwaymen Scholars

The Imam narrates that Bishr al-Ḥāfī ﷺ said that Allah ﷻ had revealed to Dāwūd ﷺ: "O Dāwūd! Do not place between Me and you a deluded scholar; such that his delusion repels you from the path to My Love. Surely, they are the highway robbers of My worshipers."

These highwaymen stop or distract the slaves of Allah from reaching Him, much like a highwayman stops the traveller from completing his journey. Sometimes, some of the shaykhs, what they do is they very much concentrate on the letter of the law of the Shariʿa, and they don't comprehend the spirit of the Shariʿa. So they will almost exclude a lot of the aspects of which actually are righteous acts which aim to bring people closer to Allah ﷻ, towards loving Him and loving the Prophet ﷺ by just saying this is *ḥarām*, or this is *bidʿah*, and "don't do this" or "don't do that". They end up closing the avenues for people who want to get to Allah ﷻ. So, indeed they are like highwaymen stop people from reaching Allah ﷻ.

Bishr is giving this quotation and not saying exactly where he got it from, but he must've got it through some sort of chain, as he wouldn't just make it up.

An example of this. There are days that are recommended to fast, and sometimes you will find a shaykh who will sway people against fasting for a clear misconception. Some learned people understood the prohibition of not fasting Saturdays as an absolute prohibition. So, they gave *fatwā* to not to fast the Day of ʿArafah or ʿĀshūrā' if they were to fall on Saturdays. Despite this matter being easily resolved, but they continue to preach this understanding. Now consider how many people they have prevented from getting good benefits related to these blessed days.

Another example, which you might be surprised by is the whole concept of remembering Allah ﷻ, which is known as the circles of *dhikr*; the circles in which Allah is remembered. Now, the word "circle of the remembrance" of Allah ﷻ are both mentioned in a hadith. The Prophet ﷺ said:

إذا مررتُمْ برياضِ الجنةِ فارْتَعُوا قالوا: وما رياضُ الجنةِ؟
قال: حِلَقُ الذكرِ

"When you pass by the meadows of *al-Jannah*, then graze there!"

They said, "What are the meadows of *al-Jannah*?"

He said, "**The circles of remembrance.**"[129]

There's the famous *qudsī* hadith:

إنَّ للهِ مَلائكَةً يَطُوفُونَ في الطُّرُقِ يَلْتَمِسُونَ أَهْلَ الذِّكْرِ، فإذا وجَدُوا قَوْمًا يَذْكُرُونَ اللَّهَ تَنادَوْا: هَلُمُّوا إلى حاجَتِكُمْ قالَ: فَيَحُفُّونَهُمْ بأَجْنِحَتِهِمْ إلى السَّماءِ الدُّنْيا قالَ: فَيَسْأَلُهُمْ رَبُّهُمْ، وهو أعْلَمُ منهمْ، ما يقولُ عِبادِي؟ قالوا: يقولونَ: يُسَبِّحُونَكَ ويُكَبِّرُونَكَ ويَحْمَدُونَكَ ويُمَجِّدُونَكَ قالَ: فيَقولُ: هلْ رَأَوْنِي؟ قالَ: فيَقولونَ: لا واللَّهِ ما رَأَوْكَ؟ قالَ: فيَقولُ: وكيفَ لو رَأَوْنِي؟ قالَ: يقولونَ: لو رَأَوْكَ كانُوا أشَدَّ لكَ عِبادَةً، وأَشَدَّ لكَ تَمْجِيدًا وتَحْمِيدًا، وأَكْثَرَ لكَ تَسْبِيحًا قالَ: يقولُ: فَما يَسْأَلُونِي؟ قالَ: يَسْأَلُونَكَ الجَنَّةَ قالَ: يقولُ: وهلْ رَأَوْها؟ قالَ: يقولونَ: لا واللَّهِ يا رَبِّ ما رَأَوْها قالَ: يقولُ: فَكيفَ لو أنَّهُمْ رَأَوْها؟ قالَ: يقولونَ: لو أنَّهُمْ رَأَوْها كانُوا أشَدَّ عليها حِرْصًا، وأَشَدَّ لها طَلَبًا، وأَعْظَمَ فيها رَغْبَةً، قالَ: فَمِمَّ يَتَعَوَّذُونَ؟ قالَ: يقولونَ: مِنَ النَّارِ قالَ: يقولُ: وهلْ رَأَوْها؟ قالَ: يقولونَ: لا واللَّهِ يا رَبِّ ما رَأَوْها قالَ: يقولُ: فَكيفَ لو رَأَوْها؟ قالَ: يقولونَ: لو رَأَوْها كانُوا أشَدَّ مِنْها فِرارًا، وأَشَدَّ لها مَخافَةً قالَ: فيَقولُ: فَأُشْهِدُكُمْ أنِّي قدْ غَفَرْتُ لهمْ قالَ: يقولُ مَلَكٌ مِنَ المَلائِكَةِ: فيهم فُلانٌ ليسَ منهمْ، إنَّما جاءَ لِحاجَةٍ. قالَ: هُمُ الجُلَساءُ لا يَشْقَى بهِمْ جَلِيسُهُمْ.

Allah has angels who roam the paths, searching for the people of *dhikr*. If they find people remembering Allah, they call out to each other: 'Come to your need.' So, they surround them

129 *Ḥasan:* Hadith narrated by al-Tirmidhī and Ahmad

with their wings up to the lowest heaven. So, their Lord asks them – and He is more informed than them – 'What do My slaves say?'

They say, 'They glorify You, magnify You, praise You and honour You.'

He will say, 'Have they seen Me?'

They will say, "No, by Allah. They have not seen You.'

He said, "So, how will they be had they seen Me?'

They will say, 'Had they seen You, they would have been more intense in their worship of You; and more intense in their honouring and praise of You, and more glorification of You.'

He will ask, 'So, what do they ask of Me?'

They will reply, 'They ask of You: *al-Jannah*.'

He will say, 'And have they seen it?'

They will say, 'No. They have not seen it.'

He will then say, 'So, how will it be if they had seen it?'

They will reply, 'Had they seen it, they would be more eager for it, and more intense in their seeking of it and wanting it.'

He will say, 'And from what do they seek refuge of?'

They will say, 'From the Fire.'

He will say, 'And have they seen it?'

They will say, 'No. They have not seen it.'

He will then say, 'So, how will it be if they had seen it?'

They will reply, 'Had they seen it, they would be more escaping of it and more intense in fearing it.'

So He will say, 'I witness you that I have forgiven them.'

So, an angel from the angels will say, 'Among them is so-and-

so. He is not of them. He only came for a need.'

Allah will say, 'And for him, I have forgiven. They are the people to be sat with. Whoever sits with them will not be sad'."[130]

So even he who has no intention of remembering Allah ﷻ will benefit from that. Now this hadith and other hadiths clearly state the virtue of sitting in circles and remembering Allah ﷻ together. Now there are some *'ulamā'* who would have come and they looked at some people who distorted the whole concept of *dhikr*, by making it like a ceremony. Some people would come and start nodding their heads frantically; others would just jump up and down. Others started to put music and others started to swirl around (the swirling dervishes), and others incorporated snakes into it and so on.

So, they distorted the process of *dhikr*. So, you have some of these other scholars who came in the middle and said any gathering for *dhikr* is *ḥarām* and it is *bid'ah*: it's not accepted. So, they prevented a whole good practice which is documented in the hadith because some people distorted the practice. Rather, they should have said: this is a wrong practice, don't do it this way, but do it in a correct way.

What happened is they prevented people from doing it. So it's almost like they cut people off on this benefit of remembering Allah ﷻ together. They robbed people of the reward.

Another example is the middle of Sha'bān.

That's why it's always important that sometimes when an action is good and some people distort it, we don't ban everything. Like the English saying: "Don't throw the baby out with the bathwater," just correct the problem and carry on with the accepted. So, this is an example of the application of how some *'ulama'* are in their attempt

130 *Ṣaḥīḥ:* Hadith narrated by Imam al-Bukhārī

to try to give people a certain understanding; they might actually end up cutting people off from acts which are acceptable, which are halal and documented.

08

Pieces of Advice for the *ʿĀrif*

Then, the Imam mentions a few other things relating to knowledge.

The Imam narrates that al-Shāfiʿī said: "You should practise abstinence! Asceticism on an ascetic is better than jewellery on a young woman[131]."

Abstinence is about abandoning or reducing worldly possessions, a term known as *zuhd*. The practice of *zuhd* is core to a person being aware of Allah, as he is more focused on the Next Life and preparing for it than this life and its allurements.

On the authority of al-Shāfiʿī who said: "He who is overwhelmed by the intensity of lust for the *dunyā*, shall be enslaved to its people. And he who is happy with subservience [to Allah], subjugation [to others] will be dispelled away from him."

On the same lines, we have the saying of Mālik ibn Dīnar: "Whoever seeks to marry the *dunyā*, it will not accept any less than his *dīn* as the *mahr*."

Allah praised the paupers who do ask others anything, to the extent that some people will think that they are rich. If you are in need, you can ask: there is nothing wrong with that: it is not *ḥarām*, but

131 The precise translation of nāhid is a "full breasted woman" which is a symbol of beauty. Allah mentions this as well as a description of the women in al-Jannah. See the Chapter of the News 78:33

then what is your link to Allah?

On the matter of those people who are not asking from others; there is a story about a man who was begging. Someone passed by him and didn't give him anything. The beggar said, "Where are the people who would give preference to others over themselves, even though they have their own needs?" He was quoting from the Quran (59:9).

So the other guy replied – also quoting Quran (2:273): "Those people have disappeared along with the people who don't ask others persistently."

People Will Either Love You or Hate You

Al-Muzanī ⁕ said: I heard al-Shāfiʿī ⁕ say: "There isn't anyone who doesn't have those who love him and those who despise him. So, if there is no other option, let one be among the people of obedience to Allah ⁕."

Avoid Belittling Small Matters

The next narration deals with someone being aware of what he is taking, in terms of *muḥāsabah*. This is a very powerful narration and should be a very frightening one for all who are conscious of Allah ⁕.

The narration comes from the Imam through his chains to Ahmed ibn Abi al-Ḥawārī who that said he wished to see Abu Sulaymān al-Dārānī in a dream. Indeed, and after one year he saw him and asked: "Teacher! What has Allah done to you?"

He said: "O Ahmad! I came out from the small gate, and I found a sack of barley, so I took a stick from it. I can't remember [what I did with it]: I cleaned in between my teeth with it or I threw it. Because of it, I am being accounted for a whole year till this night."

Why? because he took a stick from somebody.

Imam al-Nawawī said to look at how important it is to fear Allah in belittling matters and others' possessions and how to use things.

The Prophet of Allah ﷺ warned us of belittling the small sins, as well as the good deeds. He said:

إيَّاكم ومُحقَّراتِ الذُّنوبِ فإنَّما مُحقَّراتُ الذُّنوبِ كمَثَلِ قوم نزَلوا بَطْنَ وادٍ فجاء ذا بعُودٍ وجاء ذا بعُودٍ حتَّى جمَعوا ما أنضَجوا به خُبزَهم وإنَّ مُحقَّراتِ الذُّنوبِ متى يُؤخَذْ بها صاحبُها تُهلِكْه

"I warn you of the belittled sins. For the example of belittled sins is like a group of people on journey who camped in the middle of a valley. So, one person went and brought a stick; and then another person went and did the same thing; until they had gathered enough [wood] to light something which would bake their bread. The belittled sins, whenever their doer is accounted for them, they will destroy him."[132]

And in regards to good deeds, he said:

لا تَحْقِرَنَّ مِنَ المَعروفِ شيئًا، ولو أنْ تَلْقَى أخاكَ بوَجْهٍ طَلْقٍ

"Do not belittle of the goodness anything, even if it is to meet your brother with a cheerful smiling face."[133]

132 *Ḥasan:* Hadith narrated by Imams Ahmad and al-Ṭabarānī
133 *Ṣaḥīḥ:* Hadith narrated by Imam Muslim

The believer should never belittle any of his sins; and should not belittle anybody's properties or possessions because everything you take or consume you have to be aware: of your heart and your intentions, and be aware of what you're taking as well as picking up.

This was the practice of the righteous people, starting from the Prophet ﷺ where he used to find a date on the path but he would not take it, saying that this date could be from charity[134] and he and his family were not allowed to consume something that was for charity. You will see this through many examples. One I will mention is that of 'Omar ibn Abdul 'Azīz ﵁ when he was the Caliph. He would have a lamp / candle which he lit for official business. When that business was over, he will extinguish it saying that this is not our money to spend.

The bottom line is the story that has been narrated here and how simple it is yet you will be accountable for a long time.

The Poet Ibn al-Mu'taz said:

خل الذنوب صغيرها وكبيرها ذاك التقى ،
واصنع كماش فوق أرض الشوك يحذر ما يرى ،
لا تحقرن صغيرة إن الجبال من الحصى

Abandon the sins, small and large; for that is piety

And act like one walking on thorny ground,
bewaring of what can be seen.

Don't belittle anything small; the mountains are of pebbles.

134 *Ṣaḥīḥ:* Hadith narrated by Imams al-Bukhārī and Muslim

Maʿrūf al-Karkhī is among the righteous people. They passed by him during the days of *fitnah*[135] (strife) going to fight; and he would say to them: "Pass by, may Allah accompany you! Pass by, May Allah bless you!"

He was told that they are going out to fight!

He said: "If Allah accompanies them, they will not fight."

It's a beautiful aspect that the Imam is giving here, which if one is aware of Allah, then Allah will guide him to what is best. Even in matters of battle and killing, they will be guided to do what is right. The secret being is that you make Allah your companion on your path.

Beware of Backbiting

Another narration which is also from Maʿrūf is what the Imam narrated from Ibn Abi al-Dunyā saying that some people sat down in the presence of Maʿrūf, and one of them back-bit another man. So he [Maʿrūf] said to him: "Oh So-and-so! Remember the day when cotton will be placed on your eyes[136]."

Here is it about being aware of what you are losing out of good deeds by backbiting others. In my book "Don't Judge!" I mention that when you are judging others, then you are losing out by making lots of errors, in addition to the fact that you are missing out on reforming your self, which is a great loss.

This is why AbdUllah ibn al Mubārak ﷺ said, "If I was going to backbite anybody, I would backbite my parents because at least they will be taking my good deeds."

135 *Ṣaḥīḥ:* Hadith narrated by Imam Muslim
136 Reference to death, as you will be washed on the table

Because when you backbite someone, they will take your good deeds of you on the Day of Judgement.

It was said to Imam al-Shāfiʿī that so-and-so is backbiting you. So he sent a plate of a sweet dish to the guy who was backbiting with a message saying, "I heard that you have given me some of your good deeds, so I thought I would repay you with something in this life."

This was the kind of attitude that they used to have, they were looking from that perspective.

Matters That Do Not Concern You

The Imam now tells us a few sayings from the great Imam and Shaykh Maʿrūf al-Karkhī who was the great scholar of Baghdad, and was quite prominent in terms of his bearings in the world.

His contribution here is: "The mark of Allah Almighty's despise for a slave is that you see him occupied with what does not concern him."

Why is this the case? Because when you concern yourself with things that do not concern you, it shows that you are falling into two problems:

1 - You are attaining lots of bad deeds because you are talking about people, gossiping about them; you are judging people and you are doing things that bring about badness.

2 - You are wasting the opportunity to do good things. Because if you are doing bad things and engaging in bad actions, you are not going to be concerned about yourself and if you're not concerned about yourself then you are losing the opportunity to correct and better yourself.

Calling unto Allah

Another attribute that the Imam mentioned about Ma'rūf was his supplication:

يَا مَالِكُ، يَا قَدِير، يَا مَن لَيسَ لَهُ نَظِير

"O Supreme Owner! O Able! O You who has no counterpart!"

Fear of Undue Praise

We have been narrated to on the authority of Ahmad ibn AbdUllah, who said: The [Quran] reciters of the people of Kūfah met in the home of al-Hakam ibn 'Otaybah. They unanimously agreed that the most prominent reciter of the people of Kūfah was Ṫalḥah ibn Muṣarrif.

So when he [Ṫalḥah] heard of this, he went to sit [as a student] with al-'A'mash and recite onto him, in order that this title would no longer be attributed to him!

He didn't want to have that kind of title, because of fear of having the wrong intention. Our Prophet ﷺ has already warned us about the type of people who will be resurrected on the day of judgment. And the first of these people who will be thrown in the Hell-fire will be the one who has learnt the Quran and recited it so that he would be called *qārī*.

Proximity to Allah

On the authority of al-Shāfiʿī ﵀ who said that Fuḍayl ibn ʿIyāḍ said: "How many a person circumambulates[137] this House; whilst another is distant from it yet rewarded greater than him [the former].".

Some people are in Makkah, near the Kaʿbah in the Sacred Masjid, in the holiest sites, which is a place to be spiritually engaged: they are really close, physically. However, if you compare them with others who are physically distant, the latter are of higher status and higher in rewards than them. Meaning that the connection is not about the physical; it is more about where your heart is and how you really connect to Allah ﷻ and not just about being in the House of Allah ﷻ.

You will find people are doing *ṭawāf* around the House, and they are more interested in looking at their mobile phone messages or making a call. They are distracted and their hearts are distant. From a different perspective, when I went to hajj I met a taxi driver, who, despite living in Makkah all his life, hadn't performed hajj. And I'm guessing that he isn't unique in that.

Actions – Not Lineage

On the authority of al-Shāfiʿī who narrates from the authority of Fuḍayl who said: "Dāwūd the Prophet ﵇ said: 'My God! Be for my son Sulaymān after me as You have been for me!'

So, Allah Almighty revealed to him: 'O Dāwūd, tell your son Sulaymān to be to Me as you were to Me, I will be to him as I was to you'."

137 To do *ṭawāf*

Tell your son to act the same way as you have acted and I will treat him in the same way as I have treated you. This statement tells us that you will only get as much as you put in. And from another perspective, understand that lineage isn't going to benefit you *per se*. Just because your father is a prophet or a shaykh or a righteous man, it doesn't mean anything.

'Ibrāhīm ﷺ asked Allah ﷻ to bless his progeny with prophethood and imamship, but Allah advised him that it's about righteousness, not lineage.

﴿ إِذِ ابْتَلَى إِبْرَاهِيمَ رَبُّهُ بِكَلِمَاتٍ فَأَتَمَّهُنَّ قَالَ إِنِّي جَاعِلُكَ لِلنَّاسِ إِمَامًا قَالَ وَمِن ذُرِّيَّتِي قَالَ لَا يَنَالُ عَهْدِي الظَّالِمِينَ ﴾

﴿ And when his Lord tested 'Ibrāhīm with some words, and he fulfilled them; He said, 'Truly I shall make you an Imam for the people.' He said, 'and from my offspring?' He said, 'My covenant shall not reach those who have transgressed'.﴾[138]

And we know that Nūḥ's ﷺ son was not among the believers. The Prophet ﷺ also advised his family the same, and he succinctly summarised this:

وَمَن بَطَّأَ بِهِ عَمَلُهُ، لَمْ يُسْرِعْ بِهِ نَسَبُهُ

"Whoever's actions have slowed him down, his ancestry will not excel him."[139]

138 Holy Quran: Chapter of the Cow 2:124
139 *Ṣaḥīḥ:* Hadith narrated by Imam Muslim

Raise Your Needs

The Imam narrates from the authority of al-Shāfi'ī ﷺ who said: Hishām ibn Abdul Malik said to al-Fuḍayl: "Raise your need to me!"[140]

He said: "I have raised it to the Most Munificent, Most Generous."

Sālim ibn AbdUllah ibn 'Omar; meaning the grandson of 'Omar ibn al-Khaṭṭāb ﷺ was in the Masjid al-Ḥarām, and he was doing *ṭawāf*. Hishām ibn Abdul Malik recognised Sālim. He approached him and said, "Do you need anything?"

Sālim was very harsh with him and replied, "Do you have no shame asking me if I need anything while we are in the House of Allah ﷻ!?"

So, Hishām backed off. But then, as they left the *masjid*, Hishām approached him again and asked him again, "Do you need anything? Do you have any needs?"

This time Sālim replied, "Do you mean the needs of this life or the needs of the Next?"

Hishām, "I mean from this life."

So, Sālim replied eloquently: a reply from someone who is aware of Allah, "I didn't ask the needs [of this life] from the One who owns them; so why should I ask it from someone who doesn't!"

The essence of both these stories is all about how a person links to Allah ﷻ. Because being aware of Allah is about knowing – with firm conviction – that only Allah is the One who can help you in achieving what you want. He is the One who hears the call, and only He can answer.

These two righteous figures also further cement the concept of

140 Denoting a form of application for support.

not taking worldly favours from the rulers, as that would corrupt one's *dīn*.

Roughen Up

The next aspect here is about looking after one attitude in terms of culture and also in terms of drinking and clothing. This is the advice of ʿOmar ibn al-Khaṭṭāb ﷺ.

The Imam tells us that one of the best disciplines with which one can use to discipline oneself in abandoning care of the sense of clothing, food and drink, and the like; is what we have been narrated to from the Commander of the Faithful ʿOmar Ibn al-Khaṭṭāb ﷺ. Abu ʿOthmān al-Nahdī ﷺ said:

"While we were in Azerbaijan with ʿUtabah ibn Farqad, we received a letter from ʿOmar ibn al-Khaṭṭāb [which read]:

As for then:

Wear the *'izār*[141], the *ridā'*[142] and sandals; and throw away the *khuffs*[143].

Abandon the pants (trousers); and dress in the dress of your father Ismāʿīl ﷺ.

Beware of [indulging in] luxuries, and beware of wearing the clothes of the non-Arabs[144].

I advise you with the sun: for it is the bath of the Arabs.

Wear the clothes of your father: Maʿad.

Roughen up, and balance [your stature].

141 Wraparound, worn on the lower part of the body
142 The Upper cloak for the upper part of the body
143 *Khuff* is like a leather sock or shoe
144 In this context, refers to the Persians.

Cut up the [horses'] stirrups[145].

Throw the arrows, and mount the horses by leaping [on their backs]."

The *'izār* and *ridā'* are basically the clothes one wears when going to do hajj in the state of *'iḥrām*; they are the two pieces of cloth. The lower is called the *'izār* and the upper is called *ridā'*. Today, many countries still wear these as part of their clothing, like Bangladesh, Yemen, Emirates, Somalia and so on.

So, he is advising these types of clothes. Then he advises to wear sandals and not to get used to wearing leather socks, which is also a form of boot. There is a medicinal aspect in all of this also, as the foot needs to breathe. But he is saying to them that basically don't lose the traditions that you have in terms of clothing. Another thing is don't get used to finding the easy way in practice. So, in regards to the *khuff* and wiping on it, is like to cut out the washing of the feet in the *wuḍū'*.

Then he said don't wear the trousers, and wear the clothes of your father ('Ismā'īl ﷺ). The Muslims got used to wearing wide clothes which don't reveal the body, and have health benefits, which for the man is important if he wants to have children!

Then he says beware of having too much of an easy life, seeking the luxuries. So, beware of dressing similar to the non-Arabs and here the word "similar" is referring to the clothes of your traditions and make sure you don't lose the benefits of having that.

He then advises them to seek the Sun, because it is the bath or a form of treatment that the Arabs used to seek. We know that the Sun is not the ideal place to spend a long time due to the dangers of Ultra Violet light, but we also know that there is benefit of getting some sunlight which helps the body to produce vitamin D. If you expose yourself to too much Sun then there is danger, but avoiding

145 Part of the saddle in which the rider's feet are placed; provides support and leverage to the rider

it, is also harmful in depriving your body of the vitamin.

Then he says that you should follow the footsteps of your father Maʿad ibn ʿAdnān one of the forefathers of the Arabs, who was renowned for living a harsh life. And that's why he summed up by saying that they should not seek an easy life. Always look for the hardships don't get used to the luxuries even if you have the means. Always look out for the hardship, and there is a narration which is: (اخشوشنوا فإنّ النعم لا تدوم) which translates as "Toughen up; for the blessings will not last."

This is not a saying of the Prophet ﷺ but is a wise narration. If you get used to the luxuries and the mod-cons, and not used to living in hardships; then there will come a time when you will not have these things and therefore you will find yourself in a bit of a pickle, because you are not used to a different way of life. A grave example of this in our modern times is what happened to the Kuwaiti people when Saddam Hussein invaded their country in 1990. Within days, even hours, many Kuwaitis were fleeing, and they found themselves as refugees in other countries. Astonishingly, a friend of my father's tells me that prior to the invasion, one preacher was giving a reminder in the Old Brompton Mosque (Earl's Court), and he was talking about how situations and affairs can change suddenly. It was strange that as he saw some people from the Gulf, he referred to them saying that the people in the Gulf are living a comfortable life; yet if Allah wills, they may all of a sudden become refugees. At the time, the comment seemed so far-fetched and some even smirked at such an absurdity. This happened a few months before Saddam sent his army across the border. The point being, the people of Kuwait found that they had to deal with a harsh life for the coming several months.

Previously, we mentioned the saying of Bishr al-Ḥāfī: "The people of the past didn't use to eat out of delicacy, and they didn't used to wear out of leisure or luxury."

These people of high status didn't use to wear clothes, to find the luxury of clothes. As today people wear the best and softest clothes and check the label, how much cotton, how much polyester and that kind of thing. The people of the past used to wear clothes to cover their nakedness. This was the path of the Prophets and the righteous. This is how their attitude was to food, to clothes, and so on. It was to serve a purpose in this regard.

It is narrated that AbdUllah ibn 'Omar ﵁ for a long time desired to eat fish. His family were aware of this; and after some effort and many months, his family got hold of some fish as a surprise for him. They prepared and cooked it for him. Then they presented it to him for supper. He saw it and was shocked. "What's this?" he exclaimed.

They informed him that they knew of his desire to eat fish; and that he had mentioned that.

On this, he replied, "Not every time, my *nafs* desires something, I have to oblige it. Take it away and give it to some needy person!"

Today one of the diseases we have in society is that people want to satisfy their desires. One of the main reasons for obesity is because we keep feeding our desires. We see a nice cake or a delicious meal; and we have to eat it or we eat too much of it. When it comes to clothes, handbags (for men as well as women), shoes, entertainment and so on.

The key to a healthy balanced life is to deny your *nafs* what it fancies or wants. You have to be in control of it, and not it in control of you.

Also, 'Omar ﵁ was saying to them that you should not get used to a luxurious life. Rather be prepared and keep physically active. One form is when it comes to mounting your horses, don't just mount them by using stirrups, but learn to jump onto the horses.

And continue to be active, learn to throw and to shoot arrows. It's all about keeping physically fit. However, do not lose sight of where you are in terms of preparing physically, being able to have those skills because if you think only about a luxurious lifestyle, then you will lose those skills and all of a sudden you might find yourself heavy and not being able to deal with difficulties in this life. We know that having an active lifestyle is also key to good health.

That was the advice given by 'Omar ibn al-Khaṭṭāb ﵁. The Imam narrates this to us from Abu 'Othmān al-Nahdī. Abu 'Othmān was one of the Followers, and he is considered as a *mukhaḍram*.

Levels of Companionship of the Prophet ﷺ

We have three distinct levels:

1 - *Ṣaḥābī* (companion): someone who saw the Prophet ﷺ, believed in him (i.e., became a Muslim) and died on Islam.

2 - *Tābi'ī* (follower): a Muslim who saw a *ṣaḥābī*, studied with him/her, or at least took some knowledge from him, and died on Islam. Simply seeing a *ṣaḥābī* doesn't make you a *tābi'ī* automatically. There would have to have been some studying or transfer of knowledge.

3 - *Tābi'ī mukhaḍram*: is a *tābi'ī* who existed during the time of the Prophet ﷺ, but did not meet him, for some reason.

Abu 'Othmān al-Nahdī is of the third category. The Imam said that he was a great man and had lots of great things related to him. He lived for a long time, saying about himself "I lived for a long time: for a hundred and thirty years and everything I saw I have found it changing except my *'aml* (hope / aspiration) it has not changed.

When al-Husayn ibn 'Alī ﵁ was killed, he left al-Kūfah and went to live in al-Baṣrah, saying "I am not going to live in a country in which the son of the daughter of the Prophet ﷺ was killed."

He died in the year 95AH or 100AH.

The Story of Jābir and Shihāb ﵁

The Imam narrates up from the authority of Jābir ibn AbdUllah al-'Anṣārī ﵁ that a man came asking him about the veiling of the believer.

I [Jābir] said, "I am not that person. Rather that is a man called: Shihāb."

So, Jābir walked with him to go to the Governor[146] of that town- a man named: Maslamah. He approached the door, and said to the guard: "Tell the Ruler to come down to me!"

The guard entered whilst smiling, and the Governor said to him: "What's the matter with you?"

He said: "There's a man at the door on a camel and he said: 'Tell the Ruler to come down to me!'."

He said: "Didn't you ask him who he is?!"

So, the guard returned to him and asked him. He said, "I am Jābir ibn AbdUllah al-'Anṣārī."

The guard returned and informed the Governor, who sprung from his seat, and leaned out [of the window]: "Come up!"

Jābir said: "I don't want to come up, but tell me where is Shihāb's home?"

He said: "Come up, and I will send for him to come and fulfil your need."

146 Meaning the governor of the town

He said: "I do not want your messenger to go to him; for if the Messenger of the Ruler came to a man, it may alarm him. And I would hate for a Muslim man to be startled because of me."

So, the Governor came down, joined Jābir and walked with him until he came to Shihāb. Shihāb leaned out and said: "Either you come up or I come down to you?"

Jābir said: "I don't want you to come down to us, and we don't want to go up to you! But narrate to us the hadith that you heard from the Messenger of Allah ﷺ regarding the veiling of a believer."

He said: I heard the Prophet ﷺ say:

مَنْ سَتَرَ عَلَى أَخِيهِ الْمُؤمِنِ فَكَأَنَّمَا أَحيَاه

"Whoever veils his believing brother; then it is as if he has given him life."[147]

Many lessons can be derived from this beautiful narration.

Firstly; the eagerness of the *Ṣaḥābah* in learning hadith. "Hadith" can be a synonym for knowledge.

Secondly; the eagerness of the *Ṣaḥābah* to spread knowledge, through teaching and directed learning.

Thirdly; the understanding of the importance of hearing first-hand, where possible.

Fourthly; following from "thirdly" if not first-hand, then as closest as possible to the source of knowledge.

147 This hadith is narrated by Imam Abu Nu'aym in his book "Knowing the Companions". Shihāb ؓ is not known, except as one of the Companions. Not knowing a companion isn't problematic, as our belief is that all the companions are trustworthy and they do not lie.

Fifthly; the humility of the scholars, as Jābir was not arrogant in merely sending this man on his quest, but he accompanied him, walking with him to achieve his objective.

Sixthly; the importance of helping others in fulfilling their needs and answering their requests.

Seventhly; the goodness of some governors is not to be refuted. There are governors who have good morals and not all are tyrants and wicked.

Eighthly; the nobility of the Companions in the eyes of others, as demonstrated by the reaction of the Governor.

Ninthly; consciousness of not startling another person, by aiming to do things in the best palatable way.

Tenthly; value of time, as Jābir had no time to waste to sit and chat. He was on a task and wanted to carry that out, in order to get back to what he was doing.

Eleventhly; a good governor knows his flock. He knows where they live and so knows their needs and addresses them.

Twelfthly; some people lack basic common sense. The guard didn't ask the name of the person requesting the Governor. More so, he was amused that a person would even make a request like that.

Thirteenthly; the guard embodied a well know Arab saying: (الذي لا يعرف الصقر: يشويه) "the one who doesn't know [the value of] the falcon, will barbeque it." He didn't know who Jābir was and thought who is this common man asking an audience with the governor.

Lastly; the importance and virtue of veiling other people, be that their shortcomings, their errors or their status.

These lessons are the main ones that come to mind; and Allah knows best.

09

Honouring those because of their relation to the beloved

We are now in the chapter where the Imam talks in general about how people should be venerated due to a certain association. He said in regard to those who are venerated because of a link to a beloved one.

This is loving people because they have a particular status. We love the Prophet ﷺ and because we love him, we love his family because of their link to him and that's why we have reserved such a high status in Islam for them to the extent that in our prayer we remember them.

Some of the poetry he mentions here as an example of this point which he is trying to establish.

ألا حيِّي الديارَ بُسعْدَ إنِي أُحِبُّ لحب فاطمةَ الديارا

Alas, salute the dwellings in Su'd for truly,

I love those dwellings for Fātimah loves them

We don't know who Fātimah is, but he is demonstrating here that if you love somebody who loves something, then you love that thing because of your love for them.

Qays (known as *majnūn*) was someone deeply in love with Layla; and they had romantic stories and poetry regarding these two. He is noted to have said:

أمرُ على الديار ديار ليلى   فأقبل ذا الجدار والجدار

وما حب الديار شغفن قلبي   ولكن حب من سكن الديار

I pass by the dwellings: the dwellings of Layla.

So, I kiss this wall and I kiss that wall.

It is not the love of the dwellings that have captured my heart;

Rather, the love of who lives in those dwellings.

There are several amusing stories relating to this couple. It was said there were some people praying in *jamā'ah* (congregation). Qays who is lost in his love passes in front of the imam without turning around or whatever. During the *ṣalāh* the people are rattled, and they came to him after *ṣalāh* and said to him, "What have you done, you came in front of us while we were praying, did you not see us?"

He said, "I was so entrenched in my love for my beloved that I did not notice you guys. And yet you are claiming that you love Allah and are devoted to Him. Yet in your prayer, you are more obsessed with me coming in front of you, so what kind of love is that?"

This is the general concept. If you love Allah ﷻ then you will love what Allah loves and you will hate what Allah ﷻ hates, and if you love the Prophet ﷺ you will love whatever he loves and so forth. And disobeying them in any way is contrary to the love that you should show.

Imam al-Shāfiʿī ﷺ said in prose[148]:

تعصي الإله وأنت تظهر حبه   هذا مَحال في القياس بديع
لو كان حبك صادقا لأطعته   إن المحب لمن يحب مطيعُ

You disobey God and you outwardly show your love [to Him].

This is impossible to equate: a unique practice.

If your love was true, you would have obeyed Him;

For truly the lover is obedient to whom he loves.

There is another poem here where he says:

أُحِبُّ الأيامَى إذ بثينةُ أيِّمٌ   وأحببتُ لمَّا أنْ غنيتِ الغوانيَ

I love the spinster women as Buthaynah is a spinster

As I love those who are married, when you will get married.

So, the point of this small section is to make you aware of the importance of identifying whom you love: you will make extra effort and you will love things because of them. The *Ṣaḥābah* would fall in love with the things the Prophet ﷺ used to do it; they loved him so much that they would imitate his actions and sometimes beyond one's perception. There is a narration, that once on journey going to hajj, AbdUllah ibn ʿOmar ﷺ at a specific point lowered his head as he was on his mount. Those around him were surprised at what he did and questioned him. He said, "The Prophet ﷺ on passing this point lowered his head, and I am imitating him ﷺ." Now, when the Prophet ﷺ did that, at the time, there was a tree branch, and so he lowered his head to avoid hitting the branch. At

148 Some have attributed these two lines to Maḥmūd al-Warrāq (may Allah have mercy on him)

the time of AbdUllah, the branch was no longer there, but sill he wanted to imitate his beloved. And there are many other incidents which demonstrate this love.

The Imam also narrates that Ahmad ibn Abi al-Ḥawārī said: I heard Abu Sulaymān say: "We do not love those whom we love except for their obedience to their tutors. Yet you disobey me, I have commanded you to extend your fingers[149]."

In the narration of al-Tirmidhī [it reads]: "to grasp".

By tutors, he means those who teach others; mentors or teachers. And he was talking to one of the students. He said to him to extend his fingers, but the student kept disobeying him. This probably was in relation to *ṣalāh* because in *ṣalāh* when you sit in the *tashahhud*, you can either open the finger or you could grasp them back. He was teaching him to extend his fingers but his student was going against him. So, he was questioning what kind of love does the student have.

And this also falls in line with what has been mentioned in this section in regards to your relationship with Allah ﷻ because if your relationship with Allah ﷻ is a subtle relationship, as people would be loved according to their relationship with Allah ﷻ. Because if you love Allah ﷻ and you have that obedience to Allah ﷻ, Allah ﷻ will love you and He will allow others to love you; so there is that bigger impact with that.

Eloquence of the Arabic Language

As an aside, the Imam adds a little bit of knowledge relating to the eloquence of the Arabic language. He commented on the aforementioned line of poetry that it is a form of novel writing, as

149 Meaning in *ṣalāh*, during *tashahhud*.

it changes from the third person to the second person. As he said (Buthaynah) then he said: (you will get married).

It has equivalents in the Holy Quran, as in the Almighty's saying:

﴿ عَبَسَ وَتَوَلَّى، أَن جَاءَهُ الأَعمَى، وَمَا يُدرِيكَ لَعَلَّهُ يَزَّكَّى ﴾

﴿ He frowned and turned away. That the blind one had come to him. And what do you know that he may be purified...﴾[150]

And Allah Almighty said:

﴿ الحَمدُ لله رَبِّ العَالَمِين ﴾

﴿ Praise be to Allah, Lord of the worlds﴾[151]

Until He said:

﴿ إِيَّاكَ نَعبُدُ ﴾

﴿ It is You; we worship ﴾[152]

Its reversal, which is the return from the second person to the third person, is demonstrated in what the Almighty said:

﴿ حَتَّى إِذَا كُنتُم فِي الفُلكِ وَجَرَينَ بِهِم ﴾

﴿...till when you were in the ark, and we ran them into...﴾[153]

The Imam narrates from his chains up to al-Fuḍayl ibn ʿIyāḍ ﵀ who said: "You ask Paradise of Him, yet you do what He despises. I

150 Holy Quran; Chapter of He Frowned 80:1-3.
151 Holy Quran; Chapter of The Opening 1:2.
152 Holy Quran; Chapter of The Opening 1:5.
153 Holy Quran; Chapter of Yūnus 10:22.

have not seen anyone having a lower opinion of himself than you."

Because it shows a kind of contradiction in yourself: you are asking Him for *al-Jannah* and yet you do things that He dislikes.

It's the very similar to the saying of the Prophet ﷺ:

فَإِنَّ الجَنَّةَ لا يَنَامُ طَالِبُهَا ... وَالنَّارُ لا يَنَامُ هَارِبُهَا

"How bewildering is the Hell Fire! The one who wants to escape it does not sleep. And how bewildering is *al-Jannah*! The one who seeks does not sleep."[154]

So, if you seek *al-Jannah* you are going to do things that will cause you to enter into *al-Jannah*, and that is through the love of Allah ﷻ and His Messenger ﷺ and being obedient to them.

We can also contemplate on the hadith that Allah ﷻ has surrounded *al-Jannah* with hardships. The heart cannot see the essence of *al-Jannah* without going through hardships.

So what happens is that you have eyes to see the material things, and you have the heart to see the non-material things, through *yaqīn*. Those that can see with their hearts, will actually be able to see beyond the borders and that is why in the Quran, Allah ﷻ says:

﴿ كَلَّا لَوْ تَعْلَمُونَ عِلْمَ الْيَقِينِ، لَتَرَوُنَّ الْجَحِيمَ، ثُمَّ لَتَرَوُنَّهَا عَيْنَ الْيَقِينِ ﴾

﴿ Nay! If you have the *'ilm* of *yaqīn* (true certainty). Then you will surely have seen the Hell Fire. Then, truly you will see it with the eye of *yaqīn* ﴾[155]

154 *Ḍa'īf:* Hadith narrated by Imam al-Ṭabarānī and others
155 Quran: Chapter of Mutual Increase 102 5-7

If your heart isn't pure nor clean, it will not see the Hell nor will it see *al-Jannah*. In the case of *al-Jannah*, it will see hardships and it retreats back. In the case of the Hell, it will see the desires and be allured by those matters.

It therefore remains that a person has to work on his heart, so that he can attain that sort of level of geniality.

On a lighter note, 'Omar ﷺ once observed a Bedouin; who prayed 2 *rak'ahs* very quickly and after which he made the following *du'ā'*: "O Allah! Marry me to one of the *ḥūr*."

So 'Omar commented, "Your *khiṭbah*[156] is very precious, but the *mahr* that you have offered is very poor."

There is another narration relating to Sulaymān al-Dārānī who said:

"Once I was praying *qiyām al-layl* and while I was praying, I felt so tired that I fell asleep in *sujūd*. Then, I felt somebody kick me and I woke up and there was this beautiful woman standing in front of me. She said, 'If you seek me, this is not the time to sleep'."

156 *khiṭbah* means proposal; and here it refers to whom you seek to marry.

10

Consequences of Mockery

The Imam goes on to another topic which is almost the opposite of the previous chapter. He mentions of the narrations of people who made mockery of the *dīn*, and he goes on and mentions a few stories here. He mentions them with his chains of narration to show that these are picked up from different places because in the past you would have people who are known as *al-Qaṣāṣīn* (storytellers). These people would sit down in meeting places and they would just tell stories. Some are true, but many are made up. Their main objective was to attract attention and to make money from it.

An incident relating to this category of people was related to me by a Somali friend. He said that once, one of these storytellers was sitting, and around him had gathered a crowd to listen to what he had to say. Before he started, he said, "You have a black cow; yet from this black cow comes white milk! How does this happen? There is a secret behind this? Do you know this secret?"

The crowd said in chorus, "No. Tell us!"

He repeated it and asked, "Can anyone tell us this magnificent secret?"

Again, the crowd had blank faces. He then passed around his cap, and asked for money in exchange for him revealing this baffling secret. After the cap has gone round and returned to him full to the brim with money, he revealed the secret:

"It is the Power of the Almighty Allah!"

The Imam narrates from somebody called Zakariya ibn Yaḥyā al-Sājī who said, "We were walking in the alleys of al-Baṣrah to the door of some of the [Hadith] narrators, so I hurried in my walk. A heretic in his religion was accompanying a man among them. The heretic said mockingly, 'Lift your feet from the wings of the angels, so you do not break them!'

After saying this, he became fixated in his place, his legs having frozen and he fell!"

This man was mocking the *dīn*, by making fun of the Prophet's ﷺ saying:

إِنَّ الملائكةَ لتَضَعُ أجنِحتَها لطالبِ العِلمِ؛ رِضًا بما طَلَبَ

"Truly, the Angels lower their wings for the one seeking knowledge, out of content for what he seeks."[157]

Some said that the lowering of their wings is literal, as the Angels descend to join in to hear the knowledge. Whilst others said that this is a metaphor for their delight and honour for those who seek the knowledge, and a metaphor for their humility to them.

The narrator of the previous narration said that when the mocker said what he said, his legs froze up meaning that he became paralyzed and just fell. The Imam said that the Hadith Master Abdul Ḥāfiẓ said: The chain of transmission of this story is as if one were to find it, or like seeing it with one's own eyes, because its narrators are renowned imams.
Another similar story which he narrates from Imam Abu Dāwūd, one of the Hadith Masters. He narrates a similar incident which

157 *Ḥasan:* Hadith narrated by Imams Ahmad, Abu Dāwūd and al-Tirmidhī.

he says, there was a person who used to mock the *dīn* and he also heard of the hadith about the Angels laying down their wings for the one who seeks knowledge. So, he put nails in his sandals and he said I want to step on the wings of the Angels. In this incident, the mocker was later affected by gangrene in his feet. Gangrene is a form of disease which could make you lose a part of the body.

Imam Muhammad al-Taymī ﷺ stated this story in his book explaining *Ṣaḥīḥ* Muslim. There, it reads: "His legs were paralyzed, as were his arms and all his limbs."

He said: In some accounts, I saw that it read "...and his physique deteriorated!"

The Imam said: In some stories, I read that one of the innovators had heard the saying of the Prophet ﷺ:

إذا اسْتَيْقَظَ أَحَدُكُمْ من نَوْمِه، فلا يَغْمِسْ يَدَهُ في الإناءِ
حتَّى يَغْسِلَها ثَلاثًا؛ فإنَّه لا يَدْرِي أَيْنَ باتَتْ يَدُهُ.

"When one of you wakes up from his sleep, let him not dip his hand in the container until he has washed it, for he does not know where his hand has remained overnight."[158]

The innovator said, as a matter of cynicism, "I know where my hand has remained overnight: in bed!" He awoke with his hand in his anus, all the way up to his forearm!

In this narration, the Prophet ﷺ instructed to wash one's hands thrice before dipping it in a bowl of clean water; if there is any *najāsah* (impurity) on the hand, then it will make that water impure. However, it is not obligatory, because the presence of *najāsah* being on the hand is doubtful, i.e., it's not established because you don't know for certain. If you knew for certain then it would be a must to wash your hands. So, this guy was a person of *bid'ah* he made fun

158 *Ṣaḥīḥ: Hadith narrated by Imam Muslim*

saying, "Well, actually I do know where my hand is, it is underneath my pillow!". He was trying to mock this hadith. The people who narrated this story said that when he woke up in the morning, his hand was in his anus, all the way up to his forearm!

Al-Taymī said: "Let one beware with regards to degrading the *Sunan*[159] and matters of fixed legislation. See how the despicable nature of their actions ended."

This is true, because as humans we are continuously upgrading and updating our knowledge. There are things which for us seem strange or unclear or don't make sense. However, with time, those irregularities in the human mind may be explained and become clear. One example I bring here is in relation to the fly's wing. The Prophet ﷺ said:

إِذَا وقَعَ الذُّبَابُ فِي شَرَابِ أَحَدِكُمْ فَلْيَغْمِسْهُ ثُمَّ لِيَنْزِعْهُ،
فَإِنَّ فِي إِحْدَى جَنَاحَيْهِ دَاءً والأُخْرَى شِفَاءً، وفي رواية: دواء.

"If a fly falls into the drink of any one of you, then let him dip it, then remove it; for in one of its wings there is illness; and in the other: there is healing."[160]

In other versions of the hadith, the Prophet ﷺ said "medicine" instead of "healing". And in further versions, he said that the fly protects itself with the wing that has the illness; meaning it falls on that wing, and that's why you should dip it whole in the liquid.

Now, one can imagine how a hadith like this seems so strange and bizarre for those who think themselves scientifically educated. It had led many to mock this hadith narration; and even some learned Muslim activists refuted the authenticity of such a hadith, based on their ill-judged logic, simply because in their "rational" minds, it didn't make sense.

159 Plural of sunna; and refers to the acts of the Prophet ﷺ.
160 *Ṣaḥīḥ:* Hadith narrated by Imam al-Bukhārī

However, with the advancement of science and more research[161], today we know as a fact that the fly has antibiotics in one of its wings. This is one example of many.

An important principle to note here is that Islamic notions or facts may either be concretely evident or uncertain in terms of their narration, as are "scientific" principles, which may be concretely proven or based on strong theses. The concrete principles of either of the two classes will never conflict; it is impossible for an established scientific fact to contradict an authentic Islamic notion. However, a conflict may happen if one or both of them are uncertain. If one of them is uncertain, then it should be reinterpreted so as to remove the contradiction. If both are uncertain, then the uncertain Islamic principle should be given precedence over the uncertain scientific notion until the latter is proven. Understanding this principle can remove much of the issues that people have, as like the matter of the fly's wing.

Back to the story of the man who woke up with this hand up his anus, the Imam says that the meaning of this hadith, as what Imam al-Shāfiʿī and other scholars ﷺ have said is that the sleeping person's hand floats over his body during his sleep; he cannot guarantee that it does not pass over an impurity such as blood from a pimple, or a lice or insect; or the place of *istinjā'*[162], and the like. And Allah knows best. It is a form of precaution.

We can see that mockery of the *dīn* is well narrated in the Quran of how people mocked their Messengers; and indeed, our Messenger ﷺ. An example of this is in Surah al-Kauthar.

161 Eldesoukey, Rehab. (2014). Microbiological studies on fly wings (Musca domestica) where disease and treat. World Journal of Medical Sciences 11 (4): 486-489
162 Refers to one's frontal and rear passages

Allah says:

﴿ إِنَّ شَانِئَكَ هُوَ الأَبْتَرُ ﴾

﴿ The one who hates you is the one who is cut off ﴾[163]

This relates to the person who mocked the Prophet ﷺ by saying that he has no sons, and he will soon be forgotten after this.

However, Allah promised the Prophet that He will raise his mention[164]:

﴿ وَرَفَعنا لَكَ ذِكرَك ﴾

And indeed, the mention of the Prophet ﷺ has remained so.

There is a narration of a Bedouin, and this was at the time of the Companions. He was advised to say the *du'ā'* of riding/mounting, as was taught in the Quran:

﴿ سُبحَـٰـنَ الَّذِي سَخَّرَ لَنَا هَذَا، وَمَا كُنَّا لَهُ مُقرِنِين
وَإِنَّا إِلَى رَبِّنَا لَمُنقَلِبُون ﴾

﴿ Glory be to the One who has subjected this to us and without it we would not have been able to control it ﴾[165]

This Bedouin said while riding his camel, "As for me, I am in control of this animal." When he said that, the camel threw him off its back and stomped on him.

The last story that the Imam narrates which is also a bewildering one but it is there, nonetheless.

163 Holy Quran; Chapter of the Abundance 108: 3
164 Holy Quran; Chapter of the Solace 94: 4
165 Holy Quran: Chapter of the Ornaments 43:13

The Imam said: Another narration which falls into the same category is what was observed in our time and the news was multiply transmitted and confirmed with the judges: that a man in the village of Bosrā[166] - in the early years of 665AH - had a bad opinion and suspicion in the people of goodness. He had a son who believed in them.

One day, his son returned from a righteous shaykh and with him was a *siwāk*[167].

He said - mockingly: "What's that your shaykh has given you?"

He said: "This toothbrush."

So, the father took it from him and put it in his anus as a sign of contempt for him!

A period passed by, when the man who inserted the toothbrush in his anus, egested a small pup from his anus, closely resembling a fish. The man killed it. Then he died immediately, or two days later.

I am not sure what the exact explanation is, but reading the descriptions, it sounds like he had some sort of parasite in his gut, like a tapeworm or maybe something worse; and that is what came out of his backside with some blood clots giving it a strange resemblance. And Allah knows best.

May Allah Almighty relieve us of His calamities, and may He guide us to honour the *Sunan* and to venerate His rituals!!

These are some of the stories that the Imam has given to show. It is almost here, that he is trying to make the distinction between the attitude of people who love Allah and His Messenger and thus will love whatever they ask them to do and those people who hate Allah and His Messenger, and hate what they love, and this is their reality: either they will be mocked in this life or they will be shamed in the Next.

166 Not to be confused with Baṣrah, the latter being a city in Iraq, and the former a city in present day Syria.
167 Toothbrush

11

Important Perspectives

Impoverishment to Allah

Sahl ibn AbdUllah said, "There is no thicker veil between the slave and Allah than a [false] claim! And there is no nearer path to Him than impoverishment."

Da'wah here means to proclaim something about yourself. The more you praise yourself the more you are satisfying your *nafs* and it is opposite of what you should be towards Allah. Your relationship between you and Allah is that of a servant to Allah. The closest person to Allah is someone who has humility and is impoverished. That is why Allah has praised the Prophet ﷺ as the slave of Allah ﷻ; as mentioned in few verses of the Quran.

Allah said:

﴿ سُبْحَانَ الَّذِي أَسْرَى بِعَبْدِهِ لَيْلًا مِنَ الْمَسْجِدِ الْحَرَامِ إِلَى الْمَسْجِدِ الْأَقْصَى الَّذِي بَارَكْنَا حَوْلَهُ لِنُرِيَهُ مِنْ آيَاتِنَا إِنَّهُ هُوَ السَّمِيعُ الْبَصِيرُ ﴾

﴿ Glory be to the One Who took His slave by night from the Sacred Mosque to the Farthest Mosque whose surroundings We have blessed, so that We may show him some of Our signs. Indeed, He is the All-Hearing, All-Seeing ﴾[168]

﴿ وَأَنَّهُ لَمَّا قَامَ عَبْدُ اللَّهِ يَدْعُوهُ كَادُوا يَكُونُونَ عَلَيْهِ لِبَدًا ﴾

﴿ Yet when the Slave of Allah stood up calling upon Him, the pagans almost swarmed over him ﴾[169]

﴿ تَبَارَكَ الَّذِي نَزَّلَ الْفُرْقَانَ عَلَى عَبْدِهِ لِيَكُونَ لِلْعَالَمِينَ نَذِيرًا ﴾

﴿ Blessed is the One Who sent down the Criterion onto His Slave, in order that he may be a warner to the whole world ﴾[170]

The Judge ʿIyāḍ ﷺ sang these lines of poetry said:

ومما زادني شرفاً وفخراً وكدت بأخمصي أطأ الثريا

دخولي تحت قولك يا عبادي وأن صيّرت أحمد لي نبيا

And what has increased me in honour and pride,

Such that I could have stepped with my sole on the Thurayya[171] [star].

Is being among Your title: "O My Slaves".

And that you have sent to me Ahmad as a Prophet.

Impoverishment means that you announce your need to Allah Most Exalted.

168 Holy Quran: Chapter of the Night Journey 17:1
169 Holy Quran: Chapter of the Jinn 72:19
170 Holy Quran: Chapter of the Criterion 25:1
171 The Pleiades, also known as the Seven Sisters and Messier 45, is an open star cluster It is among the star clusters nearest to Earth, and is the cluster most obvious to the naked eye in the night sky. They have been known since antiquity to cultures all around the world; and hence its usage in this prose.

Allah said:

﴿ يَا أَيُّهَا النَّاسُ أَنْتُمُ الْفُقَرَاءُ إِلَى اللَّهِ وَاللَّهُ هُوَ الْغَنِيُّ الْحَمِيدُ ﴾

﴿ O Mankind! It is you who stand in need of Allah;
and Allah is the Self-Sufficient, Praiseworthy ﴾[172]

And Mūsā ﷺ said:

﴿ "My Lord! I am truly in desperate need of
whatever You may send down on me of goodness." ﴾[173]

وَيُعجِبُني فَقري إِلَيكَ وَلَم يَكُن لَيُعجِبُني لَولا مَحَبَّتُكَ الفَقرُ

And I am delighted with my impoverishment to you,

And being in need of You, would not have delighted me

Had I not loved You.

Focus on Worship

We have been narrated to with authentic chains on the authority of Abu Yaḥyā al-Bakrāwī who said: "I did not see anyone more worshiping of Allah than Shu'bah, to the extent his skin dried off his bone, as there was no flesh between them."

Shu'bah al-Ḥajjāj (d. 160AH) was the famous Imam and Hadith Master ﵀ who was so dedicated to the worship of Allah that he even denied his self and stopped looking after himself. He is

172 Holy Quran: Chapter of The Originator 35:15
173 Holy Quran: Chapter of the Stories: 28:24

mentioned here in terms of reaching such a state of focus on his worship, that he forgets to properly look himself. Shuʿbah was not the type of guy who was not doing anything; rather he was one of the Hadith Masters who had the title *Amīr al-Muʾminīn* of hadith. He studied lots and presented a lot.

Piety

Al-Shāfiʿī ﷺ said: "The most beneficial of munitions is piety; and the most harmful of it is aggression."

If you feel the need to attack somebody, it shows a lack of substance because if you are in the right then you don't need to attack somebody or mock them.

Al-Shāfiʿī ﷺ said: The best actions are three:

1 - The remembrance of Allah Almighty.

2 - Consoling brothers.

3 - Being fair to people.

It means these three are of the best works.

Hypocrisy

The Imam narrates that al-Shāfiʿī said: "Hypocrisy is not known except by a sincere one."

Meaning that one cannot know its reality and see its hidden aspects, except he who seeks sincerity. He strives for a long time searching, thinking and excavating for it, until he knows it or some of it; this does not occur to everyone; rather, this happens to the select.

As for an ordinary person who claims that he knows hypocrisy, then he is ignorant of its reality. The Imam offers us with the gift that he will mention in a chapter in this book – *in shāʾ Allah* Almighty - you will see in it wonders which will bring satisfaction to your eyes, *in shāʾ Allah*.

The one who can really know *riyāʾ* which is showing off is the sincere one. *Riyāʾ* is one of the hidden diseases of the heart. The one who truly knows it, is the person who is sincere because that person is the one who has the ability to recognize it and to be aware of it.

It is like when you are expecting a thief: somebody warns you that there are thieves around coming to rob houses, and he describes those thieves to you; maybe they are from this ethnicity, they come around in groups of three, the time that they usually come around. You will become much more in tune to what to expect of these thieves. Also, you will be better prepared because if you know that they come at certain time you may say I'm going to install this kind of alarm, I'm going to make sure that somebody is at the house at this kind of time etc. So the more a person is awakened to something, the more they will be prepared for that something.

The more a person is talking about *riyāʾ*, *kibr*, and *ikhlāṣ* and intention, the more he is going to be in tune. [Even for myself, as I have been teaching these lessons in the past it has allowed me to consciously increase my thinking about the whole concept of *ikhlāṣ* and *niyyah*, and intentions. I am thinking more about even the small acts, now and again, that I am doing; what my intentions are; let me think about my intention. So, talking about these things you will, no doubt, attain more.]

So this is similar to the saying which was said by al-Ḥasan al-Baṣrī ﷺ

مَا أَمِنَهُ إِلَّا مُنَافِقٌ، وَمَا خَافَهُ إِلَّا مُؤْمِنٌ

"Hypocrisy: the one who feels secure from it, is the hypocrite and the one who is afraid of it the believer."

It is like the believer is always thinking about what can nullify his *īmān*, what are the hidden aspects and he is always aware of *nifāq* (hypocrisy). He is always scared of falling into hypocrisy. Whereas the person who is not really thinking about it, and the kind of guy who feels that "this is not going to happen to me", is more likely to fall into it.

Ibn Abi Mulaykah ﷺ said, "I met thirty of the Companions of the Prophet ﷺ: all of them feared for their selves from [falling into] hypocrisy. None of them would say their *īmān* is like the *īmān* of Jibrīl or Mīkā'īl."

So, the Imam continues explaining what Imam al-Shāfi'ī said that the *mukhliṣ*[174] will spend a lot of time thinking, contemplating, looking at aspects of *riyā*', what is classified as *riyā*' and what can't be *riyā*' so that he knows it more than the general public. A person who doesn't think about it, is not likely to know about it. That's why he said anybody from the general public who claims that he knows *riyā*', wouldn't be correct. The average[175] person who doesn't think about it and doesn't consider it, they are not going to know it. As *riyā*' can be very specific, very fine and hidden.

To cement all that has been aforementioned, the Imam narrates a beautiful saying as related by 'Ustādh al-Qushayrī in his message "al-Qusharyriyyah" who narrates that Abu Yazīd [al-Bustāmī] ﷺ said:

174 *Mukhliṣ:* Someone who has *ikhlāṣ*
175 Commoners

"For twelve years I was the blacksmith of my soul. For five years I was the mirror of my heart. And for one year I was observing in between the two. [I realised] in my middle was an apparent/outward girdle; so I worked for twelve years to cut it, thinking how to remove it. [And I realised] I had an internal girdle; so I worked for five years to cut it, thinking of how to remove it.

It was then made apparent to me, and I looked at the creation, and I saw them dead. So, I pronounced on them four *takbīrs*[176]!"

The Imam explains what he said here, because it seems full of riddles. He said if you think about what he has said here, there is a lot of beautiful words which talk about the whole concept of *riyā'* and how hidden *riyā'* is; making it difficult to spot.

When he said that he saw everybody as dead, meaning that he considered everyone as dead; the Imam said that this is a very precious and beautiful description which rarely will you find outside the words of the Prophet ﷺ. It is like a unique phrase. So, what does he mean by it?

When he talks about all these years working as a blacksmith for himself, he said he was doing as the Prophet ﷺ mentioned in different narrations which is the whole concept of *jihād*, struggling against oneself. Fighting against one's self and trying to get control of the *nafs*. He spent all this time fighting with himself, working hard, trying to hammer himself down to the extent that he was able to overcome the self. A lot of the *'ulamā'* who talk about knowing Allah ﷻ and being aware of Allah ﷻ they address the *nafs*. If you want to control your *nafs*, you have to subdue it. The usual way to do that is denying its needs and not giving it everything that it desires. To be in control of it, you have to prevent it and deny it from all the desires that it wants. And this comes about by reducing all the luxuries that it wants and thrives on: the food, the leisure, recreation, sleep and so. The more you deny it, the more you will be able to control it.

176 Indicative of the funeral prayer

That's why Allah ﷻ talks about:

﴿ وَنَهَى النَّفْسَ عَنِ الْهَوَى ﴾

﴿ He prevented the *nafs* from desires ﴾[177]

When you do this, then you can control the *nafs* and it will come under your guidance.

When he said that I saw everybody as dead, he meant that they have the same reality like dead people. So, the Imam explains that reality.

The reality of dead people is that they do no harm to anybody, and they do not benefit anybody. They don't give nor do they prevent. They have no ability to give life nor do they take away life. They don't connect with others nor do they break the connections. They don't make things closer nor do they distant things away. They don't make people happy nor do they make people sad. They don't provide for others nor do they hold back their provision. They don't hold for themselves anything.

So, when he considered them as dead, it means that he knows the reality and it's almost like a harsh reality meaning that the people in his perception have no weight in terms of how they will benefit or harm him. Therefore, you should not fear them nor should you anticipate anything from them, nor should you seek to get what they have, nor should you show off to them, nor should you flatter them, nor should you occupy yourself with them, nor should you despise them, nor should you mock them.

Because at the end of the day they are not going to do anything, so why would you give them extra advantage when they don't have it. The same goes with talking about their negatives, looking at their mistakes: they are dead why would you go and search for their

177 Holy Quran: Chapter of Those who Extract 79:40

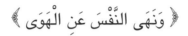

mistakes, or try to envy them, or try to look at what they have, or try to get what they have, because nobody wants to gain what they have. So, at the end of the day, treating or considering them dead, the end result is that you treat them as you would treat dead people. And, usually, what do we do when we hear about dead people? We say "*raḥimahu Allah*". We ask Allah ﷻ to have mercy on them. We make *du'ā'* for them. We usually feel empathy for them, we feel sorry for them, etc. Similarly, you should have that same kind of attitude towards others; you will feel that *raḥmah* for them like in the same way that you will do for the dead. That is the summary of what it means when he considers the others be dead.

And then he said, after that, the reality is that if you give too much weight to people's opinions, then obviously they will influence you, and they will affect you: this is like a summary of all we have spoken about all up to now. That being the fruit of *ikhlāṣ*, which is not to be concerned with others but to be concerned with Allah ﷻ and to think about how Allah ﷻ looks at you, your heart, your intention and your actions. And if you do this you will get the goodness in this life and the next life.

These are the words of Abu Yazīd al-Bustāmī. It isn't the scope of this book to go into details regarding the biographies; I will defer that to another book, if Allah permits.

However, I can say that he is a little bit of a strange character, because he has some very beautiful words and sayings, at the same time, some people attribute some strange things to him as well. They say that he has said some things which actually might seem very problematic. But when you look at his biography by people like Imam al-Dhahabī and Imam Ibn Kathīr they speak well of him and they said he is actually one of the Sultan of al-'Ārifīn: the head of those who are aware of Allah ﷻ because he said some deep things.

He began to describe himself as a blacksmith; that person who works hard heating and hammering metal to shape it. Lots of heat is generated, lots of work, lots of time. So, he said for twelve years he was doing that to himself. This was followed by holding up a mirror to his heart, examining it and reflecting on its reality: what is wrong with it, what is polluting it and how can it be cleansed and purified.

Then, he mentioned two girdles. As for the outward girdle, then this is about a person's attitude towards depending on Allah ﷻ and his attitude towards other people. He was saying that the girdle that was holding him back was his relationship with others. So, he needed a long time to work on that to cut that off.

As for the internal girdle; that is about looking at yourself from inside, how you view yourself. How you view yourself can also hold you back. Sometimes you are happy with your affairs, you think "I'm such a good person", "I'm coming to the *masjid*", "I'm doing this" and "I'm doing that"; that in itself maybe a girdle that holds you back, because you are no longer concerned with Allah, but with your own ego. You think that you have *ikhlāṣ* and honesty, when in reality there is a problem within yourself.

Amongst the sayings that he also said is in regards to gifts (*karāmāt*) [which we will talk about at a later stage *in shā' Allah*] "If you saw somebody having these gifts to the extent that he is flying, don't be deceived by that person until you look at what kind of reality they have in terms of the orders of Allah ﷻ, the prohibitions of Allah ﷻ, and the limitations and the shari'a."

This is something that the Imam will address later on in the book in the Chapter of the *Karāmāt*. However, it is good to know how this statement further cements the correct perspective of Sufism; which is that it is bound by the orders of Allah ﷻ, and not according to the whims of men.

Make the Most out of Your Youth

The Imam goes on to mention in his narration to al-Qushayrī ﵀ where he narrates that al-Junayd, narrates that his uncle al-Sarī al-Saqaṭī ﵀ said: "O Youth! Be serious in your efforts before you reach my stage; then you will weaken and fall short as I have fallen short."

By "my stage" he means old age; meaning that you will become weak and you will fall short like I have fallen short. Al-Junayd is relating this, and he said at that time when he gave that advice, already the youth couldn't even match his *'ibādah* even though he was old. He was already at that stage and he was saying I have become weak and I have fallen short, and obviously he was being very humble as well.

There is a narration that once he was sitting in the *masjid* and he was reading and praying then he extended his legs. He said "I heard somebody say, 'Ya Sarī, is this how you will sit in front of the kings?" So, he said, "I pulled my legs in" and he never stretched his legs again after that.

This reminds me of an incident in which I was sitting in my flat (when I was living in Sheffield) with this person I knew. It was a small room, and in it, we had a narrow bookcase and there were some books, and there were some *maṣaḥif* there as well. This person was just sitting with his legs right in the front of the books.

I said "Brother, the Quran is there! And there are books of hadith." He exclaimed, "Where is the hadith that says I shouldn't do that? Give me the evidence!"

I was quite shocked with his reply; and so I said to him bluntly, "If now I put my feet in your face; where is the hadith to say that there is anything wrong in putting my feet in front of your face?

Some things are basic *'adab*; you don't have to have hadith to tell you this."

Giving and Taking Condolences

Imam al-Shāfi'ī narrates here in regards to al-Ḥusayn ibn 'Alī, the grandson of the Prophet ﷺ. One of his sons died. After he died al-Ḥusayn wasn't seen sad; people looked at him they didn't see him sad or depressed or grieving. So, he was asked, "How come you are not grieving for the loss of your son?"

He said, "We are *Ahl al-Bayt* (the family of the Prophet ﷺ); we ask Allah ﷻ so He gives us. So, on the occasions that He wants something from us which we don't like, we have to also accept it."

We cannot then complain and show that we are upset with this. Our situation has to be the acceptance of Allah ﷻ. If He gives us, we are happy. If He doesn't give us, we should not become sad! This is how to treat Allah ﷻ.

Sa'īd ibn Jubayr رضي الله عنه was of the Followers and a student of Ibn 'Abbās رضي الله عنه. He once looked towards his son and he said to him, "I know a characteristic that you have."

He said, "What is it?" He said, "You will die and then I will anticipate that" meaning that there will come a time when you will die and I am alive, I will anticipate the reward of being patient for losing you so there is reward in that as well.

In a similar narration, Mūsā ibn al-Muhtadī comforted 'Ibrāhīm ibn Muslim saying, ""[He is] Your happiness: yet he is a trial and tribulation. [He is] Your sadness: which are prayers and mercy." The Imam said: A man wrote to one of his brothers comforting him with the loss of his son:

"As for then; the child for his parent is sorrow and strife for as long as he is alive; and if he precedes him, he is prayer and mercy. So, do not despair on what you have missed of his sorrow and his tribulation, and do not lose what Allah Almighty has compensated you of his prayers and mercy."

He was saying that the happy time that you think is happy, is in fact a trial for you, they are alive and you see them: yet they are trials, *fitnah* and tests for you. When they die, there is a *ṣalawāt* and *raḥmah*, mercy from Allah ﷻ if you are patient. So, you are between *fitnah* (trial) on one hand and *ṣalawāt* and *raḥmah* on the other hand, so don't be upset on losing somebody.

The Imam also narrates a saying that is attributed to a Bedouin woman that when she lost her son, she wasn't aggrieved that much. They commented: "How good is your grief for your son!"

She replied with such a beautiful romantic response. She said, "After I lost his father - meaning her husband - that loss has made me forget all the other calamities and misfortunes that follow." It is almost like measuring and anticipating the different aspects.

And that's why in some narrations, the Prophet ﷺ reminded us of the greatest calamity is the calamity in losing him. We can extend this meaning given by the Bedouin woman to the one who remembers the affliction with the loss of the Prophet ﷺ.

The Prophet ﷺ said:

إذا أصيب أحدكم بمصيبة فليذكر مصيبته بي فإنها أعظم المصائب

"If any one of you is afflicted with a tragedy, then let him be reminded of his tragedy in [losing] me, for it is the greatest of tragedies."[178]

178 *Ṣaḥīḥ:* Hadith narrated by Imams al-Dārimī and al-Ṭabarānī

And he said:

يا أيها النَّاسُ أي ما أحدٌ مِنَ النَّاسِ أَو مِنَ المؤمنِينَ أُصيبَ بِمُصيبةٍ فَلْيَتَعزَّ بمصيبتِهِ بي عَنِ المصيبَةِ التي تُصيبُهُ بغيري، فإنَّ أحداً من أُمَّتي لَن يُصابَ بمصيبةٍ بَعدي أَشدَّ عَلَيه مِن مصيبتي

"O People! Whoever among the people or believers has been afflicted by a tragedy, then let him be consoled with my tragedy from the tragedy of being afflicted with another. For none of my ʾ*ummah* will be affected by a tragedy after me more severe on him than my affliction."[179]

Ibn Abd al-Barr ﵀ said, "The Prophet ﷺ is true in what he has said, for the calamity and tragedy in losing him is the greatest of all tragedies that afflict a Muslim after him until the Day of Resurrection, for the revelation was cut off and Prophethood ended."

Consequence of Sin

Ahmad ibn Abi al-Ḥawārī said: I heard Abu Sulaymān say: "I remained twenty years not having a wet dream. I enacted in Makkah an act; so I woke up having had a wet dream."

I said to him, "What was the act?"

He said: "I missed the *'Ishā'* prayer in the Sacred Mosque in congregation."

So he considered that as a sin, the punishment of which was that he had a wet dream. And we know that a wet dream is not under the control of a person, but they used to consider that as something that was belittling for them.

179 *Ṣaḥīḥ:* Hadith narrated by Imam Ibn Mājah

12

Laḥin in Action and Speech

The Arabs have something called *laḥin*; which is when a person speaks Arabic (or any language in fact) and they don't speak correctly, to the extent that they change the words or the grammar. Because the Arabic language is very precise in terms of the subject and the object; and whether the word is affected by a proposition or the like. A small change in the vowel character at the end of the word, can render the whole meaning different.

Take as an example the following verse:

﴿ وَكَلَّمَ اللهُ موسى تَكلِيما ﴾

The vowel sound on the word (الله) is *ḍammah* (ُ) which means that Allah is the subject of the word (كَلَّم) which is to speak / spoke. The verse therefore translates as:

﴾ And indeed, Allah spoke to Musa; affirmed ﴿[180]

However, if instead of the *ḍammah* (ُ) on the word (الله) we had a *fatḥah* (َ), then the verse would translate to:

"And indeed, Allah was spoken to by Musa, affirmed."

180 Holy Quran: Chapter of the Women 4:164

So, you can see how this would affect the meaning. In this specific example, it would impact on a theological issue relating to whether Allah speaks or not.

Laḥin started to happen more frequently once there were more conquests and the Arabs interacted with a lot of the non-Arabs. Their language became diluted as non-Arabs started to speak broken Arabic.

The Arabs considered their language (and rightly so) as a superior language. They were somewhat arrogant in this perspective, because the word "Arab" comes from the root word *'a'rabah* (أعرَب) which means that the person can express himself: he can speak and is able to convey and talk. On the contrary, they termed the non-Arab as *'ajam*; which means someone who can't express themselves, can't speak or dumb. The Arab is the one who can speak whereas the *'ajam* is somebody who cannot speak well. And that's why they even labelled animals as *'ajam* meaning that they cannot speak or express themselves. You may be detecting some arrogance there, but it goes back to the etymology of these words, and after Islam came, this dissipated as Muslims realised that it's not your language or ethnicity that offers you special status, rather it is your God consciousness.

One might argue that it's okay for the Arabs to be arrogant in this case because the Arabic language is eloquent and is an advanced language, and that's why the Quran was revealed in this language; it was preserved in the oral transmission because of its preciseness. And when you read the Quran and you look at the way that words are used, you can realise its beauty.

One of the powers of the Quran is in how the Quran has been written. It is written in one way, but it encompasses different pronunciations.

The classic example is in the Chapter of al-Fātiḥah with the words Malik (مَلك) and Mālik (مَـٰلك) which mean king and owner respectively.

Another example you have the word *kitab* (كتب); it can be read as *kitab* (book) or *kutub* as plural.

Or you might have *ya'lamūn* (يَعلَمون) and *ta'lamūn* (تَعلمون), which is "they know" and "you know".

Or you might have *al-'Ālamīn* (العالَمين) and *al-'Ālimīn* (العالِمين), meaning "the worlds" and "those have knowledge".

You will see that there is so much eloquence in the Quran.

Anyhow, as time progressed people started to lose that beauty of the Arabic language and they started to mess up the language.

It is narrated that on one occasion, a man came to the judge complaining that his father had passed away, and his brother had consumed the inheritance of their father and has taken all the wealth.

He said it in an extremely broken Arabic, with some grammatical errors.

The Judge replied, "Your loss in your language is a much greater loss than the inheritance that your brother has taken!"

It is narrated that a Persian guy excelled in the Arabic language to the extent that whenever he would sit in a gathering and he would talk they would think he is an Arab. So much so, they would ask him from which [Arab] tribe are you?

He would laugh and say, "No, I'm Persian but I have mastered your language more than you."

On one occasion, someone said to him, "Go to so-and-so who is a

Bedouin and talk to him; if you manage to trick him into thinking you are an Arab, then you have truly defeated us."

The Persian was really confident, and so he went to the house of this Bedouin. He knocked on the door. The Bedouin's daughter answered the door. So, he asked her, "Where is your father?" She said:

أبي ذهب إلى الفيافي، فإذا فاء الفيء أفى

"My father has gone to the open land and when the light drops, he will come back!"

However, note that she used very proper words for "open land", "light drops" and "come back".

He said to the girl, "Sorry, can you say that again!"

So, she repeated it, and still, he couldn't understand. She could tell that he was confused because she was talking very proper Arabic.

Her mother came to the door, and said to her, "Who is at the door?"

The girl said, "I don't know, some *'a'jamī* (non-Arab) asking about my father."

So, the guy was dumbstruck. If the little girl detected that he was not an Arab, what will the father do. So, he left defeated.

With time, the Muslims – both Arabs and non-Arabs started to have *laḥin*, which means the tongue no longer speaks in the right melody. Literally, *laḥana* (لحن) is about having a melody; and it used in this context to mean going off course. The language is no longer accurate and you can detect that in the lack of melody in the language. The Arabs, being so precise in the language, they can detect when somebody is speaking badly. That's why it is as if the rhythm goes out of the language.

In this section, the Imam mentions what some of the righteous people were trying to mention, that although there was a lot of focus on the *laḥin* in the tongue, people were disregarding the *laḥin* in their actions. Meaning that amongst some, the focus was on getting the wordings right, but losing sight of getting their actions right.

That's why Imam Mālik ⬩ said, "You would meet a man and he doesn't stutter; not even a letter. However, his actions are all stutters."

Meaning that he is focused on his language, yet his actions are off course: missing their purpose.

He said we narrated something similar from some of the righteous ascetics that they said: "We expressed in our speech such we did not stutter. [Yet] we faltered in our actions such that we did not express ourselves!"

The poet said:

لَمْ نُؤْتَ مِنْ جَهْلٍ ولكننا   نستر وجه العلم بالجهل

نكره أَن نلحنَ في قولنا   وما نبالي اللحن في الفعل

We were not flawed due to ignorance, but

we conceal knowledge with ignorance.

We hate to falter in our speech,

yet we do not care about stuttering in our actions

The Imam is narrating these few incidences here to say that the reality of the matter is that there has to be focus on the action and not just on language. Because language is more of a veneer to the reality covered behind it.

This is almost like one of the aspects of hypocrisy. Why? Because a hypocrite is someone who says what he does not do.

al-Khalīl ibn Ahmad

Then, we have this narration, and it is beautiful how the Imam mentions this because he mentions one of the Masters of the Arabic language. This is al-Khalīl ibn Ahmad. Al-Khalīl was one of the famous Arabic linguists and grammarians. And it is said that he asked Allah ﷻ to give him something that nobody had attained before. So, he was given this grasp of the language. He was also a righteous person.

ʿAlī ibn Naṣr narrated to us that he said: I saw al-Khalīl ibn Ahmad - may Allah the Almighty have mercy on him - in a dream. So, I said in my dream: 'I do not see anyone more intellectual than al-Khalīl!' So I said: 'What has Allah done with you?'

He said: "Did you see where we were? For there was nothing better than *Subḥān Allah*, *al-Ḥamdu Lillāh*, *Lā 'ilāha illā Allah* and *Allahu Akbar*. "[181]

In another narration:

ʿAlī ibn Naṣr said: I saw al-Khalīl ibn Ahmad in a dream, so I said to him: "What did your Lord do with you?"

He said: "I was forgiven."

I said: "With what did you escape?"

He said: "With [the saying] *Lā Ḥawla wa lā quwwata illā billāh*[182]."

I said: "How did you find your knowledge? I mean the prose, literature and poetry?"

181 Meaning that the remembrance of Allah was what really beneficial.
182 "There is no power to move and no strength except with Allah"

He said: "I found that like scattered dust.[183]"

Sībawayh

Al-Khalīl is the teacher of Sībawayh[184], who is also a famous linguist. In fact, he embarrassed the Arabs because he was Persian, and he learnt the Arabic language and mastered it more than the Arabs.

He actually compiled a book which is known as "al-Kitāb" which is a reference for the Arabic grammar. Because the reality of the Arabic, in essence, is not about lineage or race; rather it is the tongue. So, if you are able to speak the language, you can be more eloquent than an Arab because the nature of the word *'a'raba* is to be able to convey yourself. You can understand this notion which we spoke about in regards to the words (arab) and (*'ajam*). And that makes sense because if a person understands the language and is able to convey it, he will be a master in that.

It's interesting to know that what inspired Sībawayh to become who he became was an incident relating to Imam Ḥammād ibn Salamah, whom we mentioned previously. The narration says that Sībawayh sat to learn with Ḥammād. In one sitting, Sībawayh read a hadith inaccurately by making it a subject as opposed to an exception. On hearing this, Ḥammād said, "You have made *laḥin*, O Sībawayh. It is not like that."

So, Sībawayh said, "No problem. I am going to seek a science, in which you will not say I have *laḥin* ever again." And from there, he went and learnt from al-Khalīl.

Interesting to note how what may seem like a negative moment,

183 A Quranic term referring to how big hard deep-rooted mountains become like dust, scattered by the wind
184 Sībawayh was his nickname in Persian given to him by his mother. It meant the fragrance of apples. His full name was 'Amr ibn 'Othmān al-Ḥārithī.

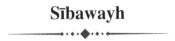

turned into rather an inspiration for this man, who became what he became, and left a legacy for many to benefit from.

Another interesting anecdote is narrated with regards to Thomas Edison[185]. It is said that his schoolmaster labelled him as "addled[186]"; which infuriated his mother, and she took him out of the school and proceeded to teach him at home. Edison said many years later, "My mother was the making of me. She was so true, so sure of me, and I felt I had someone to live for, someone I must not disappoint."

Because of this challenge, and due to this reaction, we are to benefit from the outstanding contribution of this man, labelled as "America's greatest inventor".

The Matter of the Wasp

Here I wish to share a somewhat interesting story relating to Sībawayh, which I will mention here as we have mentioned him; it demonstrates the intricacies of the language.

In the early years, two prominent schools of the Arabic Language developed. They both so happened to be in Iraq. They were the school of al-Baṣrah and al-Kūfah. Almost like the Oxford and Cambridge University rivalry in the UK today. Sībawayh was from al-Baṣrah. They have a specific way in terms of certain differences in how they apply the language. He was the master of that school. The master of the Kūfan School was al-Kisā'ī, who was also a very famous Quran reciter.

The two schools differed about a very simple matter: about the

185 An American inventor and businessman. He developed many devices in fields such as electric power generation, mass communication, sound recording and motion pictures. Also, he was one of the first inventors to apply the principles of organised science and teamwork to the process of invention.
186 unable to think clearly; confused

usage of *iyyaa* (إيّا). It was very simple if you look at it; but it was very complex in terms of the argument.

Basically, the sentence which demonstrated the difference was:

كنت أظن أنّ العقرب أشدُّ لسعة من الزنبور فإذا هو هي أو:
فإذا هو إياها؟

Translated: I used to consider that the scorpion is more severe in its sting than the wasp; so I found it, to be it.

The main difference was in the last phrase in the sentence; and it is a difference of whether we use the last reference as an object or subject. Two different positions about whether the usage of an object or a subject is more correct and proper; that was the argument.

This argument became a very famous argument. One of the ministers of the Khalifah invited them both to have a debate to put an end to it. They came and they both gave their arguments and explained their reasoning and evidences. Neither of them really won. Then Sībawayh suggested to ask the Bedouins, because their language is pure and untainted. When they went to bring some Bedouins, they found some already standing at the gate of the palace. So, they brought them in. The minister who is like the judge asked them about which one is right?

They sided with al-Kisāʾī. They said his version is the right one.

Sībawayh was very heartbroken as he lost this essential matter, he was really hurt. But what added to his heart-break was that he thought it was a plot against him. That these Bedouins were bribed to say what they said. So, he said, "Let the Bedouins pronounce this sentence". Let them read the sentence out aloud. But they refused to read it. He wanted to show that because their tongue is so accurate, they wouldn't be able to read something which is wrong. Remember what we said about the melody of the language (*laḥin*). There must have been something in play, so he left.

And because of this *simple* matter, he was so heartbroken that he went back home to Persia and he died a few weeks later. He died from being heartbroken about this matter. And that was Sībawayh.

And the matter is called, in Arabic: *al-Mas'alah al-Zunbūriyyah* (The Wasp Question).

13

'Awlīyā' of Allah

Love of pious people, respecting them, and honouring their righteousness brings one closer to Allah ﷻ. And so, it is not strange that the Imam has dedicated a long chapter on these righteous people who are close to Allah, and have been mentioned by Him ﷻ in the Quran:

﴿ أَلَا إِنَّ أَوْلِيَاءَ اللَّهِ لَا خَوْفٌ عَلَيْهِمْ وَلَا هُمْ يَحْزَنُونَ
الَّذِينَ ءَامَنُوا وَكَانُوا يَتَّقُونَ ﴾

﴿ Truly, the *'awlīyā'* of Allah: there shall be no fear over them, nor shall they grieve. [They are] Those who have believed and practise *taqwa* ﴾[187]

Honour and prestige are due to them with the conditions prescribed by the Islamic principles.

The Imam commences by quoting the above verse from the book of Allah ﷻ. It is in regards to what Allah has termed here, as *'awlīyā'* Allah. The term *'awlīyā'* is one of the words that are difficult to translate properly into English. It's one of those words that doesn't have an exact translation however you want to look at it. It is not as some people translate it as meaning "the allies of Allah ﷻ". Others translate it as being "the friends of Allah ﷻ"; and some as those

187 Holy Quran; Chapter of Yūnus 10:62-63

who are associated with Allah ﷻ. All these translations are poor translations of the word *walī*.

The term *walī* comes from a word used in the Arabic language, which directly transitions between two parties. They may be similar, or one is superior to the other. I give you an example relating to when the Arabs talk about freed slaves. If somebody owned a slave, then he emancipated that slave, the slave is known as a *mawlā*. The word *mawlā* is derived from the same root word for the one who is freeing the slave, who is also called a *mawlā*. So, it becomes that both the master and the freed slave are called *mawlā* because they have that interconnection between them. They both give each other allegiance: both help each other out, and both inherit from one another. That's why it becomes problematic to understand in English because Allah ﷻ doesn't need anybody's help, and Allah ﷻ doesn't have anybody associated with Him. Similarly, Allah ﷻ doesn't need any allies, and He doesn't need any friends because Allah ﷻ is unique. But it's almost like there is a connection, a relationship in which Allah ﷻ supports those connected with Him.

And even the Quran talks about:

﴿ إن تنصروا الله، ينصركم ﴾

﴿ If you victor Allah, He will give you victory ﴾[188]

But Allah ﷻ doesn't need anybody's victory. Or as in the hadith:

احفظ الله يحفظك

"Guard Allah; Allah will guard you."

188 Holy Quran; Chapter of Muhammad 47:7

Yet Allah doesn't need anyone to protect Him. Even when you look at the word *tawbah*, we often translate *tawbah* - in English to repentance. Repentance gives the understanding somebody who has wronged themselves or others and done a sin, he's repenting, he's coming back. He's coming back in the form of humiliation, towards the one Whom he is repenting to. However, in Arabic, "*tawbah*" is a two-way process because, in the Arabic language, the one who repents is known as *tā'ib* or *tawwāb*: which means he is returning to Allah ﷾. But Allah ﷾ is *al-Tawwāb* as well. There is a connection; you are going to Allah ﷾, but Allah ﷾ is also coming to you. You don't find that in the English language. You can't get that in the English language because there is that mutual engagement that Allah ﷾ is giving. This is the same concept that comes with the word *'awlīyā'*, which is that those who are associated with [those who have a connection with] Allah are almost like friends and helpers and supporters of Allah ﷾, but not in the way that the English language conveys.

Allah ﷾ says that those people He has named His *'awlīyā'*, there will be no fear over them, nor should they have any grief. And why should they? Because if they are associated with Allah ﷾ they have the protection of Allah ﷾ for they are connected to Him.

And who are *'awlīyā'* Allah? What is their essence? The Quran describes them as "Those who have *īmān*, and they have *taqwa*."[189]

However, *taqwa* is not something that they just do once; it's inherent within them. For them, they will have the glad tidings in this life and the *Ākhirah*. The glad tidings are the kind of support that Allah ﷾ gives to the righteous people.

The Prophet ﷺ explained that the *bushrā* (glad tidings) can also be in the form of a good dream. A person has a good dream: either he sees a good dream and he's happy with it, or somebody sees

189 Holy Quran; Chapter of Yūnus 10:63

him in a good dream. That is the *bushrā*. That is a kind of glad tidings that Allah ﷻ gives to a believer. However, it could be other things. It could be the signs that Allah ﷻ gives, for Allah might give somebody a sign to show him that he is on the right path or a gift; which Imam al-Nawawī dedicated a whole chapter to which is known as *karāmah*, an honourable gift that Allah ﷻ bestows on people of His choosing.

Now, the Imam says that the valid opinion of the *madhhab* of the people of the truth is that these gifts are real, they happen, and we affirm them. We also believe that they continue to happen. So, they are not linked to a set time or a designated place. They are not exclusive to Prophethood, but they are something that Allah ﷻ can give to whomever He wants, and this verse is evidence of that. He also says that generally – in Islam – there are two pieces of evidence. One is called *al-naql*, and the other one is called *al-'aql*. The former is that which is conveyed or transmitted. This includes the Quran and the hadith of the Prophet ﷺ and maybe extends wider than this. It's about transmitted news. What you have read, heard or received. And the other one is *'aql*, which includes the mind, the logic and the rationale. So, we have those two sources of evidence, something which is rational; it makes sense. And other which is received as transmission.

Now, there are things that the mind and the rationale can perceive, and there are things that the mind cannot perceive. For example, we cannot rationally prove that angels exist. We cannot rationally proof that *al-Jannah* exists, or maybe even jinn. These are part of the unseen (*'ālam al-ghayb*). However, we believe in them because we have evidence from the transmitted sources, as we know that Allah ﷻ exists. And we know the Quran is the truth through evidence and rational acceptance and through *īmān* (conviction). So, therefore, whatever is found there, we can also consider that as evidence. So the Imam says that this aspect of *karāmāt* is confirmed by both *'aql* and *naql*.

As for the *'aql*, then rationally, it is something that can happen. Why? Because it can happen: it is possible. It's not going to alter any aspect of the *dīn*. And because we know that Allah ﷻ is able to do all things, so He can give anybody anything. He can grant the ability to do things that go against what is considered as natural laws: the laws that Allah ﷻ has placed. So it's possible that it can happen. It doesn't go against the intellectual, rational mind. And at the end of the day, if we believe that Allah ﷻ gives everything, Allah ﷻ can do this.

As for the *naql*, he said there is much evidence to support this, either from the Quran or the Sunna.

So what is a *karāmah*? A *karāmah* is a gift is something that goes against the norms. Some might term it "supernatural". And it happens to someone righteous, and it is not associated with a claim to Prophethood. So, it's not somebody claiming to be a Prophet, although a Prophet may receive one.

Usually, a *karāmah* is an award from Allah ﷻ to support a person with his obedience. It can strengthen him, and it might also aid his *īmān*. It might also show that he is a truthful person, but it's not something that he would boast about or would display to others. As usually, a person who has this kind of thing would not be somebody who would brag about it.

So, what is the evidence that the Imam mentions from the Quran?

Maryam bint 'Imrān ﷺ

First of all, he says the story of Maryam ﷺ. Because Allah ﷻ said to Maryam:

﴿ وَهُزِّي إِلَيْكِ بِجِذْعِ النَّخْلَةِ تُسَاقِطْ عَلَيْكِ رُطَبًا جَنِيًّا ﴾

﴿ And shake the trunk of the palm tree unto you; fresh ripe dates will fall on you ﴾[190]

Maryam was heavily pregnant and was about to give birth. This is a time when a woman is quite weak and in lots of pain. At this time, Allah ﷻ commanded her to shake the palm tree and onto her will descend fresh, moist dates. So that's evidence he uses here because to shake a palm tree isn't an easy task for a well-built individual in "normal" circumstances, let alone a woman who is about to go into labour.

Also, the saying of Allah ﷻ before 'Īsā ﷺ was born:

﴿ كُلَّمَا دَخَلَ عَلَيْهَا زَكَرِيَّا الْمِحْرَابَ وَجَدَ عِنْدَهَا رِزْقًا قَالَ يَا مَرْيَمُ أَنَّى لَكِ هَٰذَا ۖ قَالَتْ هُوَ مِنْ عِنْدِ اللَّهِ ۖ إِنَّ اللَّهَ يَرْزُقُ مَنْ يَشَاءُ بِغَيْرِ حِسَابٍ ﴾

﴿ Whenever Zakariya entered onto her in the room, he found with her some provision. He would say, 'O Maryam! From where did you get this?' She said, 'It is from Allah, for Allah provides to whomsoever He wills without measure' ﴾[191]

190 Holy Quran; Chapter of Maryam 19:25
191 Holy Quran; Chapter of the Family of Imran 3:37

Maryam ﷺ had a room dedicated to *'ibādah*, which is called a *miḥrāb*. Christians have something called the chapel, which is almost like a prayer room. It's like a *muṣala*.

Today, Muslims have adopted the word *miḥrāb* to be used for the small niche in which the imam stands to lead the prayer. And what is amusing to see is that some of those who construct *masājid* and like to put some engravings and decorations, would write the above verse over the imam's niche. I found this amusing, as they have placed a verse over the niche because it contains the word *miḥrāb*, even though it is not relevant.

What is also amusing to know is that this niche – which people term *miḥrāb* - is not really a *miḥrāb* in the proper Islamic sense. This is something that Mu'āwiyah ibn Abī Sufyān ﷺ initially adopted. When 'Alī ﷺ was the Khalīfah in al-Kūfah, 'Amr ibn al-'Āṣ ﷺ was the governor in Egypt, and Mu'āwiyah was the governor in al-Shām (present-day Syria, Jordan, Palestine and Lebanon). During this time, there was a group of deviant Muslims, known as the *Khawārij*. They disagreed with all of the above three and decided to assassinate them simultaneously. They agreed that on the 17th of Ramadan, each one would go to the respective cities and assassinate them during the prayer of *al-Ṣubḥ*. At the time, 'Amr was ill, and so he didn't go out to the *ṣalāh*. The assassin came and attacked the imam, thinking that it was 'Amr, but it wasn't him. The other one attacked Mu'āwiyah, but he didn't manage to kill him. He only injured him. As for 'Alī ﷺ, the guy managed to strike fatal blows, as being a true coward, he attacked from behind. 'Alī ﷺ died a few days later from the injuries. May Allah be pleased with him.

So after that, Mu'āwiyah having sensed that there was this kind of threat; and that people were no longer trustworthy. He made this part in the *masjid* so that when the imam sits or stands here, and people are behind him he's guarded. Before, there was nothing like this. The person could just come from the side and just attack the imam. To attack the imam when he is inside the niche is going to be tricky because people will see him in the front row, and they can block him, especially if there are bodyguards or the like. This niche is called *al-maqṣūrah*, but later on, the term *miḥrāb* was superimposed.

Back to Maryam 🌸. Zakariyya ﷺ used to enter onto Maryam in her *miḥrāb*, and he would find with her some sort of *rizq* in the form of food. The Quran's explainers will say that he would either find the summer fruit in the winter or vice versa. So, Zakariyya ﷺ would ask her where did you get this? And so, you can see how this is a gift from Allah to Maryam 🌸.

Was Maryam 🌸 a Prophet?

————◆◆◆◆————

The Imam also mentioned Imam al-Ḥaramayn, who is al-Juwaynī 🌸. He said that al-Juwaynī says that there is a consensus that Maryam 🌸 was not a Prophet. He is saying this here to indicate that this is a gift for someone who is not a Prophet. However, there is a difference of opinion about this matter. And some of the *'ulamā'*, including the likes of Imam al-Qurṭubī, have favoured the opinion that Maryam was a Prophet, using additional evidence from the Quran itself. For example, in the Chapter of Maryam, Allah 🌸 mentions several stories and several names. Firstly, he mentioned Zakariyya, and then Yaḥyā; followed by Maryam and her son 'Īsā. Then 'Ibrāhīm, his son Isḥāq and his son Ya'qūb, then Mūsā and Hārūn, followed by Ismā'īl and 'Idrīs. Then, Allah says:

﴿ أُولَئِكَ الَّذِينَ أَنْعَمَ اللهُ عَلَيْهِمْ مِنَ النَّبِيِّينَ مِنْ ذُرِّيَّةِ آدَمَ وَمِمَّنْ حَمَلْنَا مَعَ نُوحٍ وَمِنْ ذُرِّيَّةِ إِبْرَاهِيمَ وَإِسْرَائِيلَ وَمِمَّنْ هَدَيْنَا وَاجْتَبَيْنَا إِذَا تُتْلَى عَلَيْهِمْ آيَاتُ الرَّحْمَنِ خَرُّوا سُجَّدًا وَبُكِيًّا ﴾

﴿ Those [aforementioned] are the ones whom Allah has blessed from amongst the Prophets from the offspring of Adam, and from those whom We carried with Nūḥ, and from the offspring of 'Ibrāhīm and 'Isrā'īl; and from amongst those whom We have guided and elevated: when the verses of al-Raḥmān are recited onto them, they fall in prostration, weeping ﴾[192]

That is an indication that everybody mentioned pre-hand was a Prophet, and Maryam was amongst those mentioned.

The counter-argument is that Allah said:

﴿ وَمَا أَرْسَلْنَا مِنْ قَبْلِكَ إِلَّا رِجَالًا ﴾

﴿ And We haven't sent before you except men... ﴾[193]

But others say that, well, what is a Prophet? A Prophet is unlike a Messenger. The latter is someone who has a message to deliver to others. There is a Quranic verse that says:

﴿ وَمَا أَرْسَلْنَا مِنْ قَبْلِكَ مِنْ رَسُولٍ وَلَا نَبِيٍّ إِلَّا إِذَا تَمَنَّى
أَلْقَى الشَّيْطَانُ فِي أُمْنِيَّتِهِ فَيَنْسَخُ اللَّهُ مَا يُلْقِي الشَّيْطَانُ ثُمَّ
يُحْكِمُ اللَّهُ آيَاتِهِ وَاللَّهُ عَلِيمٌ حَكِيمٌ ﴾

﴿ We haven't sent before of any *rasūl* nor *nabī*... ﴾[194]

Showing that there are two categories: *rasūl* (messenger) and *nabī* (prophet). The latter is more general than the former. A *nabī* is somebody who has some sort of communication from Allah ﷻ. And Maryam - without doubt - had direct communication. She has been spoken to by an angel. That's why some say that she was a Prophet.

192 Holy Quran; Chapter of Maryam 19:58
193 Holy Quran; Chapter of Yūsuf 12:109 ; and the Bees 16:43; and the Prophets 21:25
194 Holy Quran: Chapter of Hajj 22:52

Companion of Sulaymān ﷺ

Another evidence from the Quran is the story relating to the companion of Sulaymān ﷺ when he said:

﴿ قَالَ يَا أَيُّهَا الْمَلَأُ أَيُّكُمْ يَأْتِينِي بِعَرْشِهَا قَبْلَ أَنْ يَأْتُونِي مُسْلِمِينَ ﴾

﴿ O Gathering! Who among you, can bring me her throne before they come to me as Muslims? ﴾[195]

This is the story of Sulaymān ﷺ and the throne of Bilqīs. To cut a long story short, the story mentioned in the Chapter of the Ants (27) is that Sulaymān ﷺ asked those from his entourage about who of them can bring him the throne of Bilqīs. Sulaymān was based in Palestine, and the throne was in Yemen. So one of the jinn said, "I can bring it to you before you leave your gathering." which was a good few hours because he used to sit in this gathering from the early daytime until after 'Asr.

However, another person among those gathered, who was human, said that I could bring it to you before even your eyesight returns to you, meaning I can bring it to you in a blink of an eye. And when he saw that and how this guy could do it, Sulaymān ﷺ said that this is a blessing from Allah ﷻ.

The evidence here being displayed is that this man was a righteous person, and some say his name was Āṣif, [hence why a lot of Pakistanis have this name]. Āṣif was a righteous man who knew a special *du'ā'*, or some say he knew the Mightiest names of Allah, so when he made the *du'ā'* with this name, Allah ﷻ as a gift for this man answered his request and brought him the throne in a blink of an eye. And obviously, Allah's ﷻ power is great.

195 Holy Quran: Chapter of the Ants 27:38

Mother of Mūsā ﷺ

Another example that the Imam mentions is the mother of Mūsā ﷺ. There is also a difference of opinion about whether she was a Prophet or not, but not as strong as that of Maryam. The majority say that she was not a Prophet. And so, therefore they used that as evidence that she was a *walī* and that Allah ﷻ had revealed to her how to cater for Mūsā ﷺ in a way which he was protected from the killing that the Pharaoh and his soldiers had instigated on the children of Israel. The way that Allah ﷻ told her was to, first of all, not worry about him. Then, to breastfeed him and to put him in the river. All these things are gifts. Not only that, Allah ﷻ also promised her that do all of this, and We will also return him back to you. And he said, don't worry about him, put him in the box, put him in the river, we'll bring him back to you. And obviously that in itself was also evidence that it was a gift from Allah ﷻ.

Dhu al-Qarnayn ﷺ

Another example that the Imam mentioned is the story of the Dhu al-Qarnayn. And he says that this has been used by al-Qushayrī in the story of Dhu al-Qarnayn as evidence of a *karāmah* that Allah ﷻ gives to him. Dhu al-Qarnayn was also the topic of dispute amongst the '*ulamā*', whether he was a Prophet or not. He was a righteous man that Allah ﷻ had given the ability to roam the earth and bringing people back to Allah ﷻ or fighting those who have rebelled against Allah ﷻ.

Why was he called Dhu al-Qarnayn, which is loosely translated as the person of two horns?

There are over ten opinions about why he was called Dhu al-Qarnayn, all relating to how one understands the term "horns":

1 - He had a helmet or crown that had two horns.

2 - He had two pigtails. His hair was like he had two strands of hair.

3 - The sides of his head were made of copper.

4 - He had what looked like two horns in his head.

5 - He was called so because he was similar to a ram, as a ram is a metaphor for someone who keeps on knocking and hammering.

6 - He reached the two horns (limits) of the sun: where it sets and where it rises.

7 - He was king over the Romans and the Persians; or the Romans and the Turks.

8 - He advised his people, they rejected him and hit him brutally on his side (one meaning of *qarn*). He advised again and they hit him again on his side; and so he was struck twice on his two sides.

9 - He ruled the two horns of the world: East and West.

10 - That when he fought, he fought with all his limbs: arms and legs.

11 - He outlived two generations (or centuries) of people.

12 - He came from nobility on both sides of his ancestry.

13 - He was given knowledge of external and internal matters.

14 - He entered both the light and darkness.

I mention all these opinions to give the reader a flavour of the imagination of those who interpret matters. As for who he was in terms of his name and lineage; then there is just as much dispute about that, so I would leave the reader to go and investigate.

So, in his story and the way that he achieved all of these successes, is a demonstration of the great gifts for him. And that's why they used his story as evidence.

Al-Khiḍr ﷺ

The next evidence is al-Khiḍr ﷺ and even though al-Qushayrī uses him as a sign or evidence for the *karāmah*, he said the majority of people actually considered al-Khiḍr as a Prophet, so it is in contrast to the other examples. In fact, when you think about the story of al-Khiḍr, he was doing things that went against norms, and his actions are mentioned in the Chapter of the Cave (18). He wasn't someone who just happened to come across this information. He actually says this is what Allah ﷻ has taught me. So, it demonstrates that he must have been connected to Allah ﷻ through Prophethood. So, all the things that he had done there as a sign of being able to be connected with Allah ﷻ, he was given a lot of *karāmāt* in that regard.

There is a famous dispute amongst scholars about whether al-Khiḍr is still alive or not. The majority of scholars say he is still alive. Their main evidence for this is that there are multiple narrations from authentic trustworthy scholars who say that they have met with him. So here it's more like a type of *naql*, because if you trust somebody, and he is a trustworthy person, and he says that he has met al-Khiḍr and spoke to him, and then you have another one who says that, and another…it becomes multiple transmitted narrations that have been generated over many times. So, it is not likely to be a fabricated incident.

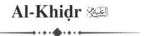

Of course, there are people who will say that he's not alive; as this means he is eternal. And they may use the evidence that it is not accepted rationally. However, it is rational because somebody can live for as long as Allah ﷻ wants. He is not immortal, as he will die, but Allah ﷻ has just extended his life, and so, it's rationally acceptable. But they use the following hadith, that the Prophet ﷺ said one month before he passed away:

ما مِن نَفْسٍ مَنْفُوسَةٍ اليَومَ، تَأْتي عَلَيْهَا مِئَةُ سَنَةٍ، وَهي حَيَّةٌ يَومَئذٍ

"There will be no living soul today, that will be alive after one hundred years."[196]

Basically, the Prophet ﷺ is saying that within a hundred years, everyone who's alive on earth will have died. So, they say that this states clearly that al-Khiḍr must have died because he is somebody. But then the basic response to that is that this hadith it what's known as *'ām* (general), and general statements can have exceptions which are known as *khāṣ*. One could say something generally, but there will be one or two exceptions. This exception doesn't mean that they break the rule, but it's like we say, every rule has an exception. So that's also acceptable from a general perspective of understanding.

The People of the Cave

He said from the examples of the *karāmāt* is the story of the people of the Cave. What happened with them is all an example of the gifts, as these were people who Allah ﷻ gave special treatment for their *īmān*. And we all know what happened to them: They slept for 309 years in the Cave and how Allah ﷻ catered for them to the extent that he would flip them over in their sleep to prevent them from being harmed. This was all generosity from Allah ﷻ.

196 *Ṣaḥīḥ:* Hadith narrated by Imam Muslim

So these examples are from the Quran. He said as for the hadith, then there are many hadith.

The Two Lanterns

One of them is what was narrated by Anas ﷺ: That there were two men who were sitting with the Prophet ﷺ and they left him one dark night[197]. As they left, they had like lanterns between their hands. So, Allah ﷻ gave them a light between their hands to see the way. They were both walking together when they departed; each one continued to have a lantern with him. So, it was like the light split. And they continued to have that light. The two men were ʿAbbād ibn al-Bishr and ʾUsayd ibn Ḥuḍayr: both of righteous people from al-ʾAnṣār ﷺ.

Blocked in the Cave

The other example is the story of the people of the cave. These were the three people who were blocked in the cave with a large rock. Each one made a *duʿā*ʾ with the most prestigious or noble action that they had done. So, every time they made a *duʿā*ʾ asking Allah ﷻ, interceding with their actions (*tawassul*), Allah ﷻ opened for them the rock a little bit until the third one said his story and made *duʿā*ʾ, then that was enough for them to escape. This story is also evidence of a *karāmah*.

197 *Ṣaḥīḥ:* Hadith narrated by Imam al-Bukhārī

Jurayj and the Newborn

Another example from the hadith is the story of Jurayj, the monk. The Israelites had falsely accused him of committing fornication, and they destroyed his house and started to beat him. His gift from Allah ﷻ was when he was accused, he poked the baby – that they alleged was his son – and asked him who is your father? So the baby spoke, informing them that Jurayj was not his father. So, that was also a *karāmah* from Allah ﷻ to aid the truthfulness of Jurayj. Despite this happening at the time of the Children of Israel, it is mentioned in an authentic hadith[198], so we know it to be sound.

'Omar ibn al-Khattāb رضي الله عنه

Another of it, is the case of 'Omar رضي الله عنه. 'Omar was considered a very special person amongst the *Ṣaḥābah* for several reasons. And one of them is the fact that he had what we call intuition in English, and in Arabic, it is called *firāsah*. It was like he could see things. The Prophet ﷺ said:

اتَّقوا فِراسةَ المؤمنِ فإنَّه ينظُرُ بنورِ اللهِ

"Beware of intuition of the believer, for he looks with the light of Allah."[199]

And he said:

198 *Ṣaḥīḥ:* Hadith narrared by Imams al-Bukhārī and Muslim
199 *Ḍa'īf:* Hadith narrated by al-Tirmidhī and others; although some said it may be pushed to the level of ḥasan

لقد كان فيما قبلكم من الأمم محدثون، فإن يكن في أمتي أحد فإنه عمر
قد كان فيمن قبلكم رجال من بني إسرائيل يكلمون من غير
أن يكونوا أنبياء، فإِنْ يَكُنْ مِن أُمَّتي منهمْ أَحَدٌ فَعُمَرُ

"There were among the nations before you people who were spoken to. If there was going to be anybody from my ʾummah [who was like that], it would be ʿOmar."[200]

"There were amongst those before, men from the Children of Israel, who would be spoken to you, yet they were not Prophets. If there were to be anyone from my nation like that, then it is ʿOmar."[201]

ʿOmar ﷺ would say things and see things, and the Quran would come down to support him in varying matters things that he had said.

Al-Suyūṭī ﷺ mentions in his book "Tārikh al-Khulafāʾ" around 20 incidents of when ʿOmar ibn al-Khaṭṭāb ﷺ mentioned an opinion, and Allah revealed some Quran to support him. He even compiled a short poem to collate these incidents.

I mention them here for the benefit of the reader:

1 - *Maqām* (station) of ʾIbrāhīm ﷺ (2:125).

2 - The captives of Badr.

3 - When two of the Prophet's ﷺ wives collaborated against him (66:5).

4 - Hijab of the Prophet's ﷺ wives (33:59).

5 - Mention of Jibrīl ﷺ (2:97).

6 - In regards to the prohibition of wine.

200 *Ṣaḥīḥ:* Hadith narrated by Imams al-Bukhārī and Muslim
201 *Ṣaḥīḥ:* Hadith narrated by Imam al-Bukhārī

7 - "Blessed be Allah, the Best of Creators" (23:14).

8 - Intimacy with wife during the nights of Ramaḍān (2:187).

9 - Your women are like harvest-producing fields (2:223).

10 - To arbitrate via the Prophet ﷺ (4:65).

11 - Do not pray [funeral prayer] on the hypocrites (9:84).

12 - "This is a false slander" (24:16).

13 - Seeking permission in entering (24:58-59).

14 - End of the verse in the Chapter of the Believers (23:118).

15 - The word "thullah." (56:13).

16 - The word "sawā'" (equal) in regards to the hypocrites (63:6).

17 - To leave to capture the caravan prior to Badr (8:5).

In addition to these, there are incidents where the Prophet ﷺ agreed with his opinion; and one occasion where he said something that was in the Torah.

Also, one of the other *karāmāt* for 'Omar was a form of telecommunication. Some may describe it as telepathy. However, telepathy refers to the ability to transmit/receive information from one mind to another. And this incident is not related to mind communication.

During his rule, 'Omar ﷺ sent an army to Iraq and appointed a man named Sāriyah as its leader. One day, during the Friday *khuṭbah* in Madinah, 'Omar on the *minbar* shouted out, "O Sāriyah, the mountain! The mountain!" The people in the *masjid* were puzzled and looked at each other bewildered as they couldn't understand what he meant.

After the *ṣalāh*, 'Ali ﷺ said, "What was that you said?"

'Omar asked, "You heard that?"

He said, "Yes! So did all the people in the *masjid*."

So ʿOmar explained that he saw an image of the army that he sent to Iraq; and could see an ambush waiting for them. So, he shouted to them to use the mountain for cover.

One month later, the army's messenger returned, and ʿOmar asked him about that.

The messenger said, "We were about to be defeated when we heard a call saying 'O Sāriyah, the mountain' three times, and so we shielded our backs with the mountain, and Allah defeated the other army.[202]

So, it is a form of telecommunication.

Khubayb ibn ʿAdī ﷺ

A similar narration to what happened with Maryam ﷺ happened to one of the Muslim captives: Khubayb-al-ʾAnṣārī ﷺ. He was captured by Quraysh who kept him as a prisoner whilst they considered what to do with him. He was held prisoner in one of the houses. The daughter of the person who was holding him prisoner said, "I didn't see a captive better than Khubayb. We would find him eating grapes. He would have grapes in his hand, even though his hands were tied in metal, and in Makkah, there was no fruit at that time."[203]

And she would add, "This was the *rizq* of Allah ﷻ that He was giving to Khubayb." So, he was getting fruit, and there was nothing there.

As you can see, the Imam says that this hadith and the other stories are many in this regard; and that is enough to satisfy this point, but you will see in this book more examples of this *in shāʾ Allah*.

202 *Ḥasan:* Hadith narrated by Imam al-Bayhaqī and others
203 *Ṣaḥīḥ:* Hadith narrated by Imam al-Bukhārī

Established Evidence

Briefly, he mentioned why he said that this is our *madhhab* because one of the Muslim sects, who are named al-Mu'tazilah, reject *karāmāt* could happen. They said that this is not possible, or it's not acceptable that they happen. Now, the Mu'tazilah were [are] a group of Muslims who are renowned for giving preference to the *'aql*, when there is a conflict with the *naql*. So, wherever there was an apparent conflict, then their preference was the *'aql*, the rationale rather than the *naql* (transmission); and they would say that there are errors in the transmission.

So, they said that it is not possible for these kinds of things to happen, and they rejected it. He mentioned here the saying of Imam al-Ḥaramayn, who is Imam al-Juwaynī. He said that their rejection is not based on any real evidence because, from the *'aql* perspective, we all know that Allah ﷻ has given His Prophets the abilities to perform acts or bring about challenges that go against the norm, to prove their Prophethood and as evidence for their Prophecy.

So, the ability to make something happen which goes against the norms like the fire not hurting 'Ibrāhīm عليه السلام; or like the changing of the stick of Mūsā عليه السلام and like the healing of the lepers and bringing people back to life with 'Īsā عليه السلام. These are all things that show that rationally it is possible for Allah ﷻ to do it by the very text of the Quran, which the Mu'tazilah do not reject. Thus, if it is possible that a Prophet does it, it's also permissible for someone who is not a Prophet, for it is Allah ﷻ who's giving that ability for the Prophet to do it, and He can also give the ability to any person to do something which goes against the natural laws.

The Imam wants to emphasize and prove the point which is the *madhhab* of *Ahl al-Sunnah* that *karāmāt* are true. Unlike the saying of the Mu'tazilah who denied *karāmāt*. They considered them more specific for the Prophets (peace be upon them), meaning that the Prophets have miracles; and so it isn't befitting for others to have *karāmāt*.

Previously, we mentioned several examples from the Quran and hadith in which the Imam says that these are examples of people who are not Prophets and yet they had honourable gifts awarded to them, going against the norm.

Between *Muʿjizah* and *Karāmah*

As previously mentioned, a *karāmah* is a gift, linguistically; and terminologically: it is a miracle. In English, we say miracle, and this doesn't equate to *muʿjizah*.

One day, I was sitting in a meeting, and one brother was talking, and he just said; the other day a miracle happened or something like that. So, another brother said, "No, brother, there is no miracle after the Prophet ﷺ!" So, he obviously confused the meaning of miracle because in English, miracle means something that goes against nature's accepted laws or the physical laws.

In Arabic we have a difference between *muʿjizah* and *karāmah*. A *muʿjizah* is derived from the word (إعجاز) *'iʿjāz*, which means to incapacitate the other: to make them incapable. *Muʿjizāt* are awarded to Prophets because it's linked to that Prophet declaring or announcing that he is a Prophet. Allah sent Prophets with clear signs as Allah ﷻ mentioned in the Quran.[204] So whenever a Prophet ﷺ comes, he will challenge people with a sign to prove that the Creator has sent him.

204 Holy Quran; The Chapter of Iron 57:25

Even some of the Prophets whose miracles might not be obvious, still had miraculous signs. Take the example of Hūd ﷺ. In the Chapter of Hūd (Chapter 11), Allah ﷻ narrates this specific incident. The story of Hūd is mentioned many times in the Quran. However, in the Chapter which carries the name of this great Prophet, Allah says:

﴿ قَالُوا يَا هُودُ مَا جِئْتَنَا بِبَيِّنَةٍ وَمَا نَحْنُ بِتَارِكِي آلِهَتِنَا عَنْ قَوْلِكَ وَمَا نَحْنُ لَكَ بِمُؤْمِنِينَ. إِنْ نَقُولُ إِلَّا اعْتَرَاكَ بَعْضُ آلِهَتِنَا بِسُوءٍ ﴾

﴿ They said, 'O Hūd! You did not bring us a clear sign, and we are not about to leave our idols just because you say so, and we do not believe in you! We say that some of our gods have afflicted you with evil'! ﴾[205]

So Hūd ﷺ gives them the sign. We are informed in the Quran that the tribe of 'Ād were all giants, they were people of gigantic stature, and they were tyrannical people. They roamed the land and spread corruption, for they had overwhelmed other people.

So Hūd's sign was to challenge them.

﴿ قَالَ إِنِّي أُشْهِدُ اللَّهَ وَاشْهَدُوا أَنِّي بَرِيءٌ مِمَّا تُشْرِكُونَ. مِنْ دُونِهِ فَكِيدُونِي جَمِيعًا ثُمَّ لَا تُنْظِرُونِ. إِنِّي تَوَكَّلْتُ عَلَى اللَّهِ رَبِّي وَرَبِّكُمْ مَا مِنْ دَابَّةٍ إِلَّا هُوَ آخِذٌ بِنَاصِيَتِهَا إِنَّ رَبِّي عَلَى صِرَاطٍ مُسْتَقِيمٍ ﴾

﴿ He said, 'Surely, I witness Allah, and I witness you that I am innocent of what you associate besides Allah. So, altogether you plot against me; and do not hesitate. For I have depended on Allah: my Lord and your Lord. There is no creature except He has taken it by its forelock. For my Lord is on the Straight Path' ﴾[206]

205 Holy Quran; Chapter of Hūd 11:53-54
206 Holy Quran; Chapter of Hūd 11:54-56

Basically, he said that I am one individual and you with all your powers do something to me: try and harm me if you can. However, the reality is that they couldn't harm him. They couldn't even touch him, and that was the miracle and the clear sign of Hūd.

So, every Prophet has a *mu'jizah*. It leaves others unable to meet that challenge. We know some of the miracles that Allah mentions in the Quran. Like for Ṣāliḥ, Allah gave the she-camel. For Mūsā, there were nine signs. For 'Īsā, the raising of the dead and curing the lepers and born blind.

The other type of miracle, which is a *karāmah* given to someone Allah chooses, does not coincide or does not correlate to the claim of prophethood. So, somebody might be awarded a miracle, but without them claiming prophethood, then this is a *karāmah*. Also, the karāmah might happen to both a Prophet and a non-prophet. A Prophet might also be given a miracle which is not a *mu'jizah* because the nature of those miracles is not to incapacitate the other side. So they were given things as honorary gifts, which go against the norm.

For our Prophet Muhammad, his *mu'jizah* is the Quran. I say "is" and not "was" because it is a continual miracle. Quraysh and the Arabs were challenged to bring something like the Quran. But they couldn't, they were incapacitated to do so.

The Imam says that the other one was that the Prophet challenged them to wish for death. The Prophet challenged them to wish for death if they were confident that they are authentic, as he said to the Jews of Madinah and as Allah relates in the Chapter of *al-Jumu'ah* (62), but they didn't, so that was also a challenge. Those were essentially the two challenges that the Prophet put forth. Everything else that the Prophet was given was generally considered as *karāmāt*.

I personally don't consider the challenge of wishing for death as a *mu'jizah*; rather it was a powerful challenge similar to how he challenged the Nazarenes of Najrān and his uncle Abu Lahab.

Karāmāt of the Prophet ﷺ

Of the *karāmāt* of the Prophet ﷺ are the following:

1 - Splitting of the Moon; which also had an element of being a *mu'jizah*

2 - Holding back the Sun from setting.

3 - Springing of the water from in between his fingers and increasing a small amount due to his *barakah*. This happened in a number of his travels. One of those incidents that were recorded was in the battle of Hudaybiyyah. There were 1400 people. They had run out of water. So they wanted water for *wuḍū'*, drinking and to water their animals. So all they had was a small amount of water. So, the Prophet ﷺ put his hands in the water and the water started to gush.

4 - Milking of the "dry" sheep during the *hijrah*.

5 - Feeding a large number from a small amount of food or milk.

6 - Speaking to the animals, and understanding their speech, like the lizard, camel, wolf, deer and others.

7 - Speaking to inanimate things like the tree stump, which cried when the Prophet ﷺ left it; and the calling to the tree to come to him. It then uprooted itself and came to him. Also, here we can include the roasted lamb shoulder warning him that it has poison in it.

8 - Mount 'Uḥud trembled when the Prophet ﷺ was on the mountain with Abu Bakr, 'Omar and 'Othmān ؓ and the Prophet ﷺ spoke to it.

9 - Curing the ill and performing healing; as he returned the eye of Qatadah ☙ back into its socket and it became sharper in vision. This also includes returning the sight of the blind, or curing eye inflammation as in the case of ʿAlī ☙. Curing those who couldn't speak. Healing the one afflicted with stroke, as well as many other incidents.

10 - Resurrecting the dead.

11 - The *barakah* of his presence or being touched by him, as in the case of his nursing parents, or seeking rain, or his sweat which was perfume, etc.

12 - The answering of his *duʿāʾ* and this has numerous examples which will take much time to explain. However, we can use an example of his *duʿāʾ* for Anas ibn Mālik ☙.

In the hadith, Umm Sulaym – the mother of Anas ☙ brought him to the Prophet ﷺ saying, "O Messenger of Allah. This is Anas, he is your servant. Make *duʿāʾ* for him."

He said, **"O Allah! Increase his wealth and his children, and bless him in what You have given him."**[207]

Anas comments on his situation saying, "By Allah, my wealth was extensive; and my children and grandchildren are more than 100[208]." And he said, "The Messenger of Allah prayed for three things for me. I saw two of them in the *dunyā* and I anticipate the third in the Final Life. And I am not aware of anyone who has been given such expansion in his life than me."

Commentators mention that he had an orchard in Baṣrah which used to yield twice a year, as opposed to once. And during the plague, he buried more than seventy of his own children.

---

207 *Ṣaḥīḥ:* Hadith narrated by Imams al-Bukhārī and Muslim
208 One narration puts it at 120

[For a more detailed insight into the *karāmāt* of the Prophet ﷺ, see al-Shifā written by Qāḍī 'Iyāḍ.]

One can see these are all *karāmāt*, they are gifts which go against the accepted norms, but they do not come to challenge people, so they are not *mu'jizāt*. People who don't announce the prophethood or do not claim to be Prophets, theirs is a *karāmah* and not a *mu'jizah* because the latter is specific for Prophets. And that's how we make the distinction.

Difference between *Karāmah* and Magic

The other distinction one might question: "how do we know that somebody has *karāmāt* as opposed to magic?" For example, some people might be practising magic, and they might claim to be close to Allah ﷻ or something like that. So, he says that it's a straightforward equation here. The *karāmah* can be noticed from someone known for his righteousness and piety, i.e., a person who has good works and so on. Whereas the *siḥir* (magic) usually comes from somebody who is *fāsiq*: somebody who doesn't adhere to the *sharī'a* and is not in adherence to the laws or the practice of Islam. This might be somebody who you may not see pray or somebody who drinks alcohol or does outward sins. Indeed, in some instances, people started to do that because the whole concept of being a *walī* or a *shaykh* had become a consumer act. It has become an opportunity to exploit others to take money from people, and food and things like that because it's all a form of trickery. Some people in their simplicity, feel they are spiritual and so when they see somebody doing this kind of spirituality, they want to get something from them, usually some sort of *du'ā'* or some kind of help. They would ask "make *du'ā'* for me, I need this"; and that is the door that sometimes Shayṭān uses to exploit some people and then lead them down terrible routes.

Some people will try to use that exploitation and might come up with certain magic to get a following and show people that they can do all these supernatural things. Whereas in reality, if they are not righteous people, then we know that these are not *'awlīyā'* and it is not a *karāmah*.

We know that a *karāmah* is a gift from Allah ﷻ where He honours one of His slaves, but it is not necessary for everybody. Some people mistakenly seek *karāmāt*, so they will say I will try and do more *'ibādah* and try to become righteous. What is your intention? To get a *karāmah*?

If your intention for your "extra" and "sincere" *'ibādah* is to get the *karāmāt*, then you have fallen at the first hurdle, because no one should be seeking a *karāmah* in itself. Al-Junayd رحمه الله has a beautiful saying in which he says, "How many of a *walī* have walked on water, but there are people who are better than them, who have died of thirst." Just because somebody has a *karāmah*, that doesn't give him a higher status. It is not directly correlated: a *karāmah* does not equate to a higher status. It is a gift that Allah ﷻ would give to someone He chooses.

The other thing - as Imam al-Qushayrī mentioned – is that a *karāmah* is a form of the sign of truthfulness for a person that Allah ﷻ awards it to him, to give him that steadfastness so he is content with that, but it is not in any way like prophethood and it is not to be used as a form of showing off or as a challenge to people. A *walī* usually does not expose his gift.

Range of *Karāmāt*

The other point that the Imam wants to mention are those aspects that need clarifying. What are the space and the range of *karāmāt* that somebody who is not a Prophet can do? He is saying the general rule, if you like, is that whatever is possible to be a *mu'jizah* for a Prophet can be a *karāmah* for a *walī*. It can be anything because at end of the day a *mu'jizah* is not from the Prophet's own making. It is something that Allah 🕮 gives him, so it can also be given to any person if Allah 🕮 chooses to give. The only difference is that he is not claiming prophethood, so any of the *mu'jizāt* that the Prophets 🕮 have done can also be considered as possible *karāmāt* for people who are not Prophets.

Fearing Allah for those with *Karāmāt*

A question which some people may ask, "If someone was given a *karāmah*, does that means that he now knows that he is a special person, a *walī*, and therefore he shouldn't have any fear?" Meaning should he feel secure that I am a chosen person. The answer is, as Imam Abu Bakr ibn Fūrak mentions that it is not acceptable for a person who has been given a gift to think that they are secure, because that goes against the essence of what a *walī* is. He gives the very simple example of the ten Companions that the Prophet 🕮 promised *al-Jannah*: those known as *al-'Asharah al-Mubasharūn bi al-Jannah*: The Ten[209] promised *al-Jannah*.

For ease of memory, one can summarise them to the four Khulafā', Sa'ad and Sa'īd, 'Abd and 'Obayd; and Ṭalḥah and al-Zubayr. So, they are:

1 - Abu Bakr al-Ṣiddīq 🕮

2 - 'Omar ibn al-Khaṭṭāb 🕮

3 - 'Othmān ibn 'Affān 🕮

4 - 'Alī ibn Abī Ṭālib 🕮

---

[209] They are named this way, because they are all mentioned in one singular hadith. However, we know from several sources, that there are many more who were promised *al-Jannah*, in addition to the ten.

5 - Sa'ad ibn Abī Waqqāṣ ﵁

6 - Sa'īd ibn Zayd ﵁

7 - Abdul Raḥmān ibn 'Awf ﵁

8 - Abu 'Obaydah ibn al-Jarrāḥ ﵁

9 - Ṭalḥah ibn 'ObaydUllah ﵁

10 - Al-Zubayr ibn al-'Awwām ﵁

So, the point is that those ten, even though they were promised *al-Jannah* by the Prophet ﷺ; meaning that they knew they will be of the people *al-Jannah*; yet that didn't change their reality in terms of their *'ibādah* and in terms of their fear of Allah. They kept doing what they were doing. And they kept fearing Allah ﷻ. They understood that their promise of *al-Jannah* was linked to them carrying on the way that they have done.

That's why we know that 'Omar ﵁ was afraid of hypocrisy, and he used to go to Ḥudhayfah ibn al-Yamān ﵁ asking him whether or not his name was on the list of hypocrites that the Prophet ﷺ gave him. Ḥudhayfah ﵁ had a secret and was not supposed to reveal it to anyone, but 'Omar ﵁ kept insisting until he confirmed to him that he was not on the list.[210]

Those people were afraid even though they were promised *al-Jannah*. However, at the same time they had firm conviction that what the Prophet ﷺ promised was true; and so when it came to death and actions were cut off, they displayed that firm belief that they were promised *al-Jannah*.

When Sa'ad ibn Abī Waqqāṣ was on his death bed, and his daughter started to cry, he said to her "Whether you cry or you don't cry, by Allah I am from the people of *al-Jannah*."

210 *Ṣaḥīḥ:* Hadith narrated by Imam Ibn Ḥajar al-'Asqalānī in Al-Maṭālib al-'Ulyah

Why? Because this shows their *īmān* as well. His saying is not arrogance or showing off; rather it is an indication of his faith in the promise of *al-Jannah* made by the Prophet ﷺ and the Prophet ﷺ has spoken the truth.

So even though somebody might be given a gift and even though he might know that he is chosen by Allah ﷻ as a *walī* it doesn't mean that they automatically think that everything is fine, because things might change. It might change for them; the situation might change, so it is a gift for them at that specific junction, if you like. At the same time, as we said before, just because somebody is a *walī* or chosen by Allah ﷻ doesn't mean he has to have a gift. Not every *walī* has a gift unlike every Prophet will have a *mu'jizah*. Every Messenger would be given the sign, but the *walī* does not necessarily need to have that.

Also, it is important that - as Imam Al-Qushayrī mentions - because when you think about everything that has been said already in Bustān al-'Ārifīn; people who know Allah ﷻ are aware of Him. These are people who are very conscious of their status with Allah ﷻ. So it wouldn't make sense that somebody who is aware of Allah ﷻ, conscious of Allah ﷻ to have that kind of feeling of assurance.

As some of the people who misinterpreted this kind of reality in the saying of Allah ﷻ:

﴿ واعْبُدْ رَبَّكَ حَتَّى يَأتِيَكَ اليَقِين ﴾

﴾ And worship your Lord until *yaqīn* comes to you ﴿[211]

They misunderstood the implication of *yaqīn* here, which means "utmost certainty". They interpreted it as when you have attained the level of certain conviction, you don't have to worship Allah ﷻ

211 Holy Quran: Chapter of The Ḥijr 15:99

after that because you have reached the *yaqīn*. They were misguided in their understanding and they went astray in that concept.

Here the verse can be explained as either:

1 - *Yaqīn* means death, because death is the absolute reality which no one denies. It is the ultimate certainty that no human differs upon whether they are Muslim or non-Muslim, whether they believe in God or don't believe: they all know that they will die, it's a certainty. So, *yaqīn* can be translated here to mean death, so worship your Lord until you die. This is supported by the following verses, in which Allah ﷻ narrates to us the saying of the disbelievers:

﴿ إِلَّا أَصْحَابَ الْيَمِينِ ، فِي جَنَّاتٍ يَتَسَاءَلُونَ ، عَنِ الْمُجْرِمِينَ ، مَا سَلَكَكُمْ فِي سَقَرَ ، قَالُوا لَمْ نَكُ مِنَ الْمُصَلِّينَ ، وَلَمْ نَكُ نُطْعِمُ الْمِسْكِينَ ، وَكُنَّا نَخُوضُ مَعَ الْخَائِضِينَ ، وَكُنَّا نُكَذِّبُ بِيَوْمِ الدِّينِ حَتَّىٰ أَتَانَا الْيَقِينُ ﴾

In these verses (39-47) of the Chapter of the Cloaked One (74), Allah informs us that the believers on the Final Day will be enjoying the pleasures of *al-Jannah*; and they will enquire about the criminals and disbelievers. They will be given a portal to engage with them. The disbelievers will say that they are in the Hell-Fire, because they didn't use to pray, they didn't feed the paupers, they used to engage in idle slanderous affairs, and they rejected the Day of Accounting. They continued to do all this until *yaqīn* came to them. And from this, we can definitely know that *yaqīn* cannot mean certain conviction because these people were disbelievers.

2 - The other meaning is related to understanding the usage of the word (حتى) *ḥattā* – (until) in the Arabic language. Because the word "until" can be used sometimes to mean when you reach a destination, or it can mean when you reach it and beyond.

This is common usage in the Arabic language. I demonstrate this to you with two examples from the Quran:

﴿ فَلَا وَرَبِّكَ لَا يُؤْمِنُونَ حَتَّى يُحَكِّمُوكَ فِيمَا شَجَرَ بَيْنَهُمْ ثُمَّ لَا يَجِدُوا فِي أَنْفُسِهِمْ حَرَجًا مِمَّا قَضَيْتَ وَيُسَلِّمُوا تَسْلِيمًا ﴾

﴿ No! By your Lord, they will not have *īmān* until they choose you to arbitrate for them in disputes which have arisen between them ﴾[212]

﴿ قُلْ يَا أَهْلَ الْكِتَابِ لَسْتُمْ عَلَى شَيْءٍ حَتَّى تُقِيمُوا التَّوْرَاةَ وَالْإِنْجِيلَ وَمَا أُنْزِلَ إِلَيْكُمْ مِنْ رَبِّكُمْ وَلَيَزِيدَنَّ كَثِيرًا مِنْهُمْ مَا أُنْزِلَ إِلَيْكَ مِنْ رَبِّكَ طُغْيَانًا وَكُفْرًا فَلَا تَأْسَ عَلَى الْقَوْمِ الْكَافِرِينَ ﴾

﴿ Say O People of the Book, you are not [founded] on anything until you establish the Torah, the Injīl and that which has been sent down to you from your Lord ﴾[213]

Both these verses give the order for continuity. In the first, you will not have *īmān* until you choose the Prophet ﷺ as an arbitrator and judge in your matters, and you continue to do so. In the second, is that the People of the Book are not founded on anything [meaning they are baseless] until they implement God's Law, and they continue to do so.

So, in this verse, the implication of its meaning will be "And worship your Lord until you attain certain conviction, and continue to do so." So, you will attain *yaqīn*, but it doesn't mean you stop at that. But it definitely does not mean worship your Lord, until you reach the level of absolute conviction, then stop, because that would be going against the guidance of the Prophet ﷺ.

212 Holy Quran: Chapter of the Women 4:65
213 Holy Quran: Chapter of the Table Spread 5:68

Types of *Karāmāt*

The next point that the Imam mentions is the different types of *karāmāt*. We mentioned the general idea that a *karāmah* can be something that is of the same nature as a *mu'jizah*. Imam al-Qushayrī ﷺ said the *karāmāt* can be different things. They could include the answering of the *du'ā'*. Somebody makes a *du'ā'*, and it is answered. An example of that is what we know of the story of the companion of Sulaymān mentioned in the Chapter of the Ants (27), and the *du'ā'* of the Prophet ﷺ for Anas.

Another example of a *karāmah* is to bring about food at a time of famine or similar; to bring water at the time of thirst or need. However, you will find that even though Allah ﷻ gives people these kinds of things, He usually makes a reason for it. So, we see at the time of the Prophet ﷺ he didn't just bring food from nothing. There would be some food, in which Allah would place the *barakah* as a form of *karāmah*.

We have the story of Jābir ibn AbdUllah ﷺ during the preparation for the Battle of the Trench[214]. He saw that the Prophet ﷺ had not eaten for three days. So, he went back to his wife to see what she had. She informed him that she had some barley and a young goat[215]. So, he ground the barley and slaughtered the goat; and added the meat to the barley to make a form of stew along with some dough kneaded to make bread. Then he went and invited the Prophet ﷺ secretly, and told him to bring a few people (3 or 4), as he considered the food not enough for any more than that. However, the Prophet ﷺ said, **"It is a lot and good!"** But he added, **"Do not remove the stew from the fire and do not bake the bread until I come!"**

214 *Saḥīḥ* narration found in the books of Imams al-Bukhārī and Muslim with slight variations
215 I avoided using the correct term "kid" as some readers may have missed the target

Then the Prophet ﷺ shouted out to all the people: "**O People of the Trench! Let's go. Jābir has made a meal for us!**" So, everyone got up to come. On seeing this large amount, Jābir's wife was extremely worried, and she was equally annoyed with her husband as she felt embarrassed that the food would not be enough, and she scolded Jābir for this.

When the Prophet ﷺ came, he went to the dough and he spat in it, as well as spitting into the cooking pot. Then, he asked Jābir's wife to get someone else to help her bake the bread; and instructed that the cooking pot should not be removed from the fire.

He also instructed the guests to enter the house without crowding each other. Slowly, small groups entered, they were served bread and stew with its meat. They ate their fill, then the next group entered; and this continued until everyone ate their fill. More so, Jābir stated that the remaining food seemed to be more than what was initially prepared. Someone hearing this narration from Jābir ؓ asked about the total number. He said, "We were around 1000 or so."

Similarly, we have many narrations about the water being blessed by the Prophet ﷺ.

Another example of a *karāmah* is to make a distance shorter. This means being able to travel long distances in a short space of time. Or another aspect is that time itself is folded. We know when we go on a journey, part of our *du'ā'* is: "O Allah! Make our journey easy for us; and fold for us the distance."

You might have noticed this or not, but sometimes you go on certain journeys and you say, "*Subḥān Allah!* That journey was very quick! I didn't notice it" and sometimes you go on the journey and it is like just taking forever. That's part of the blessing (*barakah*) that Allah bestows.

Secondly, it could be related to time. Time can be folded, in the sense that there is *barakah* in the time, such that so much is achieved in a short space of time. The Imam is going to mention a few stories later on in regards to this. However, we do have the story of the Night Journey (*'Isrā'*) and the Ascension (*Mi'rāj*) in which the Prophet ﷺ did a lifetime (or more) of a journey in what was seconds in the material perception.

Another example al-Qushayrī mentions is that somebody is freed from his enemy, or escapes being caught, as when Um Jamīl – the wife of Abu Lahab – came looking for the Prophet ﷺ and she was blinded from seeing him[216]. Another example is to hear somebody's speech from a far distance or the other way around. And he said a lot of those things are basically the matters that can all occur as *karāmāt*.

However, he said that this is the saying of Imam al-Qushayrī. There are some things which we say that cannot happen as a *karāmah*. And he gives two examples. One of them, he says, is to bring about a child or a human without two parents, as was a *karāmah* for Maryam (عليها السلام). The other one he said is to change something which is inanimate into a creature, as was the *mu'jizah* of Ṣāliḥ عليه السلام, Mūsā عليه السلام and 'Īsā عليه السلام. This is what Imam al-Qushayrī said, and there is some dispute about this, as the general notion being that what is permissible for a Prophet, can be permissible for a *walī*; and Allah knows best.

Derivation of the Word *Walī*

The next point that the Imam addresses is where is the word *walī* is derived from.

216 *Saḥīḥ:* Hadith narrated by Imam Ibn Ḥibbān

He said that there are generally two possible meanings depending on how we view the derivation of the word. It could be that a *walī* is the subject, meaning that he is the person who is doing something. Or it could be an object, meaning that he is having something done to him.

Al-Qushayrī said: The [word] *walī* may originate from two [roots]:

1 - The subject: this is if we consider the derivation of the root *fa'īl* (فعيل) which is an exaggerated form of the *fā'il* (فاعل) (subject); similar to the word *'alīm* (عليم) is to *'ālim* (عالم); and *qadīr* (قدير) is to *qādir* (قادر).

In this sense, its meaning will be: the one whose obedience is in ongoing succession without being disrupted by any sin. It means that he is always obedient to Allah ﷻ without any sins in between. So, he is called *walī* meaning that he is the subject. And he's the one who's doing that, which is consecutive, which is what the word *wālā* really means here. And that's where you got the word *tilāwah* which means the following of something after the other.

2 - The object which is the second [derivation] is *fa'īl* (فعيل) meaning *maf'ūl* (مفعول) (object); like *qatīl* (قتيل) means *maqtūl* (مقتول) and *jarīḥ* (جريح) meaning *majrūḥ* (مجروح).

In this sense, its meaning will be the one who Allah takes care of his preservation and guarding, perpetually and in succession. Such then, He does not create for him the disregard which is the ability to do an act of disobedience; rather He sustains his success, which is the ability to do an act of obedience.

So, the *walī* is the object of Allah ﷻ, meaning that Allah ﷻ is looking after him. So he's named a *walī* because he's being looked after by Allah ﷻ. And because he's being looked after by Allah ﷻ, he is being saved from doing bad things and sins and so on.

That's why Allah ﷻ said:

﴿ وَهُوَ يَتَوَلَّى الصَّـٰلِحِينَ ﴾

﴿ And He takes care of the righteous ﴾[217]

He said as for the term: *'abdun ṣāliḥun*; then this could be used for a Prophet or a *walī* as Allah ﷻ uses it for both. Because the Prophet ﷺ mentioned that and even Allah ﷻ describes His Prophets using the term *'abd*; and it can be used for other people.

Definition of *Ṣāliḥ*

What is the definition of somebody who is *ṣāliḥ*?

The Quran mentions four categories of high-ranking people.

1 - The Prophets (*anbīyā'*)

2 - Truthful and accepting the truth (*ṣiddīqūn*)

3 - Martyrs (*shuhadā'*)

4 - Righteous (*ṣāliḥūn*)

The first category includes those who have been communicated to by Allah ﷻ.

The second category includes those who have firm conviction in what the Prophets have brought. They are people who have *yaqīn*. It is a higher status than the third category because they are people whose conviction is inherent within them. This is why Abu Bakr ؓ is the highest-ranking non-Prophet, even though he didn't die as a

217 Holy Quran; Chapter of the Heights 7:196.

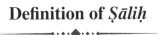

martyr in the battlefield. Some say he may have been poisoned. The third category is the *shuhadā'*, which is literally translated as witnesses.

These are people who were either killed in battle: in the way of Allah ﷻ or died in a specific way.

Shuhadā' are essentially divided into three categories:

1 - *Shahīd* in the *dunyā* and *al-Ākhirah*.

2 - *Shahīd* in *al-Ākhirah*, but not in the *dunyā*.

3 - *Shahīd* in the *dunyā*, but not in *al-Ākhirah*.

As for the **first** category: this is a *shahīd* who has been killed in a battle against disbelievers, and not in a battle against Muslims as sometimes Muslims might fight each other. If he dies in a battle, or as a result of the injuries from the battle, he is in this category.

What does it mean in the *dunyā*? It means that he is not washed, he is not dressed in the clothes of the coffin, he is buried as he is, as his blood witnesses for him. And we don't pray *ṣalātul Janāzah* for him.

The **second** category is one who is considered a *shahīd* in the *Ākhirah* but not treated as one in the *dunyā*. Meaning that he will get the reward and status of a *shahīd* in the Next Life; but in this life, he is washed, shrouded and prayed upon.

These are people whom the Prophet ﷺ mentioned as *shahīd*. This category includes people who have drowned, died from fire, died from a building collapsing on them, the one who has died from internal illness, the one who has died from plague, the woman who has died during childbirth; the person who is killed defending himself, his honour or his property; and the one killed by a tyrant for speaking out against him.

The **third** category is people who are *shahīd* in the *dunyā*, but not in *al-Ākhirah*. These are people who are treated as *shuhadā'* in the *dunyā*, by not washing them, etc. However, their reality is that they were not sincere in their actions. We thought that they are *shahīd*. They might have been killed in a battle, but Allah ﷻ knows that they were not true, their intention was not true. So, in the Next Life, they will be shamed up. And this goes back to the hadith that I mentioned in my introduction about people who do good deeds, but with the intention of wanting to get recognition from humankind.

The fourth category of high-ranking people is *al-ṣāliḥun*. He asks, what is the definition of the *ṣāliḥun*? He is a person who is resident, meaning continuously looking after the *huqūq*, the obligations towards Allah ﷻ and obligations towards the people. So as long as somebody is observing the obligations towards Allah ﷻ and towards other people then that is the basic level of somebody we can label as *ṣāliḥun*. Obviously, we don't go into too much detail, but we would have also categories of people who are considered trustworthy, as is defined in fiqh and hadith transmission.

Is a *Walī* Free from Sin?

Is a person who is given a *karāmah* protected from falling into any error? Is he *ma'ṣūm*?

Ma'ṣūm means he doesn't commit any sins: minor let alone major. The answer is, as Imam al-Qushayrī mentions that a *walī* is not *ma'ṣūm*: he is not free from falling into sin. Unlike the Prophets, who are free from errors, and they do not commit any sins. The *walī* does not have that same privilege. He might be protected from falling into sins or maybe making mistakes but that's not part of their definition. So, just because he is a *walī* doesn't mean that he would not commit sins.

Here, the Imam narrates that al-Junayd was asked about an *'arīf*, would he commit adultery or fornication?

So, he lowered his head for a while thinking about this and then he said, "and the decree of Allah ﷻ is already set." [meaning it can happen].

Thus, it might be that they will commit something like that, but as for the Prophets ﷺ they will not commit any sin. This is in contrast to the Jews and Christians who attributed sin to the Prophets ﷺ, out of blasphemy towards them. They accused Nūḥ ﷺ of drinking alcohol and becoming drunk; and he is innocent of their blasphemy. They accused Lūt ﷺ of committing incest with his daughters, and Sulaymān ﷺ of magic; we ask Allah His forgiveness for the blasphemy that they have recorded.

Even traditionally as some people attribute sin to Adam ﷺ, as they say, that Adam committed the original sin. However, when we examine the Quranic wording, we can see that that is not a sin in the general sense, although it is a sin in the sense of falling short below the expected standard, and in relation to disobedience.

And Allah ﷻ says about Adam, he says:

﴿ وَلَقَدْ عَهِدْنَا إِلَىٰ ءَادَمَ مِنْ قَبْلُ فَنَسِيَ وَلَمْ نَجِدْ لَهُ عَزْمًا ﴾

﴿ We had given the decree [in form of instruction] to Adam from before; but he forgot, and We did not find that he had the will [to disobey] ﴾[218]

So, he didn't do it willingly; or he did not have the will to disobey. So that is not a sin if somebody forgets and doesn't have the firm will or resolve to commit the sin. Because for you to be reprimanded for sin you have to, first of all, do it while you are intending and knowing: you know that this is a sin. And you are

218 Holy Quran: Chapter of Ṭā-Hā 20:115

intending intentionally to do that sin. But if you unintentionally did it or there's no will, or you forgot, then this is not considered a sin.

And if we go through the different stories of the Prophets, we will find that there are, unfortunately, people who have misinterpreted a lot of the acts of the Prophets ﷺ to make them out as if they were sins.

Here we can take a tangent, but quite relevant to explore some common errors in assessing the Prophets ﷺ. I will just make quick references here, and *in shā' Allah*, if Allah allows me, I will provide a translation for the work of one of my shaykh's shaykh who wrote a treatise in this matter.

Take Mūsā عليه السلام; he killed somebody did he not? But he didn't kill somebody as an act of aggression because what did Musa do? He was defending somebody. Two people were fighting and the Israelite asked for help against the Egyptian. So Musa went to help him; and when the aggressor tries to repel him off, Mūsā عليه السلام punched him. Normally a punch is not something that will kill somebody. It is not a usual tool of killing, but because Mūsā عليه السلام was very strong: his punch was fatal. Actually, Mūsā عليه السلام was acting nobly as he was repelling aggression and defending another person. So how can it be a sin?

And if we examine the other stories, we will find similar things with regards to Yūsuf, Dāwūd, Sulaymān, Lūṭ and 'Ibrāhīm and others ﷺ. Some people have mistakenly read matters into certain verses which could be explained away correctly.

Concept of Fear

Al-Qushayrī ﵀ addresses this, by asking who are *'awlīyā'*?

They are those - as described earlier - who are allied to Allah ﷻ; will they no longer have any fear? Are they secure from the punishment of Allah ﷻ?

He said that the reality of those senior *'awlīyā'* was that they were afraid. The reality wasn't just because they thought that they were close to Allah ﷻ in any way that they would no longer be afraid; or that they had some sort of assurance or security from the punishment of Allah ﷻ.

Even the highest-ranking Angels were afraid of Allah ﷻ. There is a narration that when the Prophet ﷺ was in the *Mi'rāj*, he noticed that the Arch Angel Mīkā'īl ﵇ was never laughing. He asked Jibrīl ﵇ about that. So, Jibrīl said ever since Allah ﷻ created the Hell Fire, Mīkā'īl has never been seen laughing[219]. So you see these are close angels; magnificent, great angels who already have assurances that they are beings who are protected by Allah ﷻ because they have no choice to disobey Allah ﷻ. Yet, even then they were afraid of Allah ﷻ. The reality as al-Qushayrī mentions is that they feared Allah ﷻ.

There might have been some people who may have shown in their practices that they did not have fear, and this might have been a rarity in their practice, but even if they did, meaning that they were comfortable with their position, that in itself is probably taken from the reality that they had good suspect of Allah ﷻ, because Allah ﷻ says:

219 *Ḍa'īf:* Hadith narrated by Imam Ahmad

أنا عند حسن ظن عبدي بي، فليظن بي عبدي ما يشاء

"I am as my slave thinks of me, so let my slave think of me as you will."[220]

And in another narration: **"If he suspects well, then good. And if he suspects bad: then bad."**[221]

Thence, if you're comfortable; and feel that Allah ﷻ is going to treat you well, He is not going to do anything wrong to you, as I believe in Allah and I am worshipping Him; and I've done this and I've done that; so why should I be afraid of the Most Generous, the Most Honourable.

However, al-Sarī al-Saqaṭī ﷺ says: "If one were to enter a garden in which there are many trees, and on every tree, there is a bird who says [to him] with an eloquent tongue: 'Peace be upon you, O *walī* of Allah!' and yet, he doesn't fear that this may be a plot, then he has fallen to the plot."

Imagine this kind of scenario. They are all doing that and yet this person is not afraid nor worried that this might actually be some sort of illusion or delusion. If he does not have those feelings, then that is in fact a delusion for him because how can he be seeing all the signs yet be reassured. The reality is he does not know his end. The Imam says there are many examples like this.

Then the Imam says if it is said; "Is it possible that the *walī* will no longer have the fear of being plotted against him? Is it possible that that kind of fear dissipates away from him?"

So, the Imam answers: "Well, if he is actually overwhelmed or he is totally engulfed from witnessing the fear, and it has been snatched from his feeling of his affair, then he is consumed in that which has

220 *Ṣaḥīḥ:* Hadith narrated by Imam Ibn Ḥibbān
221 *Ṣaḥīḥ:* Hadith narrated by Imams al-Bukhārī and Muslim

overtaken him; apparently of seeing things and being aware of them."

So, it might be that there will be occasions where he is no longer afraid and he's feeling very secure. However, the actual quality of fear is one of the qualities of those who are aware. Meaning, that whenever somebody is aware, somebody is present, somebody is thinking, then they will have that fear, and realise that his affairs may not stay the same. They are almost like in a kind of a different reality where they are feeling that security, they're feeling that contentment, that happiness, etc. but it is mixed with the fear that matters may not stay the same. So, it is possible that he's saying that the fear would go from them but usually, the reality is that they are people who are afraid of Allah ﷻ."

Status of a *Walī*

Imam al-Qushayrī ﵀ asks another question. He says, "What if it is asked, 'What is the usual status of the affairs the *walī*, when he is awake'?"

He then mentions nine points about how the state of a *walī*.

First of all; he is truthful in fulfilling the duties of Allah ﷻ. So he is not going to be somebody who is going to forsake the duties of Allah ﷻ. And there is something that I mentioned before which sometimes happens to people who actually are far away from Allah ﷻ thinking that they are close to Allah ﷻ, the closer you come to Allah ﷻ the more you will be worshipping Allah ﷻ, the more you'll be fulfilling the duties, not the other way around.

Secondly; he will have mercy and empathy towards the creation, in all his situations and states.

Thirdly; he will extend his *raḥmah* (mercy) to other people and creatures. And here it's all the creation so it's not just the Muslims or just humans, but all the creation; the animals, the insects, even the plants. There is that concept of mercy towards all of those things. And we know how the Prophet ﷺ was merciful with the inanimate objects, as well as to the animate objects; as in the case of the weeping tree trunk.

Fourthly; he is continuously trying to treat people nicely by carrying things for them. And by "carrying", it is not just physically, but also carrying their concerns, seeing what and how he can help them and so on. Also, in Arabic; it can mean that he takes on the burden of their nastiness towards him, and doesn't reciprocate.

Fifthly; he would be someone who initiates a request of goodness from Allah ﷾ towards the creation, without them even asking for it. So, he is someone who is aware of others, and he sees their situation; he will see how he can help them and obviously by asking Allah ﷾.

Sixthly; His kind of state would be that he is concerned with how to help people, how to get salvation to the creation; and that he does not want to retaliate, and get his own back, or to enact revenge on others. So, you can see the overwhelming kind of matter here is about how the mercy and dealing with people nicely.

Seventhly; he is someone who is aware of his duty towards them, but he avoids making them feel that they owe him for his goodness towards them. So, he doesn't think you need to treat me nicely because I am this or that. And at the same time, he doesn't take from their wealth and possessions, as he is not trying to get any material gain from them.

Eighthly; he does not have any greed in any way. He also holds back from extending his tongue from speaking badly towards them.

This means that he is conscious of his tongue; and more so, of not letting others feel bad in any way.

Ninthly; he shields himself from witnessing any of their misdeeds. And he is not an opponent to any of them in the *dunyā* or the *Ākhirah*.

So these are nine points that Imam al-Qushayrī mentioned of how a *walī* should be behaving. And as I mentioned, the overarching reality here is that this person is caring for them, he is aware of them, he's not trying to get anything from them for his own self neither materially, emotionally, nor physically. Rather he is trying to help them in any way he can. And the Imam said he is basically part of them and he is not asking anything from them neither in the *dunyā* nor the *Ākhirah*.

As for patience and forgiveness, Allah ﷻ said:

﴿ ولمن صبر وغفر إن ذلك لمن عزم الأمور ﴾

﴿ And for the one who is patient and forgives, then that is of the strongest of will power in affairs ﴾[222]

And Allah ﷻ also said:

﴿ والكاظمين الغيظ والعافين عن الناس والله يحب المحسنين ﴾

﴿ Those who hold back their anger, those who pardon people, and Allah loves those who are righteous ﴾[223]

The Imam says, we have been narrated to in the book of "'Amal al-Yawm wa al-Laylah" which is written by Ibn al-Sunnī with his

222 Holy Quran; Chapter of Consultation 42:43
223 Holy Quran; Chapter of the Family of 'Imrān 3:134

transmission to 'Anas ﷺ that the Prophet ﷺ asked, **"Can any one of you do as what Abu Ḍammḍamm did?"**

They said, **"O Messenger of Allah, who is Abu Ḍammḍamm?"**

He said, **"Whenever he would wake up in the morning, he would say, 'O Allah I have gifted myself and my honour to you', and so he wouldn't curse the one who curses him. Nor would he wrong someone who has wronged him. Nor would he strike someone who hit him."**[224]

So, he basically does not even want to get his right back. Allah ﷻ has given a person the right to take back anything, if he is wronged. It doesn't mean that you wrong him, but you can deal with him in the same way. If he has taken something from you, if he has mistreated you; there are processes through which you can get your right back.

This person, Abu Ḍammḍamm: his reality was that he was dealing with people in a different reality which speaks: "I'm not going to even seek for that, I am going to forgive people, because I'm dealing with Allah ﷻ. I've gifted myself and my honour to Allah ﷻ."

As for caring for others, then the Prophet ﷺ has said:

واللهُ في عَونِ العبدِ ما كانَ العبدُ في عَونِ أخيه

"And Allah is at the service of a person as long as he is at the service of his brother."[225]

224 *Ḍa'īf:* Hadith narrated by Imams Abu Dāwūd and Ibn al-Sunnī
225 *Ṣaḥīḥ:* Hadith narrated by Imam Muslim

And Imam al-Shāfi'ī ﷺ said:

لا تَمْنَعَنَّ يَدَ المعرُوفِ عَن أَحدٍ   مَا دُمتَ مُقتَدِراً فَالسَّعدُ تَارات

وَاشْكُر فَضَائِلَ صُنعِ اللهِ إذ جُعِلَت   إليكَ لا لكَ عندَ النَّاسِ حَاجَاتُ

قَد مَاتَ قَومٌ وَما مَاتَت مَكارِمُهُم   وعاشَ قومٌ وهُم في النَّاسِ أَمْواتُ

Do not hold back the hand of goodness from anyone.

As long as you are able, for happiness comes by occasionally.

And be grateful for the virtue of Allah's doing, when…

The needs of people are directed towards you, not for you

For there are people who have died,
and their nobility hasn't passed away.

Yet others have lived, and they are dead amongst the people.

Imam al-Qushayrī further goes on to tell us the highest of all the *karāmāt* for a *walī*. And this is a beautiful point, and is something that I think is key, and it's almost like the summary. Because some people think that the only *karāmāt* are things like walking on water, levitating in the air, getting this food when at a time of famine and so on. It is true, that these are *karāmāt* but the most prominent of *karāmāt* as al-Qushayrī says is that they are continuously being guided towards acts of obedience and they are protected from sins, shortcomings, or falling into errors and mistakes. And here by errors and mistakes, it doesn't mean that they don't make mistakes, but that they don't do things that go against the rules and regulations.

And here the Imam clarifies these errors and mistakes by saying these are not sins but things like *makrūh* (disliked), and that they do not do these disliked matters. And by disliked, we mean things which are not *ḥarām* such if one did them, he would not get any sin. So they keep away from these disliked things.

What Imam al-Qushayrī is saying here is that one of the greatest gifts that any *walī* of Allah ﷻ is to continue to do good deeds and to always be looking for avenues of good acts. So, whenever they are doing good, Allah ﷻ opens for them more avenues, chapters, and doors towards further goodness, and keeps them away from all things that are *ḥarām*; but also all things which are not befitting for them. And that's why, when you look at the actions of the Prophet ﷺ not only was he doing things which are the obligatory and the recommended things, he was doing things which were permissible, but he never did things which were *makrūh*. It is an important fiqh perspective because sometimes people think that you might see an action, they'll say, "Oh! The Prophet ﷺ did it so and they might label it as *makrūh*."

I'll give you an example of urinating while standing. As an act, it is *makrūh*. The correct practice obviously, is to sit down. There are many reasons for this, and most prominently, is to avail somebody from exposing their *ʿawrah* and to guard oneself from the *najāsah*, the impurity of the urine getting on your clothes. We have a narration that says that the Prophet ﷺ went to a dump yard in a certain area, and he urinated standing[226]. Somebody will say, 'well, you are saying that urinating while standing is *makrūh* and there is a hadith in this regard, so did the Prophet ﷺ do something that was *makrūh*?'

We say that when the Prophet ﷺ stood and urinated there was a reason; and what was the reason? It was that the area that he was did not allow for him to sit down to urinate. So, the reality of the situation meant that the Prophet ﷺ could not fulfil the sitting down: therefore it no longer becomes *makrūh*. The dislike has been removed for him, because now the act has become something that

226 *Ṣaḥīḥ:* Hadith narrated by Imams al-Bukhārī and Muslim

is permissible. So, the Prophet ﷺ did not do *makrūh*. He did that which was permissible because in that situation to sit down was going to be difficult. And you can measure a lot of things in that same way. If I wanted to expand, I could, but obviously that would make the book much larger.

Seeing Allah ﷻ

The Imam goes into another topic which is also associated with the aspect of *'awlīyā'* and that is about seeing Allah ﷻ. He follows on narrating a lot from Imam al-Qushayrī as you may have noticed. Al-Qushayrī asks is it possible to see Allah ﷻ with the eyesight as a form of gift? And is it one of the *karāmāt* that a person may be given to see Allah ﷻ?

Al-Qushayrī answers that the stronger opinion is that it cannot happen because there is a unanimous verdict on that. And then he said, I heard from Imam Abu Bakr Ibn Fūrak that he narrates from al-'Ash'arī ﵀ that they said there are two sayings in this matter, so there is a difference of opinion on whether a person can see Allah ﷻ. And then he says, we have said that a group of people have narrated a consensus that seeing Allah ﷻ cannot happen for the *'awlīyā'* in the *dunyā* because it's not going to happen even though, rationally, it can happen because at the end of day what prevents it from happening? It's not impossible for Allah ﷻ to do. And he said that the *Ṣaḥābah* themselves, and even those who came after them differed about did the Prophet ﷺ see Allah ﷻ his Lord, Most High on the Night Journey and Ascension: *Laylat al-'Isrā' wa al-Mi'rāj*.

So even the *Ṣaḥābah* – themselves – differed about whether or not the Prophet ﷺ saw Allah ﷻ with his eyesight in the *dunyā*, because he was still part of the *dunyā*, although one could argue that was a different realm. And here, al-Qushayrī, says that the chosen opinion amongst the majority, is that he did see Allah ﷻ during the Night Journey and that is the saying of Ibn ʿAbbās ﷺ. The Imam said that he has extended this explanation in his book "Sharḥ Ṣaḥīḥ Muslim". So, there's a difference of opinion about seeing Allah ﷻ. I don't think it's a big matter to debate or discuss. The Companions differed about whether the Prophet ﷺ saw Allah ﷻ in *Laylat al-'Isrā'*. If there is a difference amongst the *Ṣaḥābah*, then by extension, there is going to be differences on whether in this *dunyā* somebody might be able to see Allah ﷻ as a gift from Him ﷻ. Although he said that the majority of people say that this kind of thing is not going to happen, and Allah ﷻ is more knowledgeable and only He knows best.

Losing the Status of *Wilāyah*

In the next chapter, Imam al-Qushayrī questions whether it is possible that once a person becomes a *walī* and having reached the state of *wilāyah*, can he lose that status? Meaning that, can he then turn around and become a different person altogether?

Al-Qushayrī said that it is permissible that person can become a *walī*, one state, and then his reality changes. He said that whoever has made a condition of the *wilāyah* that he will be in a good state until the end, then obviously they are going to say it is not possible because if we said that the condition of being *walī* is that you continue on your path of being a good person and as an ally to Allah ﷻ it that is a condition, then it means that you are not going to change.

However, some people who said that maybe he is in that reality, in his status, he is a believer, he is a *walī*, but it is possible that his situation may change then obviously that is an acceptable opinion as well.

So, therefore it depends on how you define the word *walī* in the first place.

Therefore, Imam al-Qushayrī further goes on to say that the opinion that we choose; part of the *karāmāt* of the *walī* is that he knows his status. So, one of the *karāmāt* is that he knows that he is linked to Allah ﷻ; and that his situation or his end will not change, and therefore this matter can be a sort of addendum to what was mentioned before; that can a *walī* know that he is a *walī* or not? So, if he does know that he is a *walī* then that means that he has been given that assurance that he will remain loyal to his status with Allah ﷻ.

Gifts which are not Supernatural

The Imam adds an additional aspect to what has already been discussed of *karāmāt*. We know what *karāmāt* are. They are acts that go against the natural disposition of things, that are supernatural acts that would not happen according to the normal, natural or physical laws. In addition, there is something called *mawāhib*, which is also translated as gift or skill. Sometimes, you say this person has *mawāhib* which means he is a skilled person. Although, the word *mawāhib* comes from the word *hibah*, which is a gift. A difference between *mawāhib* and *karāmāt* is that the latter goes against the natural, whereas the former does not. Therefore, there are things that happen naturally and are physically possible, however they are just fascinating to the mind. People might question how can that happen, as it might not make sense to them. It is not that they don't believe it, it's just maybe in their normal estimation of things, it is hard for them to accept it.

Moreover, he said that this is something that certain people will have, and it's not something that is specific for the *'awliyā'* as it could be for them as well as others.

The Imam says that he is going to mention some of these *karāmāt* and *mawāhib in shā' Allah,* from the general instruction of Allah ﷻ in which He says:

﴿ وَكُلًّا نَّقُصُّ عَلَيْكَ مِنْ أَنبَاءِ الرُّسُلِ مَا نُثَبِّتُ بِهِ فُؤَادَكَ ﴾

﴿ and such We narrate onto you, the news of the Messengers, which will make your heart steadfast and confident ﴾[227]

Allah ﷻ also says:

﴿ أُولَئِكَ الَّذِينَ هَدَى اللَّهُ فَبِهُدَاهُمُ اقْتَدِهْ ﴾

﴿ They are the ones whom Allah ﷻ has guided so in their guidance you should follow ﴾[228]

Thus, the Imam is telling these stories with the aim of strengthening the reader's heart; and to relate stories in which to find motivation and inspiration.

Then he mentioned with his chain of narration, which goes all the way back to Abu Sa'īd al-Khudrī ؓ from the Prophet ﷺ who said:

لن يشبع المؤمن من خير يسمعه حتى يكون منتهاه الجنة

"The believer will never be full of listening to good things until he reaches *al-Jannah.*"[229]

227 Holy Quran; Chapter of Hūd 11:120
228 Holy Quran; Chapter of the Cattle 6:90

The Imam quotes Imam al-Tirmidhī saying that it is a sound hadith[230]. Good narrations, pleasant stories and nice words are something that a believer always seeks, and they are a form of spiritual nourishment for him.

229 *Ḍa'īf:* Hadith narrated by Imams al-Tirmidhī and Ibn Ḥibbān
230 Despite him saying that, the narration has been judged as a weak narration.

14

Stories of the Righteous

Barakah in Time

The Imam says with a transmission that extends back to Imam al-Tirmidhī who said that ʿAlī ibn Ḥajar narrates that Maslama ibn ʿAmr narrated to them saying that ʿOmar ibn Hāniʾ used to pray every day, one thousand *sajdah* (meaning one thousand *rakʿah*) and he used to glorify Allah ﷻ a hundred thousand times, (saying *subḥān Allah*).

Obviously, as we will see shortly, this is a type of *karāmah*. Allah ﷻ folds the time for this person so that he's able to perform all those acts. Because if you were to compute the time taken for those acts, then there's not even enough time in a day to perform them. So how is he able to do all of that! It must be a gift from Allah ﷻ.

Abu Muslim Al-Khawlānī

The Imam chooses to mention some narrations pertaining to one specific *tābiʿī*: Abu Muslim al-Khawlanī ؓ.

The Imam narrates the story of Abu Muslim that relates to some aspects of *karāmāt* that Allah ﷻ can give to some of His creation.

Abu Muslim's [al-Khawlānī] wife said, "O Abu Muslim! We don't have any flour."

He asked, "Do you have anything?"

She responded, "A dirham, which we got from selling some yarn."

He then replied, "Give it to me, and give me the sack."

Following that, he went to the market, and stood in front of a man selling food. A beggar stood near him. The beggar said, "O Abu Muslim, give me some charity!"

Abu Muslim ran away to another stall but the beggar kept following him saying, "Give me charity!"

Married people will understand this situation. Your wife has given you a chore to do, and you don't want to let her down. Therefore, he was quite hesitant to give away his dirham because he knows that his wife is waiting for the flour.

So, when the beggar wore him down - with his persistent begging, he gave him the dirham.

He then took the sack and filled it with sawdust (from the carpenter's workshop) and earth. He arrived home feeling worried and knocked on the door with a trembling heart. When she opened the door, he hastily gave her the sack and went away.

She opened the sack and found white refined flour, which she proceeded to knead and bake into loaves.

Later after a portion of the night had passed, Abu Muslim, with a fearful heart, returned home. When he entered, his wife served him a tray with white loaves of bread.

Surprised, he asked, "From where did you get these?"

She replied, "O Abu Muslim! It is from the flour that you brought!"

Abu Muslim started to eat, as tears flowed down his cheeks!

This is – as the Imam says – a great story, with many great benefits. Obviously, anyone who looks at that can see that. And it's important to know that stories like this were occurring, and do happen, and they are not strange to those who experience them, even though others might find it strange, but no doubt Allah ﷻ can give and He has the ability to change things. Nothing is impossible for Allah ﷻ.

The Imam says that the name of Abu Muslim, the owner of this *karāmah* ؓ is: AbdUllah ibn Thuwab, or it is said: Ibn Thawāb, or Ibn Athwab, or Ibn AbdUllah or ibn 'Awf or Ibn Yaslam. It is also said that his name was Ya'qūb ibn 'Awf. However, the correct one is AbdUllah ibn Thuwab.

He was from the people of Yemen, who inhabited the Levant in Dāriyā: the renowned village next to Damascus. Another famous person from this village is Abu Sulaymān al-Dārānī. He was among the senior Followers, and amongst their most devoted and righteous. He was one of those who have apparent *karāmāt*.

He lived during the time of the Prophet ﷺ. He had travelled to go and see the Prophet ﷺ, to be in his company. However on his way there, the Prophet ﷺ passed away. Thus, he didn't actually see him. A term that the '*ulamā*' use for this kind of people is *mukhaḍram*. They were the people who lived at the time of the Prophet ﷺ but for whatever reason, didn't have the chance to see him. Even though they lived at the same time as the *ṣaḥābah*, they are not *ṣaḥābah*, since they never saw the Prophet ﷺ. However, he managed to meet Abu Bakr al-Ṣiddīq and 'Omar ؓ.

Among his other precious gifts, as was mentioned by Imam Ahmad ibn Ḥanbal ؒ was his ability to walk on water.

Abu Muslim al-Khawlānī passed by the Tigris River whilst it was breaking off the branches of the trees on its banks. So, he walked on water and then turned to his companions saying, "Are you missing any of your equipment, so you can ask Allah ﷻ?"

He narrates it from another path [of transmission], stating that he stood on the [bank of] Tigris, while praising Allah Almighty and glorifying Him. He then mentioned His blessings, and the crossing of the Children of Israel through the sea. Thereafter he advanced his horse entering the Tigris followed by his people until all of them safely crossed the river under his *karāmah*. May Allah be pleased with him.

I watched a video that was circulating on social media that showed how the river could throw an immense amount of wood while people were trying to collect as much of it as they could.

Also, with the narration of Imam Ahmad ؒ that Abu Muslim was in the land of the Romans. The governor sent an army, and set a time for their return. When they didn't return on time, Abu Muslim became very concerned. As he was doing *wuḍū'* on the shore of a river, he spoke to himself regarding the matter. At that time, a crow landed on a tree across from him. The crow said, "O Abu Muslim! Are you worried about the army?"

He spontaneously replied, "Yes."

The crow then said, "Do not worry; for they have been victorious and they will return to you on such and such a day at such and such time."

Abu Muslim said to the crow, "Who are you, may Allah have mercy on you?"

The crow responded, "I am one who brings happiness to the hearts of believers."

After sometime, the regiment arrived at the specified day and time as was mentioned by the crow.

The speaking of animals is something that we know is real. It's not something that is made up or fake, and it's not related to Dr Dolittle either. Because we know that Sulaymān ﷺ spoke to animals and our Prophet ﷺ also spoke to animals. Indeed, animals spoke to people as in the story of the wolf and the cow.

After the Prophet ﷺ led the morning prayer, he turned to face the people. He said:

بيْنَا رَجُلٌ يَسُوقُ بَقَرَةً إِذْ رَكِبَهَا فَضَرَبَهَا، فَقالَتْ:
إِنَّا لَمْ نُخْلَقْ لِهذا، إِنَّما خُلِقْنَا لِلْحَرْثِ

"Whilst a man was leading a cow, he mounted it and struck it. The cow then said, 'We have not been created for this. We have only been created for ploughing."

The people said, "*Subḥān Allah*, a cow talking!"

So, the Prophet ﷺ said:

فإِنِّي أُومِنُ بهذا أنَا، وأَبُو بَكْرٍ، وعُمَرُ

"Truly, I believe that. I, Abu Bakr and ʿOmar." Even though they were not there.

Then he continued:

وبيْنَما رَجُلٌ في غَنَمِهِ إِذْ عَدَا الذِّئْبُ، فَذَهَبَ منها بشَاةٍ، فَطَلَبَ حتَّى كَأنَّهُ اسْتَنْقَذَهَا منه، فَقالَ له الذِّئْبُ هذا: اسْتَنْقَذْتَهَا مِنِّي، فمَن لَهَا يَومَ السَّبُعِ، يَومَ لا رَاعِيَ لَهَا غيرِي!؟

"And whilst a shepherd was among his flock, a wolf runs by and takes a sheep. The man chases it until he retrieves his sheep from it. The wolf then says to him, 'You retrieved it from me! So, who will guard it when the day(s) of the predators[231] befall: when it shall have no shepherd other than me!"

So, the people said, "*Subḥān Allah*, a talking wolf!"

The Prophet ﷺ said, **"Truly, I believe that. I, Abu Bakr and 'Omar."** Even though they were not there.[232]

We know a camel came and complained to the Prophet ﷺ[233]. We know that a pigeon also approached the Prophet ﷺ[234] to complain to him; and so on. More than that, inanimate objects also spoke to the Prophet ﷺ as in the case of salutation of the rocks[235] and the whining of the tree trunk[236].

With the authority of Ahmad ﷺ that Abu Muslim was sitting and talking with his companions in the land of the Romans. They said, "O Abu Muslim! We are craving some meat, so ask Allah Almighty that He may provide us with some."

He said, "O Allah! You have heard their saying, and You are able to do what they have requested!"

It was only then that they heard some commotion in the military camp. A stag had entered and passed by the companions of Abu Muslim and they jumped up to catch it.

So, it was his *du'ā'* that Allah responded to. This also teaches us, something that I mentioned before, that when we look for these *karāmāt* or we are looking for special things to happen, there must

231 Denoting a time when humans will be extinct, and predators will roam the Earth
232 *Ṣaḥīḥ:* Hadith narrated by Imams al-Bukhārī and Muslim
233 *Ṣaḥīḥ:* Hadith narrated by Imams Abu Dāwūd and Ahmad
234 *Ṣaḥīḥ:* Hadith narrated by Imam Abu Dāwūd
235 *Ṣaḥīḥ:* Hadith narrated by Imam Muslim
236 *Ṣaḥīḥ:* Hadith narrated by Imam al-Bukhārī

be a cause or reason. Some people think that things will just happen pretty much out of nothing.

However, it is of the *sunan* of Allah ﷻ that He will gift people, but there must be some sort of reason. When you read the story of Mūsā ﷺ as he was squeezed between the sea in front of him; and Pharaoh from behind him, Allah ﷻ could have just opened up the sea, but Allah ﷻ said:

﴿ فَأَوْحَيْنَا إِلَى مُوسَى أَنِ اضْرِب بِّعَصَاكَ الْبَحْرَ فَانفَلَقَ فَكَانَ كُلُّ فِرْقٍ كَالطَّوْدِ الْعَظِيمِ ﴾

﴾ So, we revealed to Mūsā that you should strike the sea with your staff ﴿[237]

This clearly shows that there should be an action. Although Allah ﷻ could have just opened the sea but He said, "Strike it with your staff!", this is acting as the reason. As we mentioned before regarding the *karāmāt* of the Prophet ﷺ and the dates of Hurairah ؓ.

Also, on the authority of Ahmad ؓ that a famine befell the people during the era of Mu'āwiyah ؓ. Mu'āwiyah went out with the people to ask for rain. When they arrived at the prayer area, Mu'āwiyah said to Abu Muslim:

"You have seen what has befallen the people, so pray to Allah!"

Abu Muslim replied: "I will do so."

He proceeded to mount a she-camel and stood on its back. He then uncovered his head from his *burnus*[238] and raised his arms praying:

"O Allah! We surely seek the rain from You. And I have come to you announcing my sins, so do not disappoint me!"

None of them moved until they were watered.

237 Holy Quran; Chapter of the Poets 26:63
238 A garment which has a hood attached to it.

Abu Muslim then said: "O Allah! Muʿāwiyah has placed me in a place of boasting. So, if I have any good status with You, take me unto You!"

He was a little bit anxious that he didn't want people to know about this gift of his *duʿāʾ* being answered. The narrator says that was on a Thursday and Abu Muslim died the following Thursday: only one week later.

This was the nature of these righteous people before as well. They were not looking for fame nor recognition. It is similar to the story of 'Oways ؓ.

'Oways al-Qaranī was also a *tābiʿī* from Yemen. He was not a *ṣaḥābī*, but he was quite a virtuous person to the extent that the Prophet ﷺ even mentioned him in a hadith: that is how special this person is. Not only did he mention him in a hadith, but he instructed some of the companions like 'Omar ibn al-Khaṭṭāb ؓ that if he were to meet 'Oways, then ask him to ask forgiveness from Allah ﷻ for you[239]. 'Omar is a high-ranking companion, but the fact that the Prophet ﷺ was telling him to ask this person to make *duʿāʾ* that Allah ﷻ forgives him, demonstrates the greatness of this person.

The story of 'Oways is quite fascinating if we wanted to go over it, but the point I want to mention is this. 'Omar was so fascinated by him that he wanted to give him a position but 'Oways refused. He said that I would like to be amongst the common public, and I don't want to be known. He was worried that people will occupy him. Unfortunately, people did find out about him and this really upset him.[240]

Imagine there is a hadith where the Prophet ﷺ says to ask this guy to make *duʿāʾ* for you, what's going to happen? Everyone is going

239 *Ṣaḥīḥ:* Hadith narrated by Imam Muslim
240 *Ṣaḥīḥ:* Hadith narrated by Imam Muslim

to go to this guy. So, he's not going to be able to get on with his normal life, and I think that's what happened.

There's also a narration which is narrated in regards to Abu Muslim as well. And this is probably part of the reason why Abu Muslim was given such a high status because of his station. After the Prophet ﷺ passed away, there was a guy called al-'Aswad ibn Qays al-ʿAnsī. Al-Aswad claimed to be a prophet, obviously he was a liar. And when he claimed prophethood in Yemen, he sent for Abu Muslim al-Khawlānī.

When he came to him, he said: "Do you bear witness that I am the Messenger of Allah?"

Abu Muslim said: "I can't hear!"

He said, "Do you bear witness that Muhammad is the Messenger of Allah?"

He said, "Yes."

He – then – repeated the question, and Abu Muslim repeated his answers.

Al-'Aswad ordered that a great fire be lit and stoked. He then threw Abu Muslim in it, yet it did not harm him.

It was suggested to al-'Aswad to exile Abu Muslim or else he will corrupt those who follow you, so he ordered him to leave.

Abu Muslim came to al-Madinah, and the Messenger of Allah ﷺ had passed away; and was succeeded by Abu Bakr رضي الله عنه.

Abu Muslim tied his mount at the door of the *Masjid*. He stood up praying in front of one of the pillars of the *Masjid*. He was spotted by ʿOmar who approached him.

He said, "Who is the man[241]?"

He said, "From the people of Yemen."

241 He referred to him in the third person, a form or eloquence in speech

Because 'Omar ﷺ had an intuition and inner sight, he said, "Perhaps you are the one whom the Liar burnt with fire?[242]"

He said, "That is AbdUllah ibn Thuwab."

He is playing with words, trying to avoid answering, because he doesn't want to be known, as it may become a *fitnah* that people start to know him and consider he is famous for walking out of the fire unscathed.

'Omar, again, being the clever person he is, knows the hidden aspect of this answer.

He said, "I ask you by Allah: Is it you?"

He said, "By Allah: yes!"

'Omar then embraced him and wept. He then seated him between him and Abu Bakr ﷺ. He then said, "Praise be to Allah who did not take my life before showing me amongst the nation of Muhammad ﷺ someone who had the same done to him as was done to the *Khalīl*[243] of al-Raḥmān: Abraham ﷺ."

The Imam comments that this is of the most noble of *karāmāt*, and the most precious of illuminating states. He also comments on the point when he said "I can't hear".

He said that it's possible that it means one of two things. Either (لا أسمع) "I can't hear" means (لا أقبل): "I don't accept [what you are claiming]", so he used that word to denote that, or it could mean that he actually could not hear such profanity and that Allah ﷻ may have closed his hearing from such a claim. And he said maybe both are possible. He said a lot of the Imams have said that the first option is the right one and they limited it to that, but he said I prefer the second one; that Allah ﷻ didn't allow him to hear.

242 A demonstration of 'Omar's ﷺ intuition
243 Close friend – or beloved

Abdul Wāḥid ibn Zayd

Ahmad ibn Abi al-Ḥawārī said in his Book of al-Zuhd that Abu Sulaymān narrated to me that: Abdul Wāḥid ibn Zayd ﵀, was afflicted by a stroke. So, he asked Allah Almighty to release it from him during times of ablution. So, when the time of ablution came, he would rise from his bed until he went to perform ablution; and when he returned to his bed, the paralysis [from the stroke] would return to him. And Allah knows best.

A *simple* case of the *du'ā'* being answered; but clearly demonstrates the status of this man with Allah, and how He has afflicted him with this illness. This shows that Allah will afflict His *'awlīyā'* with difficulties and hardship, as was said by the Prophet ﷺ who said:

أشدُّ النَّاسِ بلاءً الأنبياءُ ، ثمَّ الصَّالحون

"The most intense of people who are afflicted are the Prophets, then the righteous."[244]

Furthermore, it demonstrates the concern of this righteous man which was *ṣalāh*.

Fulfilment of *du'ā'*

Another example of the fulfilment of *du'ā'* is what the Imam narrated to from the authority of al-Ḥasan ibn 'Imrān ibn 'Uyaynah that Sufyān ibn 'Uyaynah told him in Muzdalifah in the last Hajj he performed: "I have fulfilled coming to this place seventy times. Each time I say, 'O Allah! Do not make it the last time in relation to this place!'

244 *Ṣaḥīḥ:* Hadith narrated by Imam Ibn Mājah

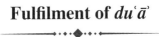

However, I am embarrassed from Allah ﷻ from the numerous times that I have asked Him."

So, he returned [home] and passed away the following year.

Every year, he would make *du'ā'* to Allah ﷻ asking him to allow him another hajj. In a way, it demonstrates his love and eagerness for Allah, to be on this ritual every year.

However at one point, he felt embarrassed of asking Allah ﷻ again and again. In that year he didn't make *du'ā'* to come back and he died.

In a way, this example shows us that certain people have a status with Allah, among them is this great man Sufyān ibn 'Uyaynah ﵀.

Sahl ibn AbdUllah

The Imam tells us that Abu Ḥātim al-Sijistānī say: I heard Abu Naṣr al-Sarrāj say: "We entered Tustur, so we saw in the palace of Sahl ibn AbdUllah ﵀ a room that people used to call the room of the predators. So, we asked people about that. They said: 'The predators would come to Sahl, and he would receive them in this room, hosting them and feeding them meat, then he would let them go!'

Abu Naṣr said: "I saw the people of Tustur all of them agreeing on this and they are a lot of people."

Those who fear Allah truly, then His creatures will fear them. Hence this approach of Sahl to the predators. Whilst it is natural to fear a dangerous animal either on oneself or on one's family or wealth, there were people who were more concerned with fearing Allah, and so were not worried about the fierce animals.

The Turkic ruler Ahmad Ibn Ṫūlūn was the tyrant who ruled Egypt, after evicting the 'Abbāsid fiscal agent. He was a wicked man who had killed thousands of people. During his reign, there was a righteous scholar by the name of Banān ibn Muhammad, and famously known as Abu Ḥasan al-Zāhid al-Ḥammāl (the Courier). This scholar went to Ibn Ṫūlūn and advised him towards good, and forbid him from the oppression that he is committing.

Being a tyrant, Ibn Ṫūlūn did not accept the advice, and was enraged that he should be given any advice at all.

So, he ordered that Abu Ḥasan be locked up. At the same time, he starved a lion for 3 days. Then, the scholar was placed in an arena and the lion was let loose on him.

The lion began to roar, and then approached Abu Ḥasan smelling him, then retreating back. He kept coming forward then retreating, until he went to a corner and sat down, not harming Abu Ḥasan.

Dazzled by what had happened, Ibn Ṫūlūn brought Abu Ḥasan and asked him, "What were you thinking when the lion was roaring?"

He said, "The lion came and smelt me, and touched my dress; and I was pondering on whether the saliva of a lion is pure or impure (*najis*)!"

He said, "Did you not fear the lion?"

He said, "Not at all, for Allah will take care of the lion."

Abu al-Khayr al-Tīnātī

The Imam tells that Ḥamzah ibn AbdUllah al-'Alawī say: "I entered on to Abu al-Khayr al-Tīnātī ﵀ and I had [within my mind] committed to myself that I would give him *salām* and leave, and not to eat food with him.

So, when I came out of his house and walked a distance, he was behind me, carrying a plate of food and said: "O young man! Eat of this, for this hour, you are no longer bound by your commitment!"

The Imam said: Abu al-Khayr is famous for his *karāmāt*. And this *karāmah* here is about reading people's mind or thoughts.

Another incident relating to Abu al-Khayr. The Imam says that it has been narrated that 'Ibrāhīm al-Raqqī said: I intended him to give him *salām*. So, he prayed *Ṣalātul Maghrib*, and he did not recite al-Fātiḥah[245] evenly! So, I said to myself: 'My travel has gone to waste!'

After I gave him *salām*, I went out for my purification and a lion sought me. So, I returned to him and told him, "The lion has sought me!"

So, he went out and shouted at the lion and said: "Did I not tell you that you should not approach my guests?!"

The lion stepped away, and I purified myself.

Then, when I returned to him, he said, "You were concerned with correcting the outwards, and so you feared the lion. Whilst we were occupied with correcting the hearts, so the lion feared us."

The Imam said: someone who tries to imitate the jurists – and yet has no fiqh – may be deceived in thinking that the prayer of Abu al-Khayr was void, due to the narrator's saying, 'he did not recite al-Fātiḥah evenly!'

This is the ignorance and stupidity of those who are confused by that, and an audacity from him to send suspicions to the *'awliyā'* of the Most Merciful. Let the sane person be wary of objecting to any of that. Rather, it is his duty if he does not understand their learned wisdom, and their renewed points of reflection, to try to understand it from those who know them.

245 Holy Quran: The Chapter of the Opening (1), an integral of *ṣalāh*

And everything that you see of this kind: of which those who have no research capabilities assume that they are violations, they are not. Rather the actions of *'awlīyā'* of Allah the Almighty must be interpreted appropriately.

As for this incident, then the answer to this is from three aspects:

The first: It does not invalidate the prayer, by agreement.

The second: He is subdued to that due to a defect in his tongue, and so his prayer was valid, by agreement.

The third: that if he had no excuse, then reciting al-Fātihah is not conditional with Abu Ḥanīfah and a group of scholars, and this *walī* does not have to adhere to the school of those who have obliged it [in the *ṣalāh*].

Whilst the Imam mentioned the third aspect, I will say that according to the school of Abu Ḥanīfah, the recitation of al-Fātiḥah is not conditional for the one being led; whereas the imam has to read al-Fātiḥah as it is obligatory. Seeing as Abu al-Khayr was leading the prayer, then this third aspect doesn't fit as a reason, and Allah knows best.

15

Enjoyable Tales

In this chapter, the Imam has collated the *karāmāt* for some people; he tells us that he has made for each one of them a purpose, so that it can be easier to attain, and easier to review and more compelling in the soul of the reader.

You must know that this section – even though it is not one of the chapters of asceticism – relaxes the soul, should it become bored. The ascetic may need the stories of others which do not affect the asceticism and may not be understood comprehensively.

For it may be that they may talk about the affairs of people and the gossip may drag them to talk about forbidden matters of backbiting and the like. If they become occupied with this matter of *karāmāt*, their souls become revitalised when they hear them and they become occupied with it rather than the ugly matters.

And in view of this, these tales that I mention – *in shā' Allah* - are not void of benefits that the seeker of the Hereafter will benefit from - and Allah grants success.

Now we are going to look at this final chapter in this book, in which the Imam has compiled some of the stories or some of the narrations which he feels are useful. And he says in the beginning of this chapter that he has compiled some of the *karāmāt* (gifts) for some of the people and I have made for each one a simple purpose so that people can understand and also refer back to, in order to have a better impact on the person who is reading.

You have to also know that he said that this chapter, even though it falls into the chapters of *zuhd*, it also helps address the *nafs*, as the soul will find some relief when it gets bored. And even the person who is *zāhid* is in need of stories or narrations which might not be found in other chapters. We also know that this was part of the Sunna of the Prophet ﷺ; as well as the *'ulamā'* of the past. As for the Prophet ﷺ then he was very keen that not all his interactions with people were about passing on knowledge through direct methods. Although he was teaching in one aspect, it wasn't just about indoctrinating with words. This is why AbdUllah ibn Mas'ūd رضي الله عنه used to sit with his students to teach them once a week on a Thursday. It was said to him, "O Abu Abdul Raḥmān! Why don't you speak to us more? Why don't you give us more lessons?"

He said, "What prevents me from giving you too much is that I'm afraid that you will get bored."

And then he said, "The Prophet ﷺ used to give us the reminders now and again."[246]

Meaning that he would choose the times for the reminders. He wouldn't just give reminders every day, because he didn't want us to get bored. And in his classes, AbdUllah ibn 'Abbās رضي الله عنه would teach people and when he saw that they had become distracted, he would say, "Bring forth the books of poetry, let us read some poetry." It was like a form of recreation to have breaks in between the lessons.

So, the Imam here is saying the same thing. He is saying sometimes if a person doesn't have these kinds of narrations, these stories, then he might end up doing other things, like speaking about trivial matters, or perhaps gossiping about others, just because he wants

246 *Ṣaḥīḥ:* Hadith narrated by Imam al-Bukhārī

something to talk about. If you don't have something to talk about, you start to gossip and then that gossiping will lead you to aspects of backbiting and other *ḥarām* acts. But if you occupy yourself with stories, which are good and useful, it actually helps to be occupied with something other than what is unacceptable.

The Imam said that these narrations also have benefits which the one who seeks the *Ākhirah* will benefit as well. And that's why Imam Abu Ḥanīfah ؒ said, "The stories of people are more beloved to me than many chapters of *fiqh*, because it conveys the *'adab* of people," meaning it tells us how people behaved and so we can learn morals and etiquette from them.

Sulaymān ibn Ḥarb

The Imam said that we have been narrated to from the authority of Imam Abu Ḥātim al-Rāzī – who is one of the pillars of hadith [narration] who said: "I attended the gathering of Sulaymān ibn Ḥarb ؒ in Baghdad. They estimated the number of people who attended his sitting to be forty thousand men.

His gathering was at the palace of al-Ma'mūn. Something similar to a pulpit was built for him and Sulaymān ascended. Al-Ma'mūn was high in his palace, and the palace door was opened, and a curtain was veiling him, whilst he was writing what Sulaymān dictated."

Abu Ḥātim said that he was not asked about any hadith except that he would narrate it to those who heard.

Al-Ma'mūn was one of the 'Abbāsī Caliphs, who was fascinated with Sulaymān. Just imagine: 40,000 people in one gathering: there are no microphones, there's no loudspeaker and they are all just gathering in one place.

I think the *karāmah* that the Imam is alluding to here is that, **first** of all, the nobility that this person had, in which the Caliph had erected for him a pulpit in his court. **Secondly**, the number of people who attended his *majlis* and they would be able to hear and listen to his narrations and hadith. Whilst this imam may not be a household name, he was known as *Shaykh al-Islam*. He was from Baṣrah and had worked as a judge in Makkah. And he was one of those people who was a highly notable person of the people of hadith. Some people said that he had taught over 10,000 hadith. The Hadith Master Abu Ḥātim (the narrator here) said, "I took from him 10,000 hadith, and I never once saw any book in his hand."

And he was narrating from his memory, which again is one of the gifts of Allah ﷻ.

Abu AbdUllah al-Muḥāmilī

The Imam says that Abu Saʿīd al-Samʿānī said that the number of people who attended the dictation sitting of Imam Judge Abu AbdUllah al-Muḥāmilī was ten thousand men.

So, it's another perspective. These were people who commanded great respect that they had a big following. Abu AbdUllah al-Muḥāmilī ؒ was one of the great scholars and *muhaddith* of Baghdad, who was born in the year 235AH and was considered one of the pillars of hadith of Iraq at that time. He was the *muftī*, as people used to come to him for fatwa for over 60 years. He was considered the reference person for fatwa.

Shihāb al-Dīn al-Suhrawardī and Jamāl al-Dīn

Another narration that Imam al-Nawawī chooses to mention as part of the stories that he narrates with the date as well. He said I saw with the Shaykh's handwriting ﷺ in varied places: I heard our shaykh and master the Imam Hadith Master Zain Uddin ﷺ twice, the last of which was on the Wednesday, the 3rd of the holy month of Ramadan in the year 657, in which he says:

The Noble Shaykh Shihāb al-Dīn al-Suhrawardī ﷺ preached in Damascus - may Allah the Exalted protect and preserve it. The Quran was recited by al-'A'azz ibn 'Ibrāhīm ibn Muhammad al-Mamdūḥ ibn 'Alī al-Rabīnī ibn AbdUllah al-Jawād ibn Ja'far. The Shaykh felt uplifted and so took off his shirt. Jamāl al-Dīn bought it for five hundred dirhams, for the blessings.

And he ﷺ did not used to waste any of his time. Rather, he continued to be engaged in prayer, recitation and remembrance ﷺ.

Our Shaykh ﷺ wore of these clothes a rag, and accompanied him for a while in Baghdad in Ribāt ﷺ.

So, the Shaykh gave some *naṣīḥah*: a kind of reminder. Another man recited some Quran during the occasion, which uplifted the Shaykh as he interacted with this reminder, and so he took off his clothes. [Obviously he didn't take off all his clothes]. He took off some of his outer clothing. It could be that the verses being recited could be verses which encouraged the reduction of the *dunyā*. A person in the audience called Jamāl al-Dīn bought those clothes for 500 dirhams. He did it impromptu. Somebody who felt spiritually uplifted with the Quran to the extent that he took off his clothes and sold it, and he found somebody who could purchase it for even a large amount like 500 silver coins. And this person was renowned for not wasting his time. He would always be occupied with something like *ṣalāh*, recitation, *dhikr* as well and he was somebody who very devout and considerate of his state in the *dunyā*. He was an Imam and a person who was well known for his piety.

Al-Ḥāfiẓ Abdul Ghanī

The Imam narrates another gift which is also among the extraordinary things. He narrates that he heard through his transmission from the righteous Imam and Jurist Shaykh Muhammad al-Birsī, who said: "We were waiting for Hadith Master Abdul Ghanī and we were a group, among us there were those who would give fatwa.

So, when he put his foot on the step of the chair, I said [secretly] to myself: 'With what thing has Allah given you virtue over us?'

He turned to me and said: 'O You who has turned away! Whoever serves is served! Whoever serves is served! Whoever serves is served!'

I said: 'I believe in Allah!'

Imam Muhammad al-Birsī was describing this incident in which the Hadith Master could read his thoughts. He said that we were a group of people sitting and waiting for the lesson to be taught. This group consisted of those who were all capable of giving fatwas so they are all colleagues, they are all on the same level of knowledge. So, he said that he was looking and when Abdul Ghanī got up to sit on the chair, meaning to narrate to them as their teacher, he questioned how Abdul Ghanī reached such a level? He said to himself "How come Allah ﷻ has given him virtue over us? We are all on the same level but he and he's sitting on the chair," and so he said to himself.

He was shocked to see that his thoughts were being read by the Hadith Master Abdul Ghanī, who addressed him as "*Ya Mudbir*!" which is an indication that he knew something about him, because he described him as someone who has turned away. We can't be sure what he was referring to exactly, but in this context, it could well mean that you are not one who is not fully engaged with the whole package of the *dīn* and seeking knowledge, etc. So, it is *you* who has turned away, and how can you rise if you are not determined!

And he clarified that by saying – thrice – that whoever serves – meaning Allah and is of service to others – then he will be served – meaning directly by Allah, who will also cause others to serve him.

This is obviously a *karāmah*, the ability to read the thoughts of others.

The Compiler of al-Muhadhdhab

Another *karāmah* that the Imam mentioned is for the person who wrote the book "al-Muhadhdhab"[247], which is a book in Shāfiʿī fiqh written by a famous scholar called al-Shīrāzī. Al-Shīrāzī worked a lot on collating the opinions within the School and putting all the different aspects in it. In fact, Imam al-Nawawī who is also known for his service to the Shāfiʿī School actually attempted to produce a commentary on "al-Muhadhdhab". Imam al-Nawawī wrote a book where he explained it, naming it "al-Majmūʿ". Basically, it was a study in comparative fiqh: he would take a section; go through each aspect and he'll say this is our *madhhab*, this is our evidence and then he'll go through the evidences of the other schools, and so the book was quite large. However, he didn't have time to finish all of it and died before the task was complete. He had asked his student Ibn

247 This is the famous fiqh book of Imam al-Shīrāzī (d. 476AH), which is considered an important reference in the Shāfiʿī School.

al-ʻAṭṭār to complete it after his death, but the latter wasn't able to do so. Instead, Imam Taqī al-Dīn al-Subkī managed to complement it, and after that Shaykh Muhammad Najīb al-Muṭīʻī.

The Imam mentions that he heard his Master Shaykh Kamāl al-Dīn Sallār, may Allah Almighty protect him – recounting from some jurists, that he put [the Book of] al-Muhadhdhab under his head and slept. He had a wet dream. He then commenced to see Abu Isḥāq the compiler of al-Muhadhdhab in the dream, who pushed him with his foot, saying to him, "Wake up! Is it not enough that you have put al-Muhadhdhab under your head, then you became impure!"

So, it was like one of the blessings for Imam al-Shīrāzī. We mentioned previously how they viewed the wet dream in the case of Abu Sulaymān.

The *Karāmah* of Increasing the Little

The Imam said: I heard our Shaykh and Master the Honourable Imam and the brilliant scholar ʻIzz al-Dīn Abu Jaʻfar ʻOmar ibn ʻAsʻad ibn Abi Ghālib al-'Ilyī al-Muftī al-Shāfiʻī ﷺ on the second day of Shaʻbān in the year 659AH in al-Rawāḥiyyah School in Damascus, may Allah guard and protect it, and the rest of the abode of Islam and its people: Āmīn.

He said: "Some of the jurists said: The Shaykh wrote the book "Nihāyat ul-Maṭlab", and I had the habit of writing a set number of papers at night. So, one night I was writing and I looked to the lantern and found the amount of oil will not be enough for me to complete my routine writing. Anyhow, I got busy with writing and ignored the lantern. I didn't realise until I had completed my routine writing. I counted the papers. When I finished counting, and mentioned my prayers, I looked at the lantern. As I turned to it, it extinguished suddenly [or he said something to that effect.]

He mentioned the gift of this Shaykh who used light from a lantern to enable him to work on his compilation. He knew that the oil in the lantern had a set timing, because in the past they didn't have electricity, the lantern they used would burn for so long and they knew that they'll be able to write so many pages during this time. So, the *karāmah* is that Allah ﷻ gave him the ability to write those extra papers by making the oil extend longer than usual. And an eloquent end, as the lantern extinguished just as he turned to look at it!

Najm al-Dīn ʿĪsā al-Kurdī

The Imam says that the Shaykh al-Faqīh Najm al-Dīn ʿĪsā al-Kurdī al-Shāfiʿī died – may Allah place His Mercy and pleasure on him - in the year 656AH, I think in Shaʿbān. He was a *faqīh* (jurist) at al-Rawāḥiyyah School in the city of Damascus – may Allah protect it, and repel any people with wrong intentions from it and may Allah preserve it and the land of Islam forever, and the entire countries of Islam and their inhabitants.

The Imam says that he saw him in a dream a few days after his death, after the night of *Jumuʿah* and I knew that he has passed away. I greeted him and said to him: "Have you been resurrected – O Najm al-Dīn – and have you returned?!"

I said to him "Al-Ghazālī said in the chapter on Death in his book "'Ihyā' 'Ulūm al-Dīn": Death is an enormous experience, and no one has come back to us after death telling us about its reality; only the one who has tasted it knows its reality."

Then, I said, "Tell us about the reality of death!"

He said: "Despite it being hard, it is only a short moment, then it passes…"

I said: "What is your condition after it?"

He said: "There – meaning with Allah – is much goodness."

It is as if he is indicating that his condition is good, due to the virtue of Allah – the Exalted – or as I understood [to that extent].

This short narration gives some reassurance to the people of *īmān* that death is not severe and intense for them. And the *karāmah* is related to this man who was seen after his death, usually a sign of reassurance to his family and students.

Duʿā for Lost Property

And we have been narrated to in the "Message of ʾUstādh Abu al-Qāsim al-Qushayrī" ﷺ in the section of the *karāmāt* of the *ʾawliyāʾ* of Allah, who said, "Jaʿfar al-Khuldī had a ring with a gem. One day, he lost it in the Tigris River[248]. He had a tried-and-tested *duʿāʾ* for returning lost property. So, he made that *duʿāʾ*, and he found his ring amongst some of his papers that he was looking through."

Al-Qushayrī narrates that Abu Naṣr al-Sarrāj said that this *duʿāʾ* is:

يَا جَامِعَ النَّاسِ لِيَومٍ لا رَيبَ فِيه، اجمَع بَينِي وَبَينَ ضَالّتي

"O You who gathers people to a Day that will undoubtedly occur, gather me with my lost [item]."

248 In Iraq.

Imam al-Nawawī said: I have tried this *du'ā'* and I have found it beneficial mostly when trying to find a lost item – quickly; and it hasn't failed.

And I heard my Shaykh Abu al-Baqā' say something similar and he is the one who taught it to me.

The Hadith Master and Imam Abu Sa'īd al-Sam'ānī said in his book of "Genealogy" regarding Ja'far al-Khuldī; that al-Khuld is a locality in Baghdad, to which Ṣubayḥ ibn Sa'īd - a narrator from 'Othmān ibn 'Affān and 'Ā'ishah ﷺ - is attributed.

The Imam tells us that Ja'far ibn Muhammad ibn Naṣr al-Khuldī al-Khawwāṣ, Abu Muhammad is one of the senior Sufis, with apparent *karāmāt*. He was renowned for his name: "al-Khuldī" because one day, he was with al-Junayd.

Al-Junayd was asked about an issue, so he said to Ja'far: "Answer them!"

So, he answered them.

Al-Junayd said to him: "Where did you get these answers from?"

He said: "From my Khuld [which means mind / heart]"

So, this name [Khuldī] stuck to him. He died in the year 348AH. He was a trustworthy hadith narrator, who the likes of al-Dāraqutnī and Abu Ḥafṣ ibn Shāhīn narrated from.

Shams al-Dīn Muhammad al-Nawawī

Another of his imams was called Shams al-Dīn Muhammad al-Nawawī ﷺ. He has the same title, because they are from the same city of Nawā.

The Imam said that in the [same] year (656AH) the Jurist Shams al-Dīn Muhammad al-Nawawī ﵀ passed away. Unto him, I read the honourable full recitation [of the Quran]. I saw him in a dream ﵀ after his death.

I said: "What is your state O Shams al-Dīn? Are you in *al-Jannah*?"

He said, "For now, we do not enter *al-Jannah*, except after the time of the Hour."

So, I said to him: "True! For the only ones who enter *al-Jannah* now are the Prophets, may Allah's prayers and peace be upon them - and the martyrs. As for others, they will be in bliss, before the Next Life; then they enter *al-Jannah* after the rise of the Hour, as the shari'a has explained."

Then I said to him: "It has been said that the soul returns to the body before the matter of Munkar and Nakīr[249]. So, when does it return to the body? After being placed in the grave, or before it whilst the body is in the coffin?"

He said: "After laying in the grave."

May Allah have mercy on him and me, our parents, our shaykhs, and whoever has benefitted us from our companions, and whomever we have offended; and for all other Muslims. *Āmīn*.

This is a beautiful narration which shows that one may benefit with some knowledge from someone who has passed away. The Imam uses this opportunity to clarify some matters which a dead person can explain.

The first one is about where the righteous dead person resides after passing away. The Shaykh clarifies that they don't enter *al-Jannah* at this time. And we know from the hadith that the first one to enter *al-Jannah* would be the Prophet ﷺ.

249 The two angels who came to a dead person after death and question him

He said:

أنا أوَّلُ مَن يقرَعُ بابَ الجنَّةِ

"I am the first to knock on the gate of *al-Jannah.*"[250]

آتِي بَابَ الْجَنَّةِ يَوْمَ الْقِيَامَةِ، فَأَسْتَفْتِحُ، فَيَقُولُ الْخَازِنُ: مَنْ أَنْتَ؟ فَأَقُولُ: مُحَمَّدٌ. فَيَقُولُ: بِكَ أُمِرْتُ لاَ أَفْتَحُ لأَحَدٍ قَبْلَكَ

"I will approach the gate of *al-Jannah* on the Day of Resurrection, and I will ask for it to be opened. The Gatekeeper will say, 'Who are you?'

I will say, 'Muhammad.'

He will say, 'To you, I have been commanded to open. None before you!'."[251]

And there are verses and hadith which tell us that martyrs are with their Lord or in *al-Jannah*. This is explained that people will enter with their spirits before the Day of Resurrection, but they will enter with their spirits and their bodies, after the Prophet ﷺ has entered.

The second matter that the Imam wanted to clarify was with regards to when the spirit re-joins the dead body. There is a hadith which says that when a person is being carried, he will start speaking to those carrying him, saying, "Where are you taking me?"[252]

So that's probably why he's asking this question for clarity.

As he mentions his Shaykh Shams al-Dīn, he narrates an incident from him.

250 *Ṣaḥīḥ:* Hadith narrated by Imam Ibn Ḥibbān
251 *Ṣaḥīḥ:* Hadith narrated by Imam Muslim
252 *Ṣaḥīḥ:* Hadith narrated by Imam al-Bukhārī

He said: I heard our companion, the Ascetic Imam, the pious knowledgeable aware Shaykh Shams al-Dīn - on Tuesday, the 21st of Jumada al-'Ūlā in the year 661AH, in the Khāniqah al-Shamīṣātiyyah in Damascus - may Allah Almighty protect it – saying:

"A few days ago, a dialogue occurred between two shaykhs who were imams, from our companions[253] in front of witnesses, whom he didn't name for me and I prefer not to mention them."

He said, "Between them a discussion arose about the Quran that is [written] in the *maṣāḥif* and [memorised] in the breasts: is it present, but not from the aspect of being omnipresent, as was said by our companions – and that the ink with which it is written is not the ancient words, rather indicative of it.

Then they sought guidance from the [books of the] Imam of the Two Holy Sanctuaries[254], to both look at what was mentioned in it, so they looked, then we left.

That night, I saw as if in the midst of a sea there was an object, and that object is what the people wanted. The Muslim scholars were standing around the shore, looking at that the object, not knowing what it is and not being able to recognise it"

He said: "I saw the Imam of the Two Sanctuaries enter between the people. He rolled up his garment and entered into that sea about fifteen cubits, then he was not able to reach it! So, he stood there where he was, and the other scholars continued as they were standing on the shore, looking at that object.

And behind the scholars, was an immense number of those who were occupied with the ancient knowledges – I mean the intellectual aspects, such as the science of body and logic, and the principles of the *dīn*. And there were those who were occupied in the matters of argument, who are known for their lack of religion, abstention of *ṣalāh* and bad concepts: and they are those I know!

253 This term usually indicates that they were from the Shāfiʿī School, the same as the two Nawawīs
254 Refers to the Sanctuary of Makkah and Madinah: He is Imam al-Juwainī

I saw them all behind the people, and there were dogs that urinated on all of them.

And someone pointed out to me a man – from amongst them, whom I know is one of those people of dispute, and was attributed and considered of those lacking *dīn*. I prefer not to name him, and I saw him drunk!" or as Shams al-Dīn said.

We ask Allah Almighty, the Generous, the One who bestows gifts, the One of Greatness and Authority, Virtue and Gratitude, The Merciful, The Compassionate, to improve our end for us, our parents, our shaykhs, our companions, those we love, and all Muslims. *Āmīn*.

One has to be careful of becoming argumentative for the sake of argument. One day I was in the Speaker's Corner in Hyde Park, where people come from different backgrounds, just to argue their points. A lot of the time, they are not interested in the truth, and they may not be religiously practicing, they just come to argue their points. And sometimes just to cause some sort of confusion. There was a Christian woman, who was arguing, and referring to a hadith narrated in al-Bukhārī about the Prophet ﷺ saying that women are deficient in mind and in *dīn*. And she was trying to make a whole case about women going to the Fire according to Islam. So, I said to her, "Well, you are not practicing your religion, because according to Christianity you should cover your head. Even in the Bible it says a woman should cover her head; otherwise, it is better that she shaves her head."

But the atmosphere there, nobody wants to listen, everybody just shouts.

Another incident was when some Christians wanted to show a contradiction in the Quran. They referred to the story of Dhu al-Qarnayn عليه السلام, in which the Quran states:

﴿ حَتَّى إِذَا بَلَغَ مَغْرِبَ الشَّمْسِ وَجَدَهَا تَغْرُبُ فِي عَيْنٍ حَمِئَةٍ ﴾

﴿ until he reached the setting [point] of the Sun,
he found it setting in a spring of murky water ﴾[255]

They argued that this is a clear contradiction, as the Sun does not set in a spring of murky water. However, I counter-argued by explaining that this is how language works, and I gave the example of someone saying, "I went to the seaside and I found the Sun setting in the sea", it doesn't mean that the Sun is actually setting in the sea, however it appears that way. And this is what the Quran is describing. Despite me repeating this more than seven times, they would not accept this point and continued to argue.

The point being is that some people look at matters of argument; they rehearse it for the sake of debate; and even if you give them clear evidence, they would not accept it.

The point of this narration is that he is saying that there are some people who argue and debate over matters which are of no real benefit. That is why it is vital to know that wasting time and effort in investigating trivial matters that will not lead to action is prohibited in Islam. This category includes debating minute aspects of rulings in cases which have never occurred, investigating the meaning of Quranic verses which are still beyond the scope of human knowledge, and differentiating between the Companions of the Prophet ﷺ or investigating the instances of disagreement that took place among them. It is important to use one's time to engage in useful activity and to seek useful knowledge. This is evident in the Quran, when Allah tells us stories; He gives us the aspects of the stories that will help us in our practice; and not matters that will not affect us at all, like the name of the dog that was with the People of the Cave, or the name of the village that Mūsā and al-Khidr عليهما السلام went to, etc.

255 Holy Quran; Chapter of the Cave 18:86

In fact, one of the biggest *fitnah* that happened in the past was the whole discussion or argument about the nature of the Quran: is it created or not? Is it the word of Allah? This debate actually didn't really have much practical application, but it was a very serious theological debate. And many people were imprisoned and tortured because of it, and some were executed. And so, sometimes the *'ummah* can get very much preoccupied with matters to the extent that they miss the whole point.

Even today, you have people who will test Muslims by asking them these theological questions to see whether or not they pass the test. They'll ask you, "Where is Allah ﷻ?" And if you don't answer according to their answer, then they cancel you out from their list.

I remember as I was teaching more and more in Kingston Mosque, one person came to me in the guise of an ignorant questioner. In a "humble" tone, he sought permission to ask me a question. When he proceeded to open his mouth with the question, I immediately knew he had been sent by someone else to test me! He wanted to see what I would answer, and use that against me. But I was open to his ploy.

Coincidently, the guy who had sent him was backbiting me to other people who wanted to come to my circles, and he would dissuade them from attending. On one occasion, we attended the graveyard for a funeral and he was there. I confronted him, and he tried to look sorrowful. But then he asked me for the name of my Shaykh, so he could "check him out" and see whether my Shaykh qualifies according to his standard.

A strange thing that happened is that he asked me for the name of my Shaykh, and he got a pen and paper to write the name. He tested the ink by scribbling with it – as one does – and the ink flowed. Then, I told him the name, and he tried to write it, but the pen wouldn't write. He then scribbled with the pen, as you do to get the ink to run. It started to write. Then he asked the name again,

I informed him; and the pen stopped writing again! Even I was surprised at what happened!

The point being is that it is important to occupy oneself with one's own affairs; rather than try to find faults with others, which is such a rotten path to tread.

Abu Yaʿqūb al-Karrāmī

The Imam then goes on to mention somebody called Abu Yaʿqūb al-Karrāmī. Abu Yaʿqūb was a good person who used to have sincerity towards others. He was someone who in today's terminology used to have a *daʿwah* table.

The Imam says that al-Samʿānī mentioned in the Book of Genealogy that the ascetic Abu Yaʿqūb Isḥāq ibn Mamshād al-Karrāmī was a good preacher. Five thousand men and women of the people of major sins and from the Magians[256] converted on his hand[257].

This is indeed among the *mawāhib* as the Imam indicated before; and it is a blessing from Allah that one can guide others to His *dīn*, as the Prophet ﷺ said:

فَوَاللهِ لَأَنْ يُهْدَى بِكَ رَجُلٌ واحِدٌ خَيْرٌ لك مِن حُمْرِ النَّعَمِ

"For Allah to guide because of you one person, is better than the red cattle."[258]

This man reminds me of a modern-day equivalent by the name of

256 Magians are an ancient pagan religion who worship fire, known also as Zoroastrians.
257 Meaning due to his effort
258 *Ṣaḥīḥ:* Hadith narrated by Imam Muslim

Mohammad Jehānī, a Libyan ex-footballer, who spent much of his later life going around talking to people about Islam and convincing them to take the step towards Allah. His technique and style very often win people over. I am told that he has a notebook which he carries. In it, he writes the names of all those who have converted to Islam due to his effort. When questioned about this notebook, he said that he wants this book to be buried with him, so it would count as a witness for his efforts on the Day of Judgement. May Allah accept from us and him.

Memorisation Abilities

A - AbdUllah ibn ʿOmar ibn Maysar

The Imam mentions also the *karāmah* of AbdUllah ibn ʿOmar ibn Maysar - Aba Saʿīd al-Ḥashamī, their mawla, al-Baṣrī, then al-Baghdādī and known as al-Qawārīrī.

Ahmad ibn Yaḥyā said that we heard 100,000 hadith from al-Qawārīrī.

Truly, it is a gift from Allah to have a great memory; and then to use it for the service of the *dīn*. Having a great memory was a feature of the people of the past. Their hearts were pure, so their minds were clean, so they memorised easily.

B - Woman who Memorised Quran

I saw in the handwriting of the Shaykh ﷺ a comment in separate places: I heard our Shaykh, the Imam and Judge – the aggregate of all sorts of goodness, the remnant of the elders and scholars: Badr al-Dīn Abu AbdUllah Muhammad ibn ʾIbrāhīm ibn Khalkān al-ʾArbīlī al-Shāfiʿī ﷺ on Wednesday, the sixteenth of Rajab in the year 660AH, say:

"I saw a woman - who I thought he said she is righteous or something to that effect – who memorised the entire Mighty Quran in seventy days!"

C - Kamāl al-Dīn Sallār

And the Imam goes on to say: I heard our Shaykh the Judge of Islam Kamāl al-Dīn Sallār ﷺ saying: "I memorised the book "al-Tanbīh"[259] in four months."

The Imam is mentioning these stories here as evidences about how people memorise. He gave us an example of quantity and speed. And obviously we saw that very evident in the early generations amongst the hadith narrators who used to memorise the hadith and they used to narrate it and they used to memorise it very precisely.

Today a person memorises the Quran and they call him a *ḥafiẓ*. However, in the olden days a *ḥafiẓ* is somebody who memorises one hundred thousand hadith with their chains. They actually memorised the whole chain with a hundred thousand of those. Imam al-Bukhārī mentioned that he memorised 200,000 chains. So, you can see that these people were blessed with this ability to memorise.

As a point to mention, the Imam mentions that Kamāl al-Dīn Sallār memorised "al-Tanbīh" in four months; and he didn't mention that he also memorised it in four months.

Compilations of Imam al-Ghazālī

The Imam said: I heard our Shaykh al-Batlīsī – may Allah preserve

259 This is the [another] famous fiqh book of Imam al-Shīrāzi (d. 476AH), which is considered an important reference in the Shāfi'ī School.

him – several times saying: "I counted the books of al-Ghazālī – may Allah Almighty have mercy on him - which he compiled, and I divided it by his lifespan; so I found that he must have compiled four notebooks every day!"

And that is the Grace of Allah, who directs it as He wills.

So basically, what he is saying is that because Imam al-Ghazālī didn't live for a long time, he only lived for 55 years, but when you think about how much he wrote, it must have been that he had compiled in his lifetime every day, at least four notebooks worth of knowledge.

Compilations of Imams al-Shāfiʿī and al-'Ashʿarī 🕮

The Imam said: Among the most well-known in multitude compilations are our Imam: Imam Abu AbdUllah Muhammad ibn 'Idrīs al-Shāfiʿī and Imam Abu al-Ḥasan al-'Ashʿarī 🕮.

Imam Abu Bakr al-Bayhaqī 🕮 enumerated the works of al-Shāfiʿī.

The Imam and Hadith Master of al-Shām – rather the Hadith Master of the *dunyā* Abu al-Qāsim - known as Ibn 'Asākir 🕮 who wrote the "History of Damascus" amongst others - in his book "Exposing the lie of the falsifier in what was attributed to Imam Abu al-Ḥasan al-'Ashʿarī", counted al-'Ashʿarī's compilations to around three hundred.

These are kind of things that the Imam mentioned here which are evidence as *karāmāt* for people because usually a person needs time to write and compile, and then revise. It takes time but these people had *barakah* in their lives to the extent that they would be able to achieve that in the past.

When we spoke about *karāmāt*, we said there is something called the folding. You have the folding of distance and you have the folding of time. One Friday, we were standing outside of *Jumu'ah* outside Feltham Assembly Hall, and we were talking and some people were saying how come we hear these narrations that this guy read the Quran in one night or he read it so many times in Ramadan. And so, it seemed that they were saying it's not rational, it can't happen. That is because they are measuring it in a material sense. And the reality is that there is a metaphysical dimension, in which Allah ﷻ can bless somebody in their time such that they can achieve a lot, even though the time may not allow.

We know that when the Prophet ﷺ went on the Night Journey and the Ascension (*al-'Isrā'* and *al-Mi'rāj*), he went and experienced so many things and did lots of things: which may easily amount to months. Yet, he did that all in one night. And it is almost like a completely different dimension that he had. So, Allah ﷻ owns time and He dictates it as He wills. There is a narration mentioned by Qāḍī 'Iyāḍ in his book "Al-Shifā" where he mentioned that on one occasion 'Alī ﷺ was occupied in battle, that he was going to miss *ṣalāh al-'Asr*. When he came back, the Prophet ﷺ made *du'ā'* that Allah ﷻ holds back the Sun. So, the Sun was held back while he prayed 'Asr before it set. This is also a *karāmah* from Allah ﷻ for the Prophet ﷺ that time was held still for a while. There are many other narrations in this regard if one wanted to look at them.

An important point to note here is as the Imam mentions those who compiled much; it is of the blessing of Allah that he – himself – is among those. When you look at how much he compiled in his short lifetime, because he only lived for 45 years, again, it was seen that there had to be some sort of *karāmah* there and *barakah* to allow so much compilation in such a short period of time. And obviously, the Imam doesn't boast this about himself.

Devotion of Abdul ʿAẓīm

In a similar way, he mentions the Noble Imam and Master, the Hadith Master and researcher, and the enlightened auditor, the precise and verifier, the compassionate and righteous, the pious ascetic, and diligent worshiper, the remnant of Hadith Masters, the Mufti, the Shaykh of Imams and Hadith narrators: Ḍiyā Uddīn Abu Isḥāq ʾIbrāhīm ibn ʿĪsā al-Murādī say on the Wednesday 6th of Shawwāl in the year 658AH at al-Bādiriyyah School in Damascus – may Allah protect and preserve it.

He said: I heard Shaykh Abdul ʿAẓīm, ﷺm, saying: "I wrote with my own hands 90 volumes, and I wrote 700 chapters, all of which are in the sciences of hadith: compilations and other." And he wrote it from his own compilations, in addition to many other things.

And he said our Shaykh, who's obviously narrating to Imam al-Nawawī, said: I have not seen nor heard of anyone more diligent than he was in work: he used to be continuous in his work, day and night.

He said: I neighboured him in the School – meaning in Cairo – may Allah protect it. My dwelling was above his dwelling for twelve years. I did not wake up in any hour of the hours of the night, in any of the nights, without finding the light of the lantern lit in his house, and he is occupied with knowledge. And even during mealtimes, the book and the books would be in front of him, as he is occupied with it!

And he further mentioned from Shaykh Abdul ʿAẓīm's verification, and the intensity of his research and his artistic touches which he was unable to express.

He said: He would hardly go out of the school neither for consolation, nor for celebration, nor for any seeking of comfort, except for Friday prayers. Rather, he would use up all his time in knowledge. May Allah Almighty be pleased with him, with our parents and the Muslims.

This narration demonstrates the blessings and gifts of Allah to this person, who managed to compile so much during such a short life. What's important to note, is that his Shaykh's dedication to the knowledge. He spent most of his life – if not all – dedicated to serving knowledge; such that his sleep and recreation were little.

Ḍiyā Uddīn Abu Isḥāq 'Ibrāhīm ibn 'Īsā al-Murādī

The Imam than says: I heard our Shaykh Ḍiyā Uddīn ⬥ say: "I wrote Ṣaḥīḥ Al-Bukhārī in six volumes with one pencil, which I used to sharpen. And with that pencil I wrote many things after al-Bukhārī in the City of Cairo – may Allah protect it.

One format of a *karāmah* is that Allah allows for something to have extended usage. In this case, one pencil was used to write six volumes, indeed a blessing from Allah ⬥. You would have read previously about the dates of Abu Hurayrah ⬥.

Abu Bakr al-Kittānī

Another narration that Imam Nawawi mentioned again this is all related to *barakah* as well; blessings in time and space. He said that Abu Saʿīd al-Samʿānī said in the Book of Genealogy: Shaykh Abu Bakr Muhammad ibn ʿAlī ibn Jaʿfar al-Kittānī completed twelve thousand times [Quran recitation] during the *ṭawāf*. He died in the year 322AH.

Probably *ṭawāf* doesn't mean that he did it in one go, but during all the times he did *ṭawāf*. And because he says here that he died in the year 322AH. So, Allah ⬥ had given him *barakah*, and he lived close to Makkah anyway. So, whenever he did *hajj* or *'umrah,* he would recite the Quran. He managed to recite 12,000 times.

'Izz al-Dīn al-'Irbilī

The Imam said that he heard his Shaykh and Master the Imam Most Learned Scholar, the Mufti, the Verifier, master of precision in all kinds of merits: 'Izz al-Dīn Abu Ḥafṣ 'Omar ibn 'Asad ibn Abi Ghālib al-'Irbilī al-Shāfi'ī ⬥ many times, most recently on Friday the 24th of Rajab in the year of 659AH say: "Every worker for Allah ⬥ with obedience, is in remembrance of Allah ⬥."

He said that he heard him saying it many times, it's like his slogan or life motto: Anyone who works for Allah ⬥ with an act of obedience, then he is someone who is remembering Allah ⬥. And it's an act of remembrance. We know that *dhikr* is something that one does with the tongue. In this instance, he is telling us that it is true, even when you are working in obedience. Whether in this case, in this scenario, it could be writing, compiling and studying; that is also a form of *dhikr* as well. Or, indeed any action in which you are aware of Allah, then that is remembrance of Allah.

And it is befitting that he ends with this narration, as the whole book is about being aware of Allah in the Garden of the Aware. And this involves that one aims to make the acts of obedience for Allah, by remembering Allah before commencement, having an intention, making that intention varied and eloquent; making that intention sincere for Allah alone.

He said I heard that many times from his Shaykh al-'Irbilī; but then he saw this written in the book "Sharḥ al-Sunnah" which is written by Imam al-Bagawī which he had taken from Sa'īd ibn Jubayr ⬥ who is one of the *Tābi'īn.* And with this our Imam and Shaykh

Imam al-Nawawī ends his book.

This is the summary that everyone who works for Allah ﷻ with his energy and effort, then he is one who remembers Allah ﷻ. And so, he ends with this beautiful phrase.

Indeed, may Allah ﷻ have mercy and be pleased with Imam al-Nawawī for this compilation, which Al-Ḥamdu Lillāh we have benefited from and we have studied a lot. And may Allah have mercy on him, his parents and all of those who have taught us, and we have benefited from, and all the Muslims. *Āmīn.*

Repeat unto me their stories, O *Ḥādī*[260]

For their tales scour the rusting heart

The Book has thus been completed with the Help of Allah and His Support.

260 The name of the one who leads the camels in the desert using poems or odes.

16

Conclusion

Thence, we have come to the end of this book. For me, it has – indeed – been a journey. A journey which has been riddled with difficulties and obstacles; but, also one which has been entertaining and educational.

Whenever one engages in the task of compiling a book, s/he will learn so much. The learning comes from the focus on what has been written and gathering one's thoughts. It comes from research and reviewing sayings and references. There is education as one opens up small – yet significant – holes into the vast vault of knowledge.

I have enjoyed this journey as I have reflected on what the Imam has collated for us in the Garden, and as I have reflected on my own experiences within life, something which I hope to able to elaborate more in future writings, if Allah extends me some time in my life.

As you would have read at the beginning, this book has been written based on the Garden that the Imam has brought to life with an array of exotic and bewildering sayings and stories: his work is a fine product of splendour in which he must be congratulated. We don't own much to give him, except that we sincerely ask Allah that He rewards him for his endeavours and his contribution to humankind.

And I have attempted to help the reader to stroll with me to enjoy the beauty of the Garden, and to indulge in the wonderful scenes and pleasant aromas. I hope that you have enjoyed my personal anecdotes which have been important stations for reflection and contemplation.

It is my aspiration to write a third part to this series, in which I can expand further on the biographies of all those who have been mentioned in the Garden, as that in itself is a large volume. That is my hope, and I put my trust in Allah, to give me the time and energy to do so.

This book "Strolling in the Garden" was thus completed on this day the Thursday 9th of Ramadan 1442AH.

May Allah the Almighty be pleased with the *walī* of Allah Shaykh Muḥyī Uddin al-Nawawī ﵀; for compiling such a beautiful compilation which is befitting to be indeed a Garden. And may Allah the Exalted extend His pleasure to the author of this work: Omer ibn Hasem El-Hamdoon al-Zubaydī al-Barīṭānī.

And may Allah extend His pleasure to our parents, our shaykhs, our companions and all Muslims. And praise be to Allah alone, and may Allah's prayers be upon our master Muhammad, and upon his good and pure family and great companions.

Glossary of terms

Note: Words which begin with "al" can be found by removing this prefix which means "the".

ʿAbd: Slave, sometimes used to refer to the human.

'Abdāl: *lit*. Substitutes or 'replaceables'. They are an elite group of righteous people, who replace one another. It is said that the world will not be void of any one of them at any one time. The notion of their existence is based on a hadith, which the hadith verifiers have disagreed on its authenticity.

'Adab: Etiquette or moral code.

Aḥādīth: *pl*. of hadith

Ākhīrah: The Final Life or the Next Life, refers to the eternal life after death.

'Akhlāq: Morals or etiquette. (*pl. of khuluq*)

'Ālam al-ghayb: World of the unseen, referring to beings and things that cannot be sensed with the physical senses.

Alḥamdu Lillāh: Praise be to Allah.

'Ālim: Scholar.

Allahu akbar: Allah is the Greatest. Used to denote that Allah is greater than all other people and objects.

Aḥkām: In general refers to any rulings, but within Islam, they are Islamic rulings pertaining to human acts.

'Aḥnāf: *pl.* for ḥanafī, one who adheres to the school of Abu Ḥanīfah ﵀

'Am: General.

Āmīn: Amen; meaning "Our Lord, hear our prayer."

'Amal: Action.

'Aml: Hope / aspiration.

'Anṣār: *lit.* Those who supported [another]. In this context, it refers to the inhabitants of al-Madīnah who received, hosted and protected the Prophet ﷺ and the Muslim emigrants from Makkah.

'Aqīdah: Doctrine or theological beliefs.

'Aql: Sound mind / rational, logic reasoning.

'Ārif: Aware or knowledgeable.

'Awliyā': *pl.* of walī.

'Awrah: Nakedness to be covered.

Badr: The name of a series of wells close to al-Madinah. It is famous for the battle between the Muslims and Quraysh which took place in its vicinity.

Barakah: Blessing(s), used to denote the gift or flow of grace and blessings from Allah.

Bid'ah: Innovation, usually relating to that in the religion.

Bismillah: In the name of Allah; used at the beginning of actions to invoke Allah's blessings and reward.

Bushrā: Good news or glad tidings.

Ḍa'īf: Weak. In the context of hadith, refers to a narration which has weaknesses in its transmission or text.

Da'wah: *lit.* an invitation to a meal. Used to denote an invite to embrace Islam.

Day of Reckoning: Day of Judgment. It is called reckoning because on that day, Allah will judge people and reckon their deeds.

Dhikr: Remembrance. It refers to the supplications or formula that Muslims say to remember Allah. Dhikr is highly encouraged and rewarded for repeating in matter to remember Allah as much as one can. *pl.* adhkār.

Dīn: Way of life or religion.

Dirham: A word originating from Persian, it was and is a unit of currency used in some Arab and Muslim lands. Traditionally it was made of pure silver.

Du'ā': Supplication or prayer.

Dunyā: *lit*. translated as "closest". It refers to the current life humans live from birth to death; in opposition with the hereafter, that the human soul accesses after death.

Faḍā'il: *pl*. of faḍīlah, which is an act of virtue or moral standing.

Fajr: Dawn. One of the obligatory daily prayers is called fajr as it is to be prayed after the break of dawn.

Fāqah: Poverty, need.

Faqīh: A person of deep understanding, and more specifically in matters of Islamic jurisprudence.

Faqīr: Impoverished or in need.

Fāsiq: Transgressor.

Fatḥ: An opening or conquest.

Fatwā: Legal Islamic ruling.

Fiqh: *lit*. understanding / comprehension; and refers to the understanding of the intricates of Islamic jurisprudence.

Firāsah: Intuition or sixth sense.

Fitnah: Trial / tribulation or strife.

Fiṭrah: The natural way instilled into the human being.

Ghanī: Rich or sufficient.

Gharīb: Strange(r). In hadith terminology it means a narration narrated with a single chain of transmission.

Ghusl: Ritual washing which encompasses all the body and hair. It is a must to perform after sexual intercourse or ejaculation; and for women: after the end of menstruation or post-natal bleeding.

Ḥadath: Ritual impurity, usually refers to the minor version which necessitates wuḍū'.

Hadī: The animal presented as part of the ritual sacrifice during hajj.

Hadith: *lit*. something new or new speech. Islamically, it refers to the narration(s) from the Prophet ﷺ or those around him. Hadith is transmitted through a chain of narration.

Ḥafiẓ: Hadith master who memorises 100,000 chains of narration or more.

Hajj: The pilgrimage to the House of Allah in Makkah. An annual recurrence, that an able Muslim is required to perform once in a lifetime.

Halal:	Permitted / allowed. Refers to what is lawful in Islam.
Ḥamd:	Praise.
Ḥanīf:	Someone who is diverted away, or inclined away. *pl.* ḥunafā'.
Ḥarām:	Prohibited / disallowed. Refers to what is unlawful in Islam.
Ḥasab:	Lineage / ancestry.
Ḥasan:	Good.
Ḥasanāt:	Good deeds.
Ḥawa:	Arabic name of Eve.
Hibah:	Gift.
Hidāyah:	Guidance.
Hijrah:	Migration.
Ḥikmah:	Wisdom. In some context, can refer to the Sunna.
Ḥuffāẓ:	*pl.* of ḥafiẓ.
Ḥuqūq:	Rights.
Ḥur:	Freeman / women. Not in bondage.
'Ibādah:	Worship. In Islam, 'ibādah has a wide implication to mean any act which is done seeking the pleasure of Allah.

Ikhlāṣ: Sincerity.

'Iḥsān: Beautification, perfection or excellence. It is a higher form of belief about attempting the best in one's behaviour and actions. The Prophet ﷺ defined it as "worshipping Allah as if you can see Him."

Ijtihad: Legal reasoning to derived to a conclusion.

'Ilm: Knowledge or science.

'Ilm al-rijāl: Science of narrators. It is the sub-branch of hadith which explores the status of the people who appear in the chains of transmission.

Imam: A leader. In Islam, it refers to a type of leadership position, most commonly used as the title of the one who leads the prayer in a mosque, or the leader of a Muslim community or people.

Īmān: Belief / conviction.

In shā' Allah: If Allah wills / hopefully.

Insān: Human.

'Iqāmah: Call to commence the prayer.

'Iqbāl: Directed attention, or focused positioning.

'Ishā': Refers to the prayer named after the timing of the day, which is the later night. It begins after the setting of the twilight and extends till the break of dawn.

ʾIsnād:	Chain of transmission of a narration.
Istighfār:	To ask for forgiveness [from Allah].
ʾIstiqāmah:	To be upright, on the straight path.
ʾIʿtikāf:	Seclusion or spiritual retreat, usually done in the masjid.
Janābah:	Major ritual impurity, necessitating ghusl.
Jannah:	*lit.* garden. In the Islamic vocabulary, it refers to Paradise: the eternal Garden of the Hereafter awarded to those who have belief and are righteous. Sometimes it is translated as "Heaven" which is not strictly correct.
Jihād:	*lit.* striving or struggling, especially with a praiseworthy aim. In an Islamic context, it can refer to almost any effort to make personal and social life conform with Allah's guidance, such as struggle against one's evil inclinations, or one's enemies be they the devils or humans. In classical Islamic law, the term refers to armed struggle against warring disbelievers.
Jinn:	Creatures of Allah that cannot be seen by the human eye. They were created before humans and also have free-will. The first jinn to be created was Satan but not all the jinn are evil. On the contrary, there are righteous amongst them.
Jumuʿah:	Friday, or sometimes used for the Friday prayer.

Kaʿbah:	The cuboid structure found in the centre of the Sacred Masjid in Makkah.
Karāmāh:	Means a nobility or generous gift. It is simply translated as a miracle: which is an extraordinary and welcome event that is not explicable by natural or scientific laws and is therefore attributed to divine agency. *pl.* karāmāt
Khāṣ:	Specific.
Khushūʿ:	Concentration in humility.
Khuṭbah:	Sermon, usually performed on Fridays, Eid and other congregational prayers.
Kibr:	Pride / arrogance.
Madhhab:	School or opinion. *pl.* madhāhib.
Maghrib:	Sunset, and refers to the prayer performed after sunset. Its time extends to the disappearance of the twilight.
Majlis:	Gathering.
Majnūn:	Mad or insane.
Makrūh:	Disliked. In foundation of fiqh, it refers to an act which if one abstains from will be rewarded, but if one carries out will not be sinning.
Manqūl:	Transmitted via textual or oral transmission.

Maqṣūrah: A niche / recess in the wall of a masjid, at the point nearest to Makkah, towards which the congregation faces to pray. See miḥrāb.

Marfūʿ: Raised. Can refer to a hadith raised to the Prophet ﷺ.

Masjid: *lit*. place of prostration. Mosque. *pl*. masājid

Maṣāḥif: *pl*. of muṣ-ḥaf.

Maʿṣūm: Protected from erring or faulting.

Mawqūf: Stopped. Can refer to a hadith which has not been attributed to the Prophet ﷺ.

Miḥrāb: A prayer room, but later used to denote a niche / recess in the wall of a mosque, at the point facing Makkah, towards which the congregation faces to pray.

Minbar: Pulpit in the masjid, where the imam stands to deliver the khuṭbah or a lecture.

Muḥaddith: Hadith scholar or hadith narrator.

Muhājirūn: Emigrants. Referring to the early Muslims, who migrated [mostly] from Makkah to Madinah, fleeing persecution.

Mukhaḍḍram: Someone who has lived through several epochs. In Islamic context refers to someone who was alive during the life of the Prophet ﷺ but never met him; and lived after him.

Muʾmin: Believer. *pl*. al-mu'minūn.

Munāfiq: Hypocrite.

Mursal: Type of hadith transmission in which the name and person of the companion narrating from the Prophet ﷺ is missing in the chain.

Muṣala: Prayer mat.

Muṣ-ḥaf: The Quranic scripture / book.

Mustaqīm: Straight.

Nabī: Prophet.

Nafs: Refers to the human's inner self or soul. Muslims are requested to tame and educate their inner-self. Sometimes referred to as the ego.

Najāsah: Physical impurity.

Najis: Physical impurity.

Naql: Transmitted textually or orally.

Nasab: Lineage.

Naṣīḥah: Sincerity. Commonly used for sincere advice.

Nifāq: Hypocrisy. One who is a hypocrite is termed a munāfiq.

Niyyah: Intention.

Nuṣuḥ: See naṣīḥah.

Qalb: *lit*. means the core or internal; and very often refers to the heart, which may be the physical or the spiritual.

Qārī: A reciter of the Quran, who also memorises the whole Quran [usually].

Qaṣāṣīn: Story tellers.

Qudsī: Divine.

Quraysh: Name of an Arab ancestor, which later became the name of the most prominent Arabian tribe residing in and around Makkah. The tribe to which the Prophet ﷺ is from.

Raḥmah: Mercy.

Rakʿah: Bowing. Also used to note one unit of prayer (ṣalāh). *pl*. rakʿāt.

Rasūl: Messenger.

Rawḍah: A garden or meadow, or it can refer to an interior garden or courtyard associated with the house or palace architecture. *pl*. riyāḍ.

Riḍā: Content / satisfaction.

Rīyāʾ: Showing off.

Rizq: Provision(s). In the Islamic context, directly refers to all that Allah ﷻ provides a person or His creatures with.

Rukūʿ: Bowing.

Ruqyah: Healing: can be physical or spiritual.

Ṣabr: Patience.

Ṣaḥīḥ: *lit*. correct; in the context of hadith means authentic. If used with a capital letter it refers to the hadith books which have carried the same name, as their authors have been vigorous in choosing the narrations. The top two Ṣaḥīḥ books are that of Imams al-Bukhārī and Muslim. The other two – which are less vigorous are that of Imams Ibn Khuzaymah and Ibn Ḥibbān.

Salaf: Predecessors.

Ṣalāh: Is translated to prayer. Its Arabic meaning is to communicate. However, it is usually used to denote a set of actions and sayings which are performed in a set way beginning with intention and ending with salutation.

Salām: *lit*. peace. In the context of ṣalāh, it refers to the salutation that exits one from the prayer. Outside prayer, it refers to the salutation or greeting among Muslims.

Ṣadaqah: Charity. Can be a synonym for zakāh. It has the same root as ṣidq.

Ṣaḥābah: Companions, and the definitive form refers to the Companions of the Prophet ﷺ. *sing*. ṣaḥābī.

Ṣāliḥīn: Righteous, good people. *sing*. ṣāliḥ.

Sayyid: Master.

Shariʿa: Islamic canonical law based on the teachings of the Quran and the Sunnah. It details aspects of personal and communal life from as basic as personal hygiene to as complex as governance and economics.

Shaykh: Refers to someone who has reached a pinnacle of something. It is therefore used for the chief of an Arab tribe, family, or village; or an old man; or someone of significant Islamic knowledge.

Shayṭān: Satan. Also, means a devil. *pl*. shayāṭīn

Shifāʾ: Cure.

Shirk: To associate or collaborate or to partner. In Islam, it often refers to associating or giving partners to Allah, which is the biggest sin in Islam.

Ṣiddīqīn: Those who have excelled in truthfulness.

Ṣidq: Truthfulness.

Siḥir: Magic.

Subḥān Allah: No precise translation; but can be understood as: "Glory be to Allah" or "Allah is Perfect" or "How Free of any Imperfection is Allah" or "May He Be Exalted".

Sujūd: Prostration.

Sunna: *lit*. the path or way. In Islam, it refers to the actions, words and affirmations of the Prophet Muhammad ﷺ as his mission was to show us the path to worship Allah and stay connected to Him. *pl*. sunan.

Surah: Chapter of the Quran. There are 114 surahs.

Tābiʿī: A follower. Someone who has studied with one or more of the Prophet's ﷺ companions.

Tafsīr: Explanation. In Islamic terminology, refers to Quranic exegis.

Ṫahārah: Purification.

Taqwa: Piety / God Consciousness.

Taṣawwuf: Practice of sufism.

Ṫawaf: *lit*. to wander or roam. In the context of hajj, it refers to walking around the kaʿbah in an anti-clockwise rotation.

Tawakkul: Dependence, usually being on Allah.

Tawarruk: A form of sitting during ṣalāh.

Tawassul: Seeking intermediary.

Tawbah: Repentance.

Tawriyah: To say something which is true, but indicates something else to the listener.

al-Tawwāb:	One of Allah's Names which means "The One who continuously and consistently accepts repentance".
Ṭayyib:	Good, pure. *pl.* ṭayyibāt.
Tazkiyah:	Process of spiritual purification.
'Uḍḥiyah:	Sacrificial animal.
'Ujb:	Feeling of pride.
'Ulamā':	Scholars, carriers of knowledge.
'Ummah:	Group of people, used for a small community or a large nation.
Walī:	A difficult word to translate. It can be translated as someone who has a wonderful connection with Allah, to the extent that he loves Allah and Allah loves him. He is guided, protected and honoured by Allah. Part of Allah's honour is to bestow on him noble gifts and extraordinary occurrences knows as karāmāt.
Wara':	Devoutness; to abstain from permissible matters out of fear that you will fall into doubt or into ḥarām.
Wuḍū':	Ablution. In Islam, it is the set of actions which include washing and wiping set parts of the body, to make ṣalāh permissible to perform.
Yaqīn:	Certainty.

Zakāh: Refers to the obligatory charity that a Muslim must give, usually every year. The two main types of zakāh are zakāt ul-fitr and zakāt ul-māl (zakāh on the annual savings).

Zāhid: Ascetic. One who practises zuhd.

Zuhd: Abstinence.

Author's Biography

Leaving Iraq at a young age, Omer El-Hamdoon was raised up in the UK. His role as a community leader has also taken him further afield in the UK and internationally. He has had a long experience of working in the Muslim community, and taken up leadership roles within the UK, including with the Muslim Council of Britain (MCB), Muslim Association of Britain (MAB), Mosques and Imams National Advisory Board (MINAB); along with other trusteeships. At the time of publication, as an imam, he is a member of the European Assembly of Imams and the British Board of Scholars and Imams (BBSI).

His passion for understanding and teaching Islam continued to increase throughout the years, and led him to delve deep into Islamic Sciences. He is doubly qualified with a Masters in each of Dentistry and Islamic Studies.

Dr El-Hamdoon is an educator and writer on Islam, as well as being an international speaker and intellectual activist. For over 25 years, Shaykh Omer has been delivering *Jumu'ah* sermons, motivational reminders and inspiring talks; as well as regular study circles and educational courses.

As a mentor and spiritual coach, he accompanies Muslims as they work on breaking the barriers standing between them and becoming their better selves, allowing their faith to radiate in every aspect of their lives.

His traditional study of Islam compiled with his knowledge of western societies make him very aware of the gap that needs bridging for Muslims living in the West; to understand and make sense of this beautiful religion within the context of their lives. Shaykh Omer combines traditional understanding of Islam with modern concepts.

He is the co-author of the book: "30 Steps Towards a Refreshing Ramadan", where he smartly conjures up some of the deepest concepts of Islam with a cocktail of technological terms, inviting the reader to dwell into the spiritual aspects of Ramadan, by relating the jargon of modern gadgets to one's inner soul (*nafs*). And he has translated other books including al-Nawawī's "Bustān al-'Arifīn", "The Hadramī Introduction" and "Meadows of the Righteous".

He speaks at varying venues and international venues; as well as appearing on a variety of TV channels speaking in English and Arabic. He also lectures on many topics, including fiqh, *usūl al-fiqh*, hadith and politics in Islam.